5 STEPS TO A

500

AP World History:
Modern
Questions

to know by test day

FOURTH EDITION

Sean McManamon

New York Chicago San Francisco Athens London Madrid
Mexico City Milan New Delhi Singapore Sydney Toronto

1 2 3 4 5 6 7 8 9   LCR   28 27 26 25 24 23

ISBN   978-1-265-02065-1
MHID   1-265-02065-5

e-ISBN   978-1-265-02078-1
e-MHID   1-265-02078-7

Contributions from former editions by Adam Stevens.

McGraw Hill, the McGraw Hill logo, 5 Steps to a 5, and related trade dress are trademarks or registered trademarks of McGraw Hill and/or its affiliates in the United States and other countries and may not be used without written permission. All other trademarks are the property of their respective owners. McGraw Hill is not associated with any product or vendor mentioned in this book.

AP, Advanced Placement Program, and *College Board* are registered trademarks of the College Board, which was not involved in the production of, and does not endorse, this product.

McGraw Hill products are available at special quantity discounts to use as premiums and sales promotions or for use in corporate training programs. To contact a representative, please visit the Contact Us pages at www.mhprofessional.com.

McGraw Hill is committed to making our products accessible to all learners. To learn more about the available support and accommodations we offer, please contact us at accessibility@mheducation.com. We also participate in the Access Text Network (www.accesstext.org), and ATN members may submit requests through ATN.

500

AP World History:
Modern
Questions

to know by test day

Also in the 500 AP Questions to Know by Test Day Series:

5 Steps to a 5: 500 AP Biology Questions to Know by Test Day
5 Steps to a 5: 500 AP Calculus AB/BC Questions to Know by Test Day
5 Steps to a 5: 500 AP Chemistry Questions to Know by Test Day
5 Steps to a 5: 500 AP English Literature Questions to Know by Test Day
5 Steps to a 5: 500 AP English Language Questions to Know by Test Day
5 Steps to a 5: 500 AP Environmental Science Questions to Know by Test Day
5 Steps to a 5: 500 AP European History Questions to Know by Test Day
5 Steps to a 5: 500 AP Human Geography to Know by Test Day
5 Steps to a 5: 500 AP Microeconomics Questions to Know by Test Day
5 Steps to a 5: 500 AP Macroeconomics Questions to Know by Test Day
5 Steps to a 5: 500 AP Physics 1 Questions to Know by Test Day
5 Steps to a 5: 500 AP Physics C Questions to Know by Test Day
5 Steps to a 5: 500 AP Psychology Questions to Know by Test Day
5 Steps to a 5: 500 AP Statistics Questions to Know by Test Day
5 Steps to a 5: 500 AP U.S. Government & Politics Questions to Know by Test Day
5 Steps to a 5: 500 AP U.S. History Questions to Know by Test Day

CONTENTS

ABOUT THE AUTHOR

Sean McManamon has a Masters in History from Hunter College, 1998. He teaches AP World History at Brooklyn Technical High School and lives in New York City with his wife, Justine, and two children, Phebe and Owen. His wife insists that he mention that both his children got 5s on their AP World History exams.

ACKNOWLEDGMENTS

I would like to thank the following people for their support: Adam Stevens, Alan Barbour, Rachel Worrell, Dr. Judith Jerome, and especially my wife, Justine Manser.

INTRODUCTION

Congratulations! You've taken a big step toward AP success by purchasing *5 Steps to a 5: 500 AP World History: Modern Questions to Know by Test Day*. We are here to help you take the next step and score high on your AP exam so you can earn college credits and get into the college or university of your choice!

This book gives you 500 AP-style multiple-choice questions that cover all the most essential course material. Each question has a detailed answer explanation. These questions will give you valuable independent practice to supplement your regular textbook and the groundwork you are already doing in your AP classroom.

Each chapter ends with a set of stimulus-based questions of the type the College Board has recently employed in its redesigned AP World History exam. As you complete these questions, use a timer and work toward completing each stimulus-based question in one minute or less. Working at this speed will prepare you for the pace you will want to maintain when taking the actual AP exam in the spring.

This and the other books in this series were written by expert AP teachers who know your exam inside out and can identify the crucial exam information as well as questions that are most likely to appear on the exam.

You might be the kind of student who takes several AP courses and needs to study extra questions throughout the year. Or you might be the kind of student who puts off preparing until the last weeks before the exam. No matter what your preparation style, you will surely benefit from reviewing these 500 questions, which closely parallel the content, format, and degree of difficulty of the questions on the actual AP exam. These questions and their answer explanations are the ideal last-minute study tool for those final few weeks before the test.

Remember the old saying "Practice makes perfect." If you practice with all the questions and answers in this book, we are certain you will build the skills and confidence needed to do well on the exam. Good luck!

— Editors of McGraw Hill

500

AP World History: Modern Questions

to know by test day

Diagnostic Quiz

GETTING STARTED: THE DIAGNOSTIC QUIZ

The following questions refer to different units in this book. These questions will help you test your understanding of the concepts tested on the AP exam by giving you an idea of where you need to focus your attention as you prepare. For each question, simply circle the letter of your choice. Once you are done with the exam, check your work against the given answers, which also indicate where you can find the corresponding material in the book.

Good luck!

DIAGNOSTIC QUIZ QUESTIONS

The Chinese conduct commercial transactions and business affairs with equity. When someone lends money to another person, he writes up a note documenting the loan. The borrower writes up another note on which he affixes an imprint of his index finger and middle finger together. Then they put the two notes together, roll them up, and write a formula at the point where one touches the other [so that part of the written formula appears on each note]. Next, they separate the notes and entrust to the lender the one on which the borrower recognizes his debt. If the borrower denies his debt later on, they say to him, "Present the note that the lender gave to you." If the borrower maintains that he has no such note from the lender, and denies that he ever agreed to the note with his fingerprints on it, and if the lender's note has disappeared, they say to him, "Declare in writing that you have not contracted this debt, but if later the lender brings forth proof that you have contracted this debt that you deny, you will receive twenty blows of the cane on the back and you will be ordered to pay a penalty of twenty million copper coins." This sum is equal to about 2,000 dinars [gold coins used in the Abbasid empire]. Twenty blows of the cane brings on death. Thus, no one in China dares to make such a declaration for fear of losing at the same time both life and fortune. We have seen no one who has agreed when invited to make such a declaration. The Chinese are thus equitable to each other. No one in China is treated unjustly.

—Account of Sulayman, the Arab Merchant in India and China.

1. The passage above supports which of the conclusions about Postclassical China?

   (A) Complex economic practices in Postclassical China
   (B) The spread of metal coinage during the Postclassical China
   (C) The openness of Postclassical China to other cultures
   (D) The taxation of Chinese agricultural crops in paper currency

2. The Ethiopian kingdom was similar to Great Zimbabwe and West African kingdoms like Mali in the Postclassical era in that they were

   (A) Stateless societies
   (B) Centralized governments
   (C) Chinese tributary states
   (D) Sub-Saharan chiefdoms

And having heard this, that a great Tartar force was coming against him, the [Great Prince] Dmitri Ivanovich gathered many soldiers and went against the godless Tartars, trusting in the mercy of God and in His Immaculate Mother, the Mother of God, the eternal Virgin Mary, calling to his aid the honourable Cross. For he entered their country beyond the Don, and there was there a clean field at the mouth of the river Nepryadva, and there the pagan Ishmaelites had ranged themselves against the Christians. And the Moscovites, of whom many were inexperienced, were frightened and in despair for their lives at sight of the great numbers of Tartars, others turned to flight, forgetful of the Prophet's saying that one shall reap one thousand, and two shall move ten thousand, if God does not abandon them. And the [Great Prince] Dmitri with his brother Volodimir ranged their troops against the pagan Polovets people, and raising their eyes humbly to heaven, and sighing from the depth of their hearts, said, in the words of the psalm: "Brothers, God is our refuge and our strength." And both forces immediately met, and there was a fierce battle for a long time, and God terrified the sons of Hagar with an invisible might, and they turned their shoulders to wounds, and they were routed by the Christians, and some were struck down with weapons, and others drowned in the river, a countless number of them.

—The Novgorod Chronicle, 1380.

3. Which of the following changes that occurred in Russia is demonstrated in the reading above?
   (A) The subjugation of Russia by pagan Ishmaelites
   (B) The introduction of new trade routes across Eurasia
   (C) The beginning of a process to end Mongol rule over Russia
   (D) The adoption of a new pagan religion of the Moscovites

Population of Western Europe, 500–1500 CE
(Estimated figures, in millions)

Date	500 CE	650 CE	1000 CE	1340 CE	1450 CE	1500 CE
Italy	4.0	2.5	5.0	10.0	7.6	11.0
Spain	4.0	3.5	7.0	9.0	7.0	9.0
Britain & Ireland	0.5	0.5	2.0	5.0	3.0	5.0
France, Belgium & Holland	5.0	3.0	6.0	19.0	12.0	18.0
Germany and Scandinavia	3.5	2.0	4.0	11.5	7.5	13.0
Total	17.0	11.5	24.0	54.5	37.0	56.0

Source: Carlo M. Cipolla. *The Fontana Economic History of Europe: The Middle Ages.*

4. Which of the following best explains the change in populations between 1340 and 1450?

(A) The Reconquista in Spain
(B) Improvements in agriculture
(C) The bubonic plague
(D) New crops such as clover

5. Based on the evidence shown in the chart above, which of the following is true?

(A) Europe's population continued its sharp decline.
(B) Europe's population bounced back up to high levels.
(C) Europe's population did not decrease in Italy.
(D) Europe's population only rose in Italy and Spain.

—Illustration of Inca farmers using a *chakitaqlla* (Andean foot plow).

6. Which of the following does NOT explain the image above?
   (A) Limited technology
   (B) Lack of work animals
   (C) Agricultural-based economy
   (D) Gold and silver mining

To have the arts of peace but not the art of war is to lack courage. To have the arts of war but not peace, is to lack wisdom ... A man who is of inner worth and upright conduct, who has moral principles and mastery of the arts is also called a samurai. A man whose purpose is learning is called a samurai ... the term samurai is indeed broad ... At court he is a statesman, in the field he is a general.

—Hayashi Razan, a scholar in the employ of the Tokugawa,
On the Mastery of the Arts of Peace and War, circa 1655.

7. The above reading is best understood in light of the following change in Japan.

   (A) The samurai class was needed more than ever in the Tokugawa era.
   (B) The samurai class were required to pass the Chinese civil service exam.
   (C) The samurai class was less needed during the Pax Tokugawa.
   (D) The samurai class was eliminated when the country was unified in 1600.

8. The text above shows a clear influence from which belief system in Japan at the time?

   (A) Shinto
   (B) Daoism
   (C) Christianity
   (D) Confucianism

—The Qutb Minar in New Delhi, India.

9. The Qutb Minar tower and building complex used stones from nearby Hindu temples that were destroyed. Which of the following related issues represents a continuity of South Asian culture?

(A) The use of statues in Hindu temples
(B) The quick introduction of Arabic script
(C) The demise of the Hindu Rajput princes
(D) The end of veneration of Sufi saints

Of the customs of Quiteve, king of the lands and river of Sofala and what occurs in the kingdom at his death:

The King of all these lands of the interior and of the river of Sofala ... heathen who adores nothing whatever, and who has no knowledge of God; on the contrary he esteems himself the god of all his lands, and is so looked upon and reverenced by his subjects, as I shall hereafter relate. He is called Quiteve, the name being common to all kings of that kingdom, who on coming to the thrown discard their former name and are never known by it again.

This Quiteve has more than a hundred wives, all with his palace, among whom are one or two of his chief wives, like queens, and the others are but concubines ...

—Portuguese account of a visit to Zimbabwe, sixteenth century.

10. Which of the following can be concluded about Great Zimbabwean society?
    (A) It had clear aspects of matriarchy.
    (B) It had clear aspects of patriarchy.
    (C) It had high levels of equality.
    (D) It had a functioning democracy.

The Governing Senate ... has deemed it necessary to make known that the land lords' serfs and peasants ... owe their landlords proper submission and absolute obedience in all matters, according to the laws that have been enacted from time immemorial by the autocratic forefathers of Her Imperial Majesty and which have not been repealed, and which provide that all persons who dare to incite serfs and peasants to disobey their landlords shall be arrested and taken to the nearest government office, there to be punished forthwith as disturbers of the public tranquility, according to the laws and without leniency. And in order that people everywhere may know of the present decree, it shall be read in all the churches on Sundays and holy days for one month after it is received and thereafter once every year during the great church festivals, lest anyone pretend ignorance.

—From Catherine II's *Decree on Serfs*, 1767.

11. Which of the following changes took place in Russia concerning serfdom?
    (A) Serfdom decreased in practice and in alignment with Western Europe.
    (B) Serfdom became more codified and harsher than it was practiced earlier.
    (C) Serfdom experienced no change and the status of serfs remained the same.
    (D) Serfdom was revived from the earlier Mongol period and Kievan Rus.

Man is born free, and everywhere he is in chains. This is because Man has given up his freedom to many masters (kings) in order to preserve his life. This primitive condition can subsist (continue) no longer. The problem now is to find a form of government which will defend and protect the life and goods of each member while still allowing each member to obey himself alone and thus remain as free as before. The Social Contract provides the solution to this fundamental (important) problem. The masses (all people) must unite together. This union of all people together is called the general will. Each person must put himself and all his power under the common control of the general will and must obey whatever the general will decides. Each member has the same power and is thus an equally important part of the whole. Through this Social Contract, man maintains as many of the freedoms he received from nature as possible. Each man, in giving his freedom to all, gives his freedom to no one. This is because there is no one over whom he does not acquire the same power as he has given (each person gives their freedom to the general will, but they also become part of the general will and have the same power as everyone else).

—Excerpts from Jean-Jacques Rousseau's *The Social Contract*, 1762.

12. The writing above by Rousseau is best understood in the context of which time and place in history?
    (A) Meiji Japan
    (B) Soviet Russia
    (C) Spanish colonial Americas
    (D) European Enlightenment

Saint-Domingue (Haitian) Constitution of 1801

TITLE II

Of the Inhabitants

Art. 3. – There cannot exist slaves on this territory, servitude is therein forever abolished. All men are born, live and die free and French.

Art. 4. – All men, regardless of color, are eligible to all employment.

Art. 5. – There shall exist no distinction other than those based on virtue and talent, and other superiority afforded by law in the exercise of a public function.

13. The statement above is best understood in the context of which of the following historical processes?
    (A) Capitalism soon replaced mercantilism as the economic philosophy of many governments.
    (B) The Industrial Revolution demanded more raw materials from nonindustrialized areas of the world.
    (C) Enlightenment principles of liberty and freedom were soon spread to non-European peoples.
    (D) Military technology of the world's armies developed deadlier ways of killing and maiming.

The prodigious extension of the several branches of the Manchester manufactures has likewise greatly increased the business of several trades and manufactures connected with or dependent upon them. The making of paper at mills in the vicinity has been brought to great perfection, and now includes all kinds, from the strongest parceling paper to the finest writing sorts, and that on which banker's bills are printed. To the ironmongers shops, which are greatly increased of late, are generally annexed smithies, where many articles are made, even to nails. A considerable iron foundry is established in Salford, in which are cast most of the articles wanted in Manchester and its neighborhood, consisting chiefly of large cast wheels for the cotton machines; cylinders, boilers, and pipes for steam engines; cast ovens, and grates of all sizes.

—Observations of a local citizen, John Aikin, in 1795.

14. The situation described in the reading above was caused by which of the following changes in British society?

   (A) Shifts in population from rural to urban areas
   (B) Increased social mobility in British class structure
   (C) The decrease in literacy and schooling for youth
   (D) Improvements in the status of women

Yesterday your Ambassador petitioned my Ministers to memorialize me regarding your trade with China, but his proposal is not consistent with our dynastic usage and cannot be entertained. Hitherto, all European nations, including your own country's barbarian merchants, have carried on their trade with our Celestial Empire at Canton. Such has been the procedure for many years, although our Celestial Empire possesses all things in prolific abundance and lacks no product within its own borders. There was therefore no need to import the manufactures of outside barbarians in exchange for our own produce.

—Qianlong Emperor, Second Edict to King George III of Great Britain, 1792.

15. What was the cause of the situation described in the account above?

   (A) The Scientific Revolution began in the Americas and Australia.
   (B) European monarchs desired more state control over religious beliefs.
   (C) Europeans began to travel to Asia in search of increased trade.
   (D) The Atlantic slave trade was increasing in volume and destinations.

—Photograph by John Warwick Brooke of a machine gun in World War I (1914–1918).

16. What was the result of this invention?

(A) The division of the world into developed and developing nations

(B) The spread of female suffrage across the Western world

(C) The conquest of the Americas by Europeans in the sixteenth century

(D) A marked increase in the extent of damage and casualties in world wars

—The American military in Haiti in 1920. Source: Times Wide World Photos.

17. Which of the following is a continuity in terms of Latin America's relationship with the United States in the twentieth century?

(A) Isolation
(B) Intervention
(C) Communism
(D) Conquest

Since return (to) Shanghai (a) few days ago I investigated reported atrocities committed by Japanese Army in Nanking and elsewhere. Verbal accounts (of) reliable eye-witnesses and letters from individuals whose credibility (is) beyond question afford convincing proof (that) Japanese Army behaved and (is) continuing (to) behave in (a) fashion reminiscent (of) Attila (and) his Huns. (Not) less than three hundred thousand Chinese civilians slaughtered, many cases (in) cold blood. Robbery, rape, including children (of) tender years, an insensate brutality towards civilians continues (to) be reported from areas where actual hostilities ceased weeks ago. Deep shame which better type (of) Japanese civilian here feel—reprehensible conduct (of) Japanese troops elsewhere heightened by series (of) local incidents where Japanese soldiers run amock (in) Shanghai itself.

—Telegram by Australian journalist Harold John Timperley that was intercepted and deciphered by American intelligence on February 1, 1938.

18. The reading above is best understood in the context of which historical event?

   (A) Japanese atrocities in the leadup to World War II in Asia
   (B) China's speeches to the Red Guards during the Cultural Revolution
   (C) Soviet Russia's territorial ambitions for Imperial Japan's Sakhalin Island
   (D) Increased tensions between the two superpowers in the postwar world

All of us, I am certain, are united by more important things than those which superficially divide us. We are united, for instance, by a common detestation of colonialism in whatever form it appears. We are united by a common detestation of racialism. And we are united by a common determination to preserve and stabilise peace in the world ... We are often told "Colonialism is dead." Let us not be deceived or even soothed by that. I say to you, colonialism is not yet dead. How can we say it is dead, so long as vast areas of Asia and Africa are unfree. And, I beg of you do not think of colonialism only in the classic form which we of Indonesia, and our brothers in different parts of Asia and Africa, knew. Colonialism has also its modern dress, in the form of economic control, intellectual control, actual physical control by a small but alien community within a nation. It is a skilful and determined enemy, and it appears in many guises. It does not give up its loot easily. Wherever, whenever and however it appears, colonialism is an evil thing, and one which must be eradicated from the earth ... .

—Sukarno, Indonesian President at the opening of
the Bandung Conference, 1955.

19. The reading above is best understood as a result of which global-wide historical process?
    (A) Cold War
    (B) World War I
    (C) Industrial Revolution
    (D) Decolonization

—Set of photos showing protesters at the Berlin Wall in 1989.

20. The destruction and eventual dismantling of the Berlin Wall above was a direct result of which of the following?

   (A) The spreading of capitalist economies due to the NAFTA agreement
   (B) The devastating loss of Germany and its allies in World War II
   (C) Wide-ranging reforms made by the Soviet premier Mikhail Gorbachev
   (D) The desire of non-Germans to reunite Germany as one country

DIAGNOSTIC QUIZ ANSWERS

1. (Chapter 1: The Postclassical Era; similar questions can be found in Questions 7 and 8 in Chapter 1: The Postclassical Era)

ANSWER: (A) Postclassical China was a time of expanding trade. Complex economic practices would have been necessary for economic growth.

2. (Chapter 1: The Postclassical Era; similar questions can be found in Questions 72 and 74 in Chapter 1: The Postclassical Era)

ANSWER: (B) Kingdoms are by their very nature centralized governments. They use monarchy, the control of trade, and religion to legitimize their rule and claim large territories.

3. (Chapter 1: The Postclassical Era; similar questions can be found in Questions 50, 118, and 119 in Chapter 1: The Postclassical Era)

ANSWER: (C) Prince Dmitry Ivanovich defeated the Golden Horde (Mongols) in battle and was the first Russian leader to openly challenge Mongol domination.

4. (Chapter 1: The Postclassical Era; similar questions can be found in Questions 38 and 93 in Chapter 1: The Postclassical Era)

ANSWER: (C) The bubonic plague devastated Europe, especially cities that were closely connected to world trade.

5. (Chapter 1: The Postclassical Era; similar questions can be found in Questions 37 and 101 in Chapter 1: The Postclassical Era, and Question 258 in Chapter 2: The Early Modern Era)

ANSWER: (B) Surprisingly, Europe's population recovered within decades of the bubonic plague. Some scholars think a period of excitement and exuberance usually follow such tragedies, as seen in the Roaring Twenties and currently in our era.

6. (Chapter 2: The Early Modern Era; similar questions can be found in Questions 66, 80, and 81 in Chapter 2: The Early Modern Era)

ANSWER: (D) The isolation of the civilizations in the Andes mountains limited their abilities and economies. Also, mining is almost always done underground.

7. (Chapter 2: The Early Modern Era; similar questions can be found in Questions 143, 144, and 149 in Chapter 2: The Early Modern Era)

ANSWER: (C) The samurai as a class were kept till the Meiji era, but many were made unemployed because, with the Pax Tokugawa, they were unnecessary. Some scholars have used the term "parasitic" to describe their status in the Tokugawa era.

8. (Chapter 2: The Early Modern Era; similar questions can be found in Questions 138 and 139 in Chapter 2: The Early Modern Era)

ANSWER: (D) The use of the terms "arts of peace," "upright conduct," "moral principle," and "purpose learning" shows a clear Confucian influence. Confucianism entered Japan during the Postclassical era along with another belief system, Buddhism.

9. (Chapter 2: The Early Modern Era; similar questions can be found in Questions 57 and 58 in Chapter 2: The Early Modern Era)

ANSWER. (A) Hindu temples always have representations of deities, humans, and animals, while Muslims have generally avoided such imagery. Qutb Minar is seen today as a symbol of Islamic triumphalism over the Hindu majority.

10. (Chapter 2: The Early Modern Era; similar questions can be found in Questions 72 and 73 in Chapter 1: The Postclassical Era and Question 254 in Chapter 2: The Early Modern Era)

ANSWER: (B) The practice of polygamy, in having multiple wives, is often a hallmark of a patriarchy. In addition, the practice of having so many wives depicts absolutism in that it shows dominance over other males.

11. (Chapter 3: The Early Modern Era; similar questions can be found in Questions 363 and 364 in Chapter 3: The Modern Era)

ANSWER: (A) Serfdom increased in czarist Russia under Catherine the Great because she felt that she needed boyar support for her reign.

12. (Chapter 3: The Modern Era; similar questions can be found in Questions 340 and 341 in Chapter 3: The Modern Era)

ANSWER: (D) Jean Jacques-Rousseau popularized the ideas of John Locke, another major Enlightenment thinker. Ideas such as the social contract and government by the consent of the governed later helped pave the way for the Atlantic Revolutions.

13. (Chapter 3: The Modern Era; similar questions can be found in Questions 324 and 325 in Chapter 3: The Modern Era)

ANSWER: (C) The Haitian Revolution broke out in 1790 when greater freedoms were demanded first among the petite blancs or lower-class whites, then the mixed race and free black populations, and finally among the vast majority of the island's population, African slaves. They key issue for this last group was the abolition of slavery.

14. (Chapter 3: The Modern Era; similar questions can be found in Questions 352 and 353 in Chapter 3: The Modern Era)

ANSWER: (A) Industrialization saw a parallel growth in cities. Manchester city in England, like other Industrial cities, grew exponentially yet lagged in political power.

15. (Chapter 3: The Modern Era; similar questions can be found in Questions 256, 257, and 260 in Chapter 3: The Modern Era)

ANSWER: (C) This letter clearly shows that the balance of power was strongly in China's favor. It had no interest and saw no benefit in changing its trading relationship with the West.

With no competition in East Asia for centuries, China had long set the terms of trade with its tribute system. However, we know that later the sale of opium will begin to alter this balance of power.

16. (Chapter 4: The Present Era; similar questions can be found in Questions 267 and 268 in Chapter 4: The Present Era: 1900–Present)

ANSWER: (D) Machine guns are sometimes described as the mechanization of death. This is a just metaphor given that they were responsible for the most combat deaths in World War I. This weapon in particular shows how the full might of the Industrial Revolution was harnessed for war.

17. (Chapter 4: The Present Era; similar questions can be found in Questions 453, 455, and 260 in Chapter 4: The Present Era: 1900–Present)

ANSWER: (B) The United States has a long history of interventions in Latin America. The United States first declared its interests in the area with the Monroe Doctrine in 1823, but with the Roosevelt Corollary, it sought to enforce this policy. It has had numerous instances of gunboat diplomacy since the late nineteenth century up until the 1983 invasion of Grenada to oust an unfavorable government. The United States has long maintained the right to interfere in its southern neighbor's affairs.

18. (Chapter 4: The Present Era; similar questions can be found in Question 390 in Chapter 4: The Present Era: 1900–Present)

ANSWER: (A) World War II differed from previous wars in its high civilian casualties. The concept of total war now meant that civilians were not just active participants but also legitimate targets.

19. (Chapter 4: The Present Era; similar questions can be found in Questions 399, 400, and 438 in Chapter 4: The Present Era: 1900–Present)

ANSWER: (D) The decolonization movement swept the world after World War II, and Sukarno was a leader of this movement. Indonesia under Sukarno was also a leader in the nonaligned movement during the Cold War in which nations, usually recently decolonized, sought to forge an independent path between the Communist and capitalist power blocs.

20. (Chapter 4: The Present Era; similar questions can be found in Questions 485 and 493 in Chapter 4: The Present Era: 1900–Present)

ANSWER: (C) Glasnost and Perestroika, the political and economic changes in the Soviet Union made by Mikhail Gorbachev, set off a desire for change in both Eastern Europe and China. The fall of the Berlin Wall was one of the many unexpected responses to Gobachev's reforms.

CHAPTER 1

The Postclassical Era:
1200 CE to 1450

Controlling Idea: Resurgence

The story here is rather simple: as we advance from the year 600 to 1200 we see that the classical civilizations have collapsed, and trade and religion lead the way in the process of recovery. The story of this unit is the story of a regeneration of centralized political authority that first matches and then surpasses levels of imperial cohesion seen in the era of classical civilizations. By 1450 a resurgence has been completed, and broadly speaking each center of civilization has recovered, consolidated, and expanded upon earlier glories. Formerly nomadic peoples have expanded, settled down, and established states. We also notice that by 1450 the major world religions are established, roughly, in the areas they hold sway until today. The great outlier when speaking in such general terms are the civilizations of the Americas, which, while developing along familiar lines seen elsewhere in the Foundations era, are not integrated into global networks of long-distance trade by 1450.

So Vanchu and Chenchu (Chinese officials), … *proceeded to communicate it to the chief people among the Cathayans (Chinese), and then by common consent sent word to their friends in many other cities that they had determined on such a day, at the signal given by a beacon, to massacre all the men with beards, and that the other cities of massacring the bearded men was that the Cathayans naturally have no beard, whilst beards are worn by the* Tartars (Central Asians), *Saracens* (Arabs and Persians), *and Christians. And you should know that all the Cathayans* (Chinese) *detested the Grand Kaan's rule because he set over them governors who were Tartars, or still more frequently Saracens, and these they could not endure, for they were treated by them just like slaves. You see the Great Kaan had not succeeded to the dominion of Cathay by hereditary right, but held it by conquest; and thus having no confidence in the natives, he put all authority into the hands of* Tartars (Central Asians), *Saracens* (Arabs and Persians), *or Christians who were attached to his household and devoted to his service, and were foreigners in Cathay.*

—The Travels of Marco Polo on his account of
a plot against the Yuan dynasty by the Chinese.

1. From the account of Marco Polo, we can conclude which of the following as true?

   (A) Marco Polo naturally sympathized with the Yuan dynasty.

   (B) The Chinese disliked facial hair or growing beards.

   (C) The Great Khan or the Yuan dynasty did not use foreigners in their employ.

   (D) Some Chinese chafed under the rule of the Mongol Yuan dynasty.

2. The Yuan dynasty tended to use many non-Han Chinese in running the government, such as Marco Polo himself, because

   (A) They had vast experience as merchants and therefore understood government.

   (B) They distrusted the Chinese who looked down upon the Mongols as barbarians.

   (C) They had connections in such far-off places as Japan and the Americas.

   (D) The Mongols could not understand the Tartar, Saracen, and Christian languages.

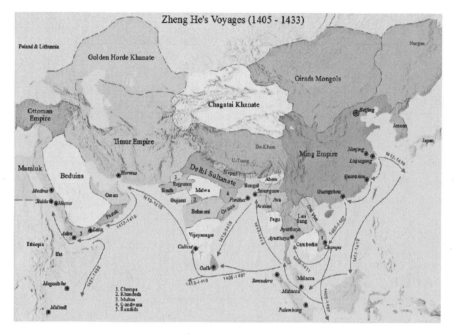

—Map showing Asian continent.

3. Which of the following best explains a historical argument on why the Chinese abandoned the commercial voyages of the Zheng He expeditions?

   (A) The trade with foreign regions was seen as unnecessary and costly with little reward for China.

   (B) The size of the fleets was so limited that they could not compete with the greater capacity of the Europeans.

   (C) Chinese navigational skills were inadequate to expand areas of expedition beyond the Pacific Ocean.

   (D) There was little of value for the Chinese to export, and the voyages were expensive to carry out.

4. China's treasure fleet voyages by Admiral Zheng He reached as far west as which of the following areas?

   (A) The Horn of Africa

   (B) The Strait of Hormuz

   (C) The Khyber Pass

   (D) The Strait of Malacca

Name of Chinese Civilizations	Dates of Rule
Song	960–1279
Yuan	1271–1368
Ming	1368–1644
Qing	1644–1911

5. The different Chinese civilizations above are most commonly defined as which of the following?

(A) Feudalists
(B) Monarchies
(C) Dynasties
(D) Shogunates

6. Which of the following philosophical innovations did traditional China develop to explain the change in ruling governments?

(A) Sinification
(B) Mandate of Heaven
(C) Three Perfections
(D) Filial piety

—Detail of a scroll painting, "Along the River During the Qingming Festival" by Zhang Zeduan.

7. The image above best supports which of the following conclusions about Song dynasty China?

   (A) The Mongol invasions devastated most Chinese cities.
   (B) There was vibrant and bustling trade in China's cities.
   (C) Buddhist beliefs spread from Central Asia.
   (D) Peasants began to migrate to Northern China.

8. Which group in Chinese society was ranked the lowest according to Confucian teachings?

   (A) Peasants
   (B) Craft workers
   (C) Merchants
   (D) Scholars

—Chinese mosque in the city of Xi'an.

9. Which of the following conclusions is best supported by the photo of an Islamic mosque with Arabic writing in the Chinese city of X'ian?

(A) Islam blended with some aspects of Chinese culture.
(B) Islamic writing was adopted by the Chinese government.
(C) Islam spread West from China to the Middle East.
(D) Chinese culture was strictly ethnocentric when it came to all outside influences.

10. Which of the following conclusions is best supported by the photo of a mosque in the Chinese city of Xi'an?

(A) China rejected Islam within its borders during the Postclassical era.
(B) Islam came to China during the Preclassical era.
(C) Islam reached China during the Postclassical era.
(D) China adopted Islam as the state religion during the Modern era.

Your servant begs leave to say that Buddhism is no more than a cult of the barbarian peoples, which spread to China in the time of the Latter Han. It did not exist here in ancient times … When Emperor Gaozu received the throne from the House of Sui, he deliberated upon the suppression of Buddhism. But at that time the various officials, being of small worth and knowledge, were unable fully to comprehend the ways of the ancient kings and the exigencies of past and present, and so could not implement the wisdom of the emperor and rescue the age from corruption. Thus the matter came to naught, to your servant's constant regret … . Now Buddha was a man of the barbarians who did not speak the language of China and wore clothes of a different fashion. His sayings did not concern the ways of our ancient kings, nor did his manner of dress conform to their laws. He understood neither the duties that bind sovereign and subject nor the affections of father and son.

—Postclassical account on Buddhism in China.

11. The attitudes above were most commonly expressed by which of the following people in traditional Chinese society?

   (A) Wandering Daoists
   (B) Muslim traders
   (C) Confucian scholars
   (D) Buddhist monks

12. Which of the following best describes the author's attitude?

   (A) Ethnocentric
   (B) Interdependent
   (C) Missionary
   (D) Warlike

Being unrepentant and lacking in shame,
I have no mind of truth and sincerity
And yet because the Name has been given by Amida Buddha
The universe is suffused with its virtues

Deeply saddening is that in these times
Both the monks and the laity in Japan
While seeking to conform with Buddhist manner and deportment,
Worship gods and spirits of the heavens and earth

—Excerpts from Shinran's Lamentation and Self-Reflection. Shinran was the founder of The Jodo (Pure Land) sect of Japanese Buddhism.

13. "Worship gods and spirits of the heavens and earth" refers clearly to the popularity of which long-standing belief system in Japan?
    (A) Daoism
    (B) Shinto
    (C) Hinduism
    (D) Buddhism

14. Which of the following is true about the arrival of Buddhism to Japan?
    (A) It took centuries to spread and gain acceptance among the Japanese people.
    (B) It helped that the Japanese spoke a form of Sanskrit, the language of India.
    (C) From Japan, Buddhism then took root in China and Korea.
    (D) With Buddhism came new technology such as gunpowder and guns.

—Buddhist Temple in Kyoto, Japan.

15. The above image proves which of the following statements?

(A) Indian Hinduism was popular in Japan.

(B) China exerted a strong influence on Japan.

(C) Buddhism was rejected by most Japanese.

(D) Islam was adopted by the Japanese court.

16. Which of the following was another area that practiced a form of Buddhism similar to that in Japan?

(A) The Philippines

(B) Polynesia

(C) Korea

(D) Pakistan

... [Daimyo] Yorimasa summoned [samurai] Watanabe Chûjitsu Tonau and ordered: "Strike off my head." Tonau could not bring himself to do this while his master was still alive. He wept bitterly. "How can I do that, my lord?" he replied. "I can do so only after you have committed suicide." "I understand," said Yorimasa. He turned to the west, joined his palms, and chanted "Hail Amidha Buddha" ten times in a loud voice. Then he composed this poem:

Like a fossil tree

Which has borne not one blossom

Sad has been my life

Sadder still to end my days

Leaving no fruit behind me.

Having spoken these lines, he thrust the point of his sword into his belly, bowed his face to the ground as the blade pierce him through, and died ... . Tonau took up his master's head and, weeping, fastened it to a stone. Then, evading the enemy, he made his way to the river and sank it in a deep place.

—Excerpts from *The Tale of the Heike*, late twelfth century.

17. The prevalence of samurai and feudal lords demonstrates which of the following historical facts about Postclassical Japan?
    (A) Japan's lack of a common culture and language
    (B) Japan's lack of political unity and government
    (C) Japan's lack of belief systems and religions
    (D) Japan's lack of access to water-based trade

18. Which of the following warrior codes was followed by the Japanese samurai?
    (A) Bushido
    (B) Kamikaze
    (C) Zen
    (D) Kamakura

19. For the Japanese samurai, which weapon was most valued as embodying the essence of the warrior?
    (A) The spear
    (B) The dagger
    (C) The bow and arrow
    (D) The sword

—Images from a Japanese scroll showing the Mongol Invasion of Japan in 1274.

20. Which of the following was a result of the Mongol invasion of Japan in 1274?

(A) It succeeded in partitioning the country into Mongol tribute states.

(B) It failed due to fierce Japanese resistance and ocean storms.

(C) It was derailed due to the death of Genghis Khan in Mongolia.

(D) It was followed by the Mongol invasion of Western Europe.

21. Which of the following later developed in Japan partly due to the Mongol Invasions in the thirteenth century?

(A) Japanese desire to engage with the world

(B) Japanese ethnocentric and xenophobic ideas

(C) Japanese cultural missions to India and China

(D) Japanese embrace of China's warrior culture

—Angkor Wat temple complex.

22. The Angkor Wat Temple in Cambodia shows a strong cultural influence from which of the following regions?
   (A) Chinese
   (B) Persian
   (C) Roman
   (D) Indian

23. The Angkor Wat Temple shows the influence from which two belief systems?
   (A) Hinduism and Buddhism
   (B) Islam and Sikhism
   (C) Jainism and Hinduism
   (D) Confucian and Daoism

Reading 1

The local people who know how to trade are all women. So when a Chinese goes to this country, the first thing he must do is take in a woman, partly with a view to profiting from her trading abilities.

—On Cambodian women.

Reading 2

When the king goes out, troops are at the head of [his] escort; then come flags, banners and music. Palace women, numbering from three to five hundred, wearing flowered cloth, with flowers in their hair, hold candles in their hands, and form a troupe. Even in broad daylight, the candles are lighted. Then come other palace women, bearing royal paraphernalia made of gold and silver … . Then come the palace women carrying lances and shields, with the king's private guards. Carts drawn by goats and horses, all in gold, come next. Ministers and princes are mounted on elephants, and in front of them one can see, from afar, their innumerable red umbrellas. After them come the wives and concubines of the king, in palanquins, carriages, on horseback and on elephants. They have more than one hundred parasols, flecked with gold. Behind them comes the sovereign, standing on an elephant, holding his sacred sword in his hand. The elephant's tusks are encased in gold.

—On a royal procession of King Indravaraman III.
—Zhao Daguan, An Account of Cambodia, circa 1300.

24. Based on Reading 1 above, which of the following is true of interaction between China and Cambodia?
    (A) Chinese traders adapted to local customs.
    (B) The Chinese aggressively began to spread their culture.
    (C) Chinese women were jealous of foreign women.
    (D) Chinese merchants forbade all contact with locals.

25. In both readings above, which is true of women in Cambodian society?
    (A) Women in Cambodia were segregated and required to stay at home with the family.
    (B) Women in Cambodia were not subject to the strict patriarchy common to much of Asia.
    (C) Women in China and Cambodia were forced to cover their face and hair when outside.
    (D) Women in Cambodia ruled over the king and men in their families.

—Photo in Vietnam, 2010.

26. The above image helps proves which of the following statements?
    (A) Buddhism promotes the monastic lifestyle for its followers.
    (B) Vietnamese men shaved their hair in respect for the Emperor.
    (C) Islamic identity is strong in northern Vietnam.
    (D) Confucian ethics are not promoted in Vietnam.

27. Which form of Buddhism was most influential in Vietnam?
    (A) Theravada
    (B) Mahayana
    (C) Zen
    (D) Shinto

Islam's success was primarily due to a process that historians term "localization," by which Islamic teachings were often adapted in ways that avoided major conflicts with existing attitudes and customs. Local heroes often became Islamic saints, and their graves were venerated places at which to worship. Some aspects of mystical Islam resembled pre-Islamic beliefs, notably on Java. Cultural practices like cockfighting and gambling continued, and spirit propitiation (appeasing a god, spirit or person) remained central in the lives of most Muslims, despite Islam's condemnation of polytheism. Women never adopted the full face veil, and the custom of taking more than one wife was limited to wealthy elites. Law codes based on Islam usually made adjustments to fit local customs.

—Essay *Introduction to Southeast Asia* by Barbara Watson Andaya.

28. Islam's coexistence with indigenous beliefs was most similar to which area of the world that also practiced Islam?
    (A) Saudi Arabia
    (B) Egypt
    (C) West Africa
    (D) Persia

29. The mention of the practice of "mystical Islam" refers most likely to which of the following?
    (A) Shia/Shiite
    (B) Sufism
    (C) Sharia
    (D) Saudi

Short-Answer Question

Whenever I visited Jerusalem I always entered the Aqsa Mosque, beside which stood a small mosque, which the Franks had converted into a church. When I used to enter the Aqsa Mosque, which was occupied by the Templars, who were my friends, the Templars would evacuate the little adjoining mosque so that I might pray in it. One day I entered this mosque, repeated the first formula, "Allah is great," and stood up in the act of praying. Then one of the Franks rushed to me, got hold of me and turned my face eastward, saying, "This is the way you should pray!" The Templars came up to him and expelled him. They apologized to me, saying, "This is a stranger who has only recently arrived from the land of Franks and he has never before seen anyone praying except eastward."

—Usamah Ibn Munqidh, twelfth-century Muslim writer on the Crusaders whom he calls the Franks.

30. Describe ONE way the reading supports the idea of conflict during the late Postclassical era.

31. Describe ONE way the reading shows cultural exchange during the late Postclassical era.

32. Describe and analyze the geographic and historical background for this reading.

—Muslim scientists in *The House of Wisdom*.

33. Based on the image above, which of the following is true of Islamic Civilization by the time of the Abbasid empire?

   (A) They taught and tested Confucian values in their schools.
   (B) They achieved great advances in the sciences.
   (C) They expanded to rule over northern Europe.
   (D) They used a Sanskrit form of writing.

34. Which city became the capital of the Abbasid Empire and a center of what has been termed an Islamic golden age?

   (A) Istanbul
   (B) Timbuktu
   (C) Seville
   (D) Baghdad

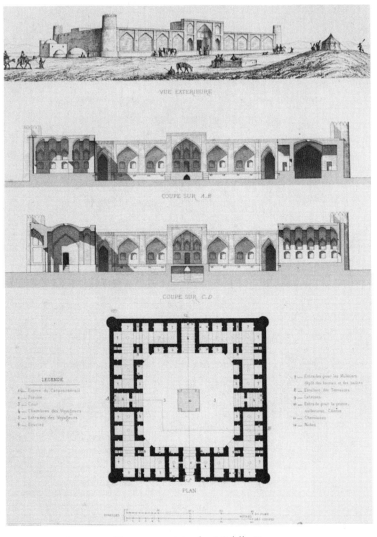

—Caravanserai in the Middle East.

35. Which of the following was a continuity in the use of the caravanserai depicted above?

(A) They provided food, lodging, and a place to conduct business along the western end of the Silk Road.

(B) They were used as military strong points and fortifications by the Arabs against the European Crusaders.

(C) They acted as centers of religious worship and helped to promote Nestorian Christianity and Judaism.

(D) These are examples of monumental architecture to glorify the local elites and give patronage to artists.

36. Which of the following historical events helped diminish the use of the buildings shown?

(A) The seven treasure fleet voyages of the Chinese admiral Zheng He
(B) The defeat of the Mongols over vast swaths of Eurasian territory
(C) Vasco da Gama's ships reaching India using an all-water route
(D) The Viking Leif Erickson founding a settlement in eastern Canada

News reached [Cairo and Syria] that the plague in Damascus had been less deadly than in Tripoli, Hama, and Aleppo. From … [October 1348] death raged with intensity. 1200 people died daily and, as a result, people stopped requesting permits from the administration to bury the dead and many cadavers were abandoned in gardens and on the roads … .

Family celebrations and marriages no longer took place … . No one held any festivities during the entire duration of the epidemic, and no voice was heard singing … . The call to prayer was suspended at many locations, and even at the most important ones, there remained only a single muezzin [caller to prayer] … .

Most of the mosques and zawiyas [Sufi lodges] were closed … .

The same thing happened throughout Egypt. When harvest time arrived, many farmers already perished [and no field hands remained to gather crops]. Soldiers and their young slaves or pages headed for the fields. They tried to recruit workers by promising them half of the proceeds, but they could not find anyone to gather the harvest. They threshed the grain with their horses [hoofs], and winnowed the grain themselves, but, unable to carry all the grain back, they had to abandon much of it … .

Workers disappeared. You could not find either water carriers, or launderers or servants. The monthly salary of a horse groom rose from 30 to 80 dirhams … . This epidemic, they say, continued in several countries for 15 years.

—*The Bubonic Plague in Syria and Egypt, 1453*
by Ahmad al Maqrizi.

37. Which of the following is true of the effects of the Black Death on the Middle East?

(A) There were outbreaks of violence against Jews and other minorities.
(B) There was an increase in the amount of people to act as a labor force.
(C) There was an increase in the wages that laborers could command.
(D) There was a prolonged decrease in trade in the Mediterranean Sea.

38. In comparison to the Black Death in Europe, the Mamluk Sultanate government's reaction to the crisis

(A) Was similar in closing down public gatherings
(B) Was different in the wages paid to laborers
(C) Was in contrast to scapegoating the gypsies
(D) Was the same in forcing soldiers into slavery

—"Preparing Medicine from Honey," depicting thirteenth-century stove technology in the Middle East.

39. The ingredients in the cookbook would reflect which of the following?
(A) The lack of foods from the New World
(B) The inclusion of foods only from the Fertile Crescent
(C) The frequent use of pork products
(D) The lack of foods from animal products

40. As referenced by the cookbook, which of the following demonstrates a strong continuity in the region?
(A) The introduction of honey as a medicine
(B) The use of Arabic script in the Middle East
(C) The spread of the Islamic religion
(D) The switch from wood stoves to clay stoves

This terminology—ancient, medieval, modern—is not used almost univer-
sally, whether appropriate or not. Those of you who are students of Islam will
certainly be aware of the famous book called "Medieval Islam" written by
one of the most distinguished scholars in the field. It is an excellent book, but
the title is an absurdity: what it means is not Medieval Islam—it means that
period of Islamic history which corresponds to the Medieval period in European
history. This classification—ancient, medieval, modern—is European; it was
invented by Europeans to classify the different phases of European history;
it was either adopted by or imposed upon the rest of the world, whether
appropriate or not.

—From the historian Bernard Lewis.

41. The secondary source on historical writing above is best understood in the
context of
(A) Medievalism
(B) Islamic exceptionalism
(C) Eurocentrism
(D) Globalization

42. In contrast with East Asia, the periodization of history there is divided into
which of the following units for study?
(A) Millenniums (1,000 years)
(B) Dynasties
(C) Empires
(D) Religions

43. According to the reasoning put forth in the reading, which historical
change begins the era in the Middle East termed "Medieval"?
(A) The birth of Jesus Christ
(B) The fall of Rome
(C) The rise of Islam
(D) The European Crusades

44. Which long-distance trade network was stabilized in the period historians term the Pax Mongolica (Mongol Peace)?

    (A) Indian Ocean routes
    (B) Triangular trade routes
    (C) East Asian sea routes
    (D) Silk Roads

45. Based on the map above, the Mongol empire stretched as far east as

    (A) Central Asia
    (B) Russia
    (C) Korea
    (D) Arabian Peninsula

46. Based on the map above, the Mongol protectorate that later became the Khanate of the Golden Horde consists of parts of the modern nation of

    (A) Russia
    (B) Iran
    (C) China
    (D) India

47. Which of the following would have been outside the sphere of Mongol control at its height?

    (A) Italy
    (B) Russia
    (C) Persia
    (D) Mesopotamia

—Ceramic piece, *Western Musicians on a Camel*, Tang dynasty.

48. Which of the following conclusions can be made?

(A) The diffusion of culture flowed from Japan to China and the rest of East Asia.

(B) Sea links existed with the East African coast using steam boats.

(C) The use of animal power was replaced by industrialization during the Song dynasty.

(D) Economic and cultural links existed between East Asia and the Middle East.

49. The image above bests supports which of the following conclusions?

(A) Transportation was suited to climate and topography.

(B) Religious beliefs governed the treatment of animals.

(C) There was a decrease in ceramic technology after the Han dynasty.

(D) There was a lack of diffusion in music from China.

Special ambassadors [reported] that a monstrous ... race of men had taken possession of the extensive, rich lands of the east ... If [the Saracens] themselves could not withstand the attacks of such people, nothing remained to prevent their devastating the countries of the West ... . [Regarding their] cruelty ... there can be no infamy [great enough] ... . The Tartar[s] ... fed upon their [victim's] carcasses ... and left nothing but the bones for the vultures.

Source: Matthew Paris, quoted in *Storm from the East.*

Their style of conversation is courteous; they ... have an air of good breeding, and eat their victuals with particular cleanliness. To their parents they show the utmost reverence ... . The order ... of all ranks of people, when they present themselves before his majesty ought not to pass unnoticed. When they approach ... [him] they show their respect ... by assuming a humble, placid, and quiet demeanor.

Source: Marco Polo, quoted in *Genghis Khan and Mongol Rule.*

50. What impact would Matthew Paris's description have on Europeans?
    (A) They would have feared the Mongols as barbaric warriors.
    (B) They would have welcomed the Mongols as fellow warrior peoples.
    (C) They would have been confused based on the different names Paris used.
    (D) They would have been felt confident that Christ would protect them.

51. Which of the following is true of the above description of the Mongols by Marco Polo?
    (A) It is a secondary source on the Mongols.
    (B) It complemented Matthew Paris's account.
    (C) It reinforced the view of the Mongols as barbaric.
    (D) It contradicts Matthew Paris's negative account.

—Mongol Passport made of iron with silver inlay. The script is Phagspa, a written language developed by Tibetan monks for the Mongolian empire. It reads:

> *By the strength of Eternal Heaven,*
> *an edict of the Emperor* [Khan].
> *He who has no respect shall be guilty.*

52. The image above is best understood in the context of which of the following?

(A) The spread of Islam to Central Asia
(B) Eurasian metallurgy technology
(C) The historical era Pax Mongolia
(D) The retraction of urbanization

53. The above Mongol passport represents which of the following?

(A) State promotion of trade activity
(B) Nonstate promotion of trade activity
(C) Merchants upset at their low status
(D) Barriers against cultural connections

54. The use of Tibetan script by the Mongols is similar to which of the following?

(A) The Mongol use of horses and Bactrian camels
(B) The conversion to Islam among most Mongol rulers
(C) The Mongol conquest of China and Russia
(D) The Mongol institution of nonhereditary rulers

—Coins from the Delhi Sultanate in India.

55. Which the following acts best as context for the image of the coins above?

(A) Roman coins were still in use by the later half of the postclassical era.

(B) Metallurgy technology for coins was still in their infancy.

(C) The Silk Road went as far east as India's Delhi Sultanate.

(D) Indian Ocean trade was largely dominated by Muslim traders.

56. Based on the image above, which of the following is true about the Delhi Sultanate?

(A) They used an Arabic writing system.

(B) They used a Chinese writing system.

(C) They used a Latin writing system.

(D) They used a Japanese writing system.

—Qutb Minar tower built to celebrate the victory of the Delhi Sultanate over the Hindu Kingdom near Delhi. The building in front with the white dome is the tomb of the saint Imam Zamin.

57. The image above represents which of the following changes in historical India in the later part of the postclassical era?

   (A) Construction using stone as building materials
   (B) The beginning of Islamic rule in Northern India
   (C) The banning of entry to lower caste families
   (D) The carving of Hindu inscriptions on monuments

58. The Qutb Minar seems to have been built to represent which of the following?

   (A) The introduction of Islam into India by sea going merchants and traders
   (B) A tall brick observatory to study astronomy, astrology, and geography
   (C) The triumph of Islam over Hinduism through monumental architecture
   (D) The collapse of Sufi Islamic practices and dome architecture

—"Dance of Sufi Dervishes." Unknown author, from the illustrated book *Divane Hafez Shirazi*, circa 1480.

59. A historical argument on the popularity of Sufi practices in India is that it was due to

(A) The division of Islam into two sects, Sunni and Shia
(B) The influence of Indian culinary traditions
(C) Constant conflict among Indian Hindus
(D) A focus on spirituality and less on doctrines

60. Which of the following terms best describes Sufi Islam?

(A) Fundamentalist
(B) Mystical
(C) Syncretic
(D) Animist

61. The Persian miniature that bears the image of Sufis dancing demonstrates which of the following misnomers about the Islamic world?

(A) Islamic beliefs and practices are not monolithic.
(B) Islamic practices do not allow for regional variation.
(C) Islamic beliefs borrow much from Zoroastrianism.
(D) Islamic texts promote the depictions of humans.

Again as in the case of West Africa, trade brought culture as well as political changes to east Africa. Like their counterparts in West Africa, the ruling elites and wealthy merchants of East Africa converted to the Islamic faith. They did not necessarily give up their religious and cultural traditions but rather continued to observe them for purposes of providing cultural leadership for their societies. By adopting Islam, however, they laid a cultural foundation for close cooperation with Muslim merchants trading in the Indian Ocean. Moreover Islam served as a fresh source of legitimacy for their rule, since they gained recognition from Islamic states in Southwest Asia, and their conversion opened the door to political alliances with Muslim rulers in other lands. Even though the conversion of elite classes, did not bring about the immediate spread of Islam throughout their societies, it enabled Islam to establish a presence in East Africa.

—Jeremy Bentley in *Traditions and Encounters.*

62. The above reading demonstrates which of the following?
    (A) The conversion to Islam in West Africa was from the bottom up.
    (B) West African rulers and elite saw clear benefits in converting to Islam.
    (C) Trade played little role in spreading Islam to West Africa.
    (D) Islam entered East Africa from Southern European traders.

63. Based on the secondary source above, in West Africa, the practice of Islam
    (A) Coexisted with previous forms of worship like animism
    (B) Completely replaced animism and other belief systems
    (C) Linked West Africa directly with Southeast Asia
    (D) Established a caste system similar to that in India

64. Which of the following trade networks is limited to the confines of the African continent?

    (A) Triangular trade routes
    (B) Indian Ocean
    (C) Mediterranean Sea
    (D) Trans-Saharan

65. Which of the following was a common unifying feature of sub-Saharan African societies in the postclassical era?

    (A) Adoption of Islam by nonelites
    (B) Broad-based expansion of literacy among the masses of the people
    (C) Common Bantu linguistic roots
    (D) Steam-powered industrial base of the economy

66. Which global force was the FIRST to consistently integrate sub-Saharan Africa into a global network of exchange of goods and ideas?

    (A) Islamic civilization
    (B) Modern globalization
    (C) Transatlantic slave trade
    (D) The Roman Empire

The women there have "friends" and "companions" amongst the men out-side their own families, and the men in the same way have "companions" amongst the women of other families. A man may go into his house and find his wife entertaining her "companion" but he takes no objection to it. One day at Iwalatan I went into the qadi's (Islamic judge) house, after asking his permission to enter, and found with him a young woman of remarkable beauty. When I saw her I was shocked and turned to go out, but she laughed at me, instead of being overcome by shame, and the qadi said to me "Why are you going out? She is my companion." I was amazed at their conduct, for he was a theologian and a pilgrim [to Mecca] to boot. I was told that he had asked the sultan's permission to make the pilgrimage that year with his "companion"—whether this one or not I cannot say—but the sultan would not grant it.

—Ibn Battuta, a Muslim traveler to Mali from
1351–1353, recounts his experiences.

67. Which of the following best describes Ibn Battuta's viewpoint toward his fellow Muslims in Mali?

    (A) Approving
    (B) Indifferent
    (C) Friendly
    (D) Critical

68. Based on the above text, what did Ibn Battuta most disapprove of in West Africa?

    (A) Gender and marriage relations
    (B) The lack of Islamic judges or qadi
    (C) The less-than-friendly nature of Malians
    (D) The long journey required of pilgrimage

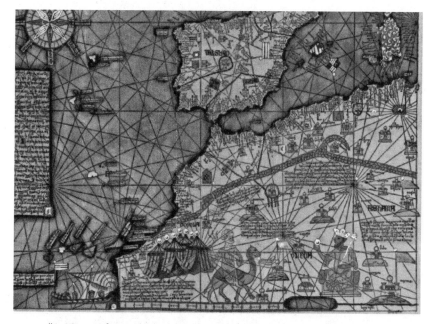

—"A West African king [Mansa Musa] holding a gold nugget" in a Spanish Catalan Atlas dated 1375.

69. Which of the following conclusions can be deduced from the map above?

(A) The African gold trade was integral to Europe during the fourteenth century.

(B) Europeans had no knowledge of camels as a method of transportation.

(C) The West African Malian king Mansa Musa was unknown to Europeans.

(D) Europeans had no interest in West Africa trade or its people.

70. Based on your knowledge of the trans-Saharan trade network of Postclassical Africa, which item was purportedly traded for gold in equal weights?

(A) Feathers

(B) Fabrics

(C) Salt

(D) Copper

71. The Malian king Mansa Musa is most famous in the West for which of the following acts?

(A) Banning the sale of Africans to Europeans or Arab slave traders

(B) His lavish fourteenth-century pilgrimage to Mecca and Medina

(C) Converting to and helping to spread Roman Catholic Christianity

(D) Boosting the local economies of North Africa and Southern Europe

Image #1: One of eight bird monoliths, made of soapstone and found in the ruins of Great Zimbabwe.

Image #2: Ruins of Great Zimbabwe, circa 1200–1400.

72. The first photo above of the ruins in southern Africa best demonstrates the existence of which of the following aspects of life in southern Africa?

(A) Small colonies of Roman craftsmen who first settled in southern Africa

(B) Nomadic groups who were skilled in the building of religious architecture

(C) A civilization with enough surpluses of food to support skilled crafts workers

(D) A strict caste society based on the worship of animal-themed deities

73. By 1500 which of the following changes occurred in Zimbabwe?

(A) It began to dominate the export of slaves in the Indian Ocean.

(B) It sent Christian missionaries north to Ethiopia and Sudan.

(C) It became a world famous center of Islamic learning.

(D) It declined due to various causes and was abandoned.

74. The Great Zimbabwe ruins had some walls that were an impressive 33 feet high. There are numerous reasons scholars have offered for this, but which of the following was the least likely explanation?

(A) They were built to deter potential attacks on the center of political power.

(B) They were built as monumental architecture to awe supporters and visitors.

(C) They were built to impress later European imperialists to show that Africa was advanced.

(D) They were built to highlight the city as an administrative and trading center.

—Spanish colonial-era drawing of a native Incan with a *quipu*.

75. The image above of the quipu shows that the Incas

(A) established contacts with ancient Egyptians
(B) had a fully formed writing system
(C) wore quipu to ritual human sacrifices
(D) developed a method of keeping records

76. The Incas developed the quipu due to which historical fact?

(A) They borrowed the quipu system from visiting Phoenician merchants.
(B) Their complex and growing empire demanded a system of record keeping.
(C) They brought the system with them when they migrated from Siberia.
(D) It was also widely used in China and adapted to the Americas.

—Nineteenth-century sketch of an Aztec-era pyramid.

77. Based on the above image, which of the following is NOT believed to be true of the ancient Aztecs?

(A) They built monumental architecture for religious purposes.

(B) They used these structures for their human sacrifices.

(C) They built these structures as palaces for their emperors.

(D) They used corvée labor as a form of taxation of their subjects.

78. Which of the following historical trends is represented by the image above?

(A) The Aztec subjects were required to give corvée labor to build public works projects.

(B) The Aztecs, ruling from their pyramid structures, conducted extensive trade with the Incas.

(C) The Aztecs brought these architectural and building technologies from their homeland in Siberia.

(D) The Aztecs initiated the building of new defensive structures to resist the invasions of the Mayans.

79. Aztec and Incan civilizations managed to construct monumental structures without which of the following?

(A) Writing systems

(B) State authority

(C) Draft animals

(D) Stone tools

—Map of South America showing topographical information and the extent of the Incan empire.

80. Based on the map above, which of the following is true?

(A) The Incas overcame difficult geographic challenges.

(B) The Incas ruled over the Amazon rainforest.

(C) The Incas were heavily influenced by the Maya.

(D) The Incas did not build cities or urban centers.

81. Which of the following best describes the region where the Inca civilization flourished?

(A) Amazon basin and rainforest

(B) Mexican plateau and highlands

(C) Andean highland and Pacific coast

(D) Yucatan Peninsula and Pampas

—Photograph of Incan terrace farming and ruins.

82. The image above of Incan terrace farming is most similar to agricultural techniques in which of the following areas of the world?

(A) Russia
(B) China
(C) India
(D) England

83. Which of the following crops were grown in the Incan Empire?

(A) Rice, corn, and cabbage
(B) Wheat, barley, and oats
(C) Sorghum, maize, and beats
(D) Potatoes, corn, and beans

84. The farming techniques shown above are labor intensive. One continuity in the labor system used by both the Incas and the Spanish conquistadors is which of the following?

(A) Slave labor
(B) Mita labor
(C) Indentured servitude
(D) Wage labor

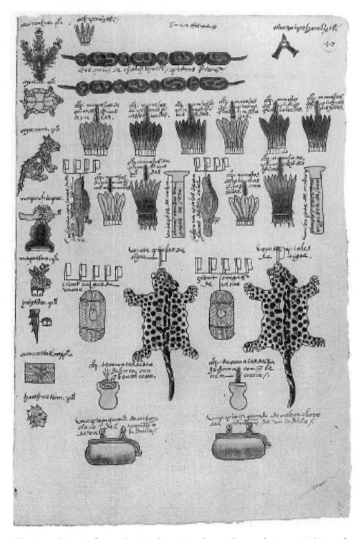

—Illustrated page from the Codex Mendoza. Created circa 1542 to show goods from neighboring cities that were delivered to Tenochtitlan, the Mexican capital. The goods include gems, feathers, jaguar pelts, and cacao.

85. Which of the following historical claims about the Aztec state can be supported based on the image?

    (A) The Aztecs kept records using a writing system borrowed from China.

    (B) The Aztecs were military dominated by the growing Incan empire.

    (C) The Aztecs were sent rare and valuable tributary goods by neighboring states.

    (D) The Aztecs traded with European states such as France and England.

86. Which of the following is a limitation of the image as an accurate source of information about the Aztec empire?

    (A) It was created by the Spanish after their conquest of the Aztecs.
    (B) It was written by the official Aztec scribes who later died.
    (C) It was biased since it was later stored in Christian monasteries.
    (D) It includes rare and valuable trade goods like bird feathers.

87. The historical situation in the image will later contribute to which of the following events?

    (A) The Spanish will easily gain Indian allies in their conquest of the Aztecs.
    (B) The non-Aztecs will soon demand better trade conditions with the English.
    (C) The level of trade between the Aztecs and neighboring states will increase.
    (D) The trade between the Aztecs and its neighbors will become seaborne.

Anthropologically classified as central-based wanderers, the Inuit spent part of the year on the move, searching for food, and then part of the year at a central, more permanent camp. Anywhere from a dozen to fifty people traveled in a hunting group. The year was divided into three hunting seasons, revolving around one animal. The hunting seasons were seal, caribou, and whale. The yearly cycle began with the spring seal hunting, continued with caribou hunting in the summer, and fishing in the autumn. A caribou hunt was also mounted in the fall. In the far north, whales were hunted in the early spring. It was a relentless cycle, broken up with occasional feasts after the seal and caribou hunts, and with summer trade fairs to which groups from miles around attended.

—Secondary source on Inuit life.

88. Which of the following best explains the geographic spread of Inuit people from Alaska to Greenland?

    (A) Their knowledge of Arctic trade winds to travel long distances
    (B) Their galleons and use of the astrolabe to navigate by
    (C) Their continuing ability to adapt to harsh environments
    (D) Their syncretic belief systems based on the geographic features

89. In comparison to the indigenous Inuit societies, the Greenland Vikings

    (A) Thrived on walrus meat for food and ivory for trade
    (B) Slowly declined due to lack of food and disease
    (C) Built up large settlements and expanded to Iceland
    (D) Enthusiastically adapted to Inuit lifestyles and culture

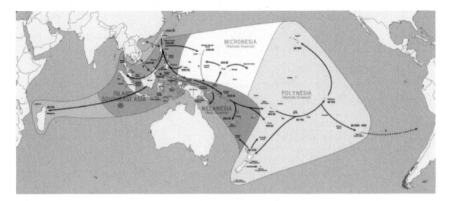

—Map showing the diaspora of Austronesian peoples across the Indo-Pacific oceans.

90. Which of the following Austronesian migrations is an unproven theory?

(A) The journey to Madagascar off the east coast of Africa

(B) The discovery and settlement of New Zealand

(C) Voyages taken across the Pacific to the Americas

(D) The colonization of the Hawaiian islands

91. The spread of the Austronesian language group is comparable to which of the following language groups?

(A) Bantu-speaking people throughout Africa

(B) Latin languages in eastern Europe

(C) Arabic languages into South Asia

(D) Siberian languages to China

92. One explanation for the extent of the Austronesian/Polynesian spread across the Indo-Pacific oceans is due to which of the following?

(A) Their search for gold and silver sources

(B) The use of the compass and navigational charts

(C) Outrigger canoes and knowledge of trade winds

(D) Land bridges and small bodies of water

Document-Based Question

Please work separately from the book on loose-leaf paper to flush out your ideas before committing your answer to space below.

93. Develop an argument on the impact of the Black Death on the world in the fourteenth century.

Document 1

Source: Lorenzo di Filippo Strozzi, *Description of the Plague at Florence in the Year 1527.*

Our pitiful Florence now looks like nothing but a town which has been stormed by infidels and then forsaken. One part of the inhabitants ... have retired to distant country houses, one part is dead, and yet another part is dying. Thus the present is torment, the future menace, so we contend with death and only live in fear and trembling. The clean, fine streets which formerly teemed with rich and noble citizens are now stinking and dirty; crowds of beggars drag themselves through them with anxious groans and only with difficulty and dread can one pass them. Shops and inns are closed, at the factories work has ceased, the law courts are empty, the laws are trampled on. Now one hears of some theft, now of some murder. The squares, the market places on which citizens used frequently to assemble, have now been converted into graves and into the resort of the wicked rabble ... If by chance relations meet, a brother, a sister, a husband, a wife, they carefully avoid each other. What further words are needed? Fathers and mothers avoid their own children and forsake them ... A few provision stores are still open, where bread is distributed, but where in the crush plague boils are also spread. Instead of conversation ... one hears now only pitiful, mournful tidings—such a one is dead, such a one is sick, such a one has fled, such a one is interned in his house, such a one is in hospital, such a one has nurses, another is without aid, such like news which by imagination alone would suffice to make Aesculapius sick.

Document 2

Source: *The Bubonic Plague in Syria and Egypt, 1453* by Ahmad al Maqrizi.

News reached [Cairo and Syria] that the plague in Damascus had been less deadly than in Tripoli, Hama, and Aleppo. From [October 1348] death raged with intensity. 1200 people died daily and, as a result, people stopped requesting permits from the administration to bury the dead and many cadavers were abandoned in gardens and on the roads ...

Family celebrations and marriages no longer took place ... No one held any festivities during the entire duration of the epidemic, and no voice was heard singing ... The call to prayer was suspended at many locations, and even at the most important ones, there remained only a single muezzin [caller to prayer] ...

Most of the mosques and zawiyas [Sufi lodges] were closed ...

The same thing happened throughout Egypt. When harvest time arrived, many farmers already perished [and no field hands remained to gather crops]. Soldiers and their young slaves or pages headed for the fields. They tried to recruit workers by promising them half of the proceeds, but they could not find anyone to gather the harvest. They threshed the grain with their horses [hoofs], and winnowed the grain themselves, but, unable to carry all the grain back, they had to abandon much of it ...

Workers disappeared. You could not find either water carriers, or launderers or servants. The monthly salary of a horse groom rose from 30 to 80 dirhams ... This epidemic, they say, continued in several countries for 15 years.

Document 3

Source: *Chronicles of Novgorod,* Russia, 1452

There was a very great plague in Pleskov. The same year envoys arrived in Novgorod from Pleskov calling the VZadyka to Pleskov to bless the people. And the Vladyka heard their prayer and went and blessed the people of Pleskov, and on his way back to Novgorod going from Pleskov he was seized with a severe illness, and died at the Uza river on the 3rd day of July, Tuesday, at nine of the day, the day of the Holy Martyr Akinf.1 The same year Vladyka Moisei erected a stone church in the name of the Assumption of the Holy Mother of God in the Volotov [field]. The same year they led Vladyka Moisei with prayers on his own throne in St. Sophia.

The same year there was a great plague in Novgorod; it came on us by God's loving kindness, and in His righteous judgment, death came upon people, painful and sudden, it began from Lady Day till Easter; a countless number of good people died then. These were the symptoms of that death: a man would spit blood and after three days he was dead. But this death did not visit Novgorod alone; I believe it passed over the face of all the land; and whom ever God commanded, that man died, and whomever he saved, him he admonished and punished, that the rest of our days we may live in the Lord virtuously and sinlessly.

Document 4

Source: The Flagellants at Doornik in 1349.

In the aforesaid year it came to pass that on the day of the Assumption of the Blessed Virgin (Aug. 15) some 200 persons came here from Bruges about [noon. These remained assembled on the market-place, and immediately the whole town was filled with curiosity as to why these folk had come. The burgesses came in small bodies to the market-place when the heard the news in order to convince them of the fact by their own eyes. Meantime the folk from Bruges prepared to perform their ceremonies which they called "penance." The inhabitants of both sexes, who had never before seen any such thing], began to imitate the actions of the strangers, to torment themselves also by the penitential exercises and to thank God for this means of penance which seemed to them most effectual. [And the people from Bruges remained in the town the whole of that day and night.]

Document 5

Source: Woodcut showing the massacre of Jews in Germany, 1493.

On Saturday - that was St. Valentine's Day-they burnt the Jews on a wooden plat-form in their cemetery. There were about two thousand people of them. Those who wanted to baptize themselves were spared. [Some say that about a thousand accepted baptism.] Many small children were taken out of the fire and baptized against the will of their fathers and mothers. And everything that was owed to the Jews was cancelled, and the Jews had to surrender all pledges and notes that they had taken for debts. The council, however, took the cash that the Jews possessed and divided it among the working-men proportionately. The money was indeed the thing that killed the Jews. If they had been poor and if the feudal lords had not been in debt to them, they would not have been burnt. After this wealth was divided among the artisans some gave their share to the Cathedral or to the Church on the advice of their confessors.

Thus were the Jews burnt at Strasbourg, and in the same year in all the cities of the Rhine, whether Free Cities or Imperial Cities or cities belonging to the lords. In some towns they burnt the Jews after a trial, in others, without a trial. In some cities the Jews themselves set fire to their houses and cremated themselves.

—An account of how the Black Death impacted the
Jewish community of Strasbourg.

Document 6

Source: *"The Origin of Quarantine" by Paul Sehdev, 2002.*

Three years later, in 1377, the first maritime quarantine was established at Venice's trading colony of Ragusa. All ships that visited the colony were required by law to anchor outside the harbor for a period of thirty days* while port authorities inspected the crew and cargo in order to determine any potential health threat.[41] The quarantine law consisted of four tenets:

(1) That citizens or visitors from plague-endemic areas would not be admitted into Ragusa until they had first remained in isolation for 1 month; (2) that no person from Ragusa was permitted go to the isolation area, under penalty of remaining there for 30 days; (3) that persons not assigned by the Great Council to care for those being quarantined were not permitted to bring food to isolated persons, under penalty of remaining with them for 1 month; and (4) that whoever did not observe these regulations would be fined and subjected to isolation for 1 month.[42]

*Eventually extended from thirty to forty days

Document 7

Source: Woodcuts of the Danse Macabre.

Figure 1: *Danse Macabre* by Michael Wolgemut, 1493.

Figure 2: Woodcut, *The Abbess* by Holbein, 1549.

—Two medieval illustrations (*August, June*) in the *Book of Hours* by Pol de Lumbourg, circa 1412–1416.

94. The image on the right of European society in the late Middle Ages is best understood in the context of which of the following truisms?

(A) The power of the Roman Catholic Church over daily life
(B) The agricultural basis for the medieval economy
(C) The strong possibility of social mobility that existed
(D) The use of vernacular languages like English and French

95. One continuity that is exemplified by the two images is one of

(A) Trade as the basis for the European economy
(B) The use of Latin as the vernacular language
(C) The lack of seasonal change in Europe
(D) Widespread social inequality

96. In the image on the right, which term best fits the individuals doing the physical labor on the land?

(A) Peddlers

(B) Serfs

(C) Slaves

(D) Sufis

97. Based on the images, one fact of European politics was the existence of

(A) A sharp religious division between Catholics and Protestants

(B) The unfair taxation policy against the nobility

(C) The formal alliances made between merchants and peasants

(D) Fortified castles that demonstrated the strength of the nobility

*I, John of Toul, make it known that I am the faithful man of the lady,
Beatrice, Countess of Troyes, and my most dear lord, Theobald, Count of
Champagne, her son against a person living or dead, except for my allegiance
to lord, Enjorand of Coucy, Lord John of Arcis and the count of Grandpre.
If it should happen that the count of Grandpre should be at war with the
countess and the count of Champagne on his own quarrel, I will aid the
count of Grandpre in my own person and will send to the count and countess
of Champagne the knights whose service I own them for the fief which I hold
of them.*

—A Vassal Pledges Loyalty, circa 1200s.

98. The text above concerning counts, vassals, and allegiances is in the context
of which system of the European Middle Ages?
(A) Mercantilism
(B) Feudalism
(C) Chivalry
(D) Chinampas

99. In the Medieval Europe system above, in return for loyalty and military
service, nobles would receive fiefs from their overlords, including land,
houses, castles, and serf peasants. This system came about primarily due to
a lack of which of the following conditions?
(A) Religious unity
(B) End of Viking attacks
(C) A centralized government
(D) A common language

100. In comparison, a similar system of land for loyalty among lords and their
vassals developed in which of the following non-European countries?
(A) India
(B) Japan
(C) China
(D) Persia (Iran)

Hanseatic League Imports and Exports* (March 18, 1368 to March 10, 1369)

*In thousands of Port Lubeck marks

Imports		Ports	Exports		Total	%
150		London/Hamburg	38		188	34.4
44		Livonian towns	51		95	17.4
	10	Riga	14			
	34	Reval (Tallinn)		14.3		
	–	Pernau		22.7		
49.4		Scania	32.6		82	15
52		Gotland, Sweden	29.4		81.4	14.9
19		Prussian towns	29.5		48.5	8.9
	16	Danzig		22.8		
	3	Elbing		6.6		
17.2		Wendish & Pomeranian towns	25.2		42.4	7.8
	5.5	Stettin		7		
	4	Stralsund		7.5		
	2.2	Rostock		4.6		
	5.5	Wismar		6.1		
4.3		Begen	–		4.3	0.8
3		Small Baltic ports	1.2		4.2	0.8
338.9		Total	206.9		545.8	100

101. Based on the table above, which of the following is true of Hanseatic League trade around the Baltic and North Seas in the 1200–1450 period?

    (A) Trade grew stagnant in this time period.
    (B) Trade was vibrant with imports and exports.
    (C) Exports were always more than imports.
    (D) London was outside its scope.

102. The Hanseatic League trade greatly contributed to which of the following historical processes?
    (A) The Italian Renaissance
    (B) The European Crusades
    (C) The Age of Absolutism
    (D) The Northern Renaissance

103. The sea-based trade of the Hanseatic cities, which then stretched to inland towns, is best understood in the context of which of the following conditions?
    (A) The end of seaborne Viking attacks
    (B) The link to India through the Silk Road
    (C) The beginning of feudal warfare
    (D) The reign of the papacy in Byzantium

The King to the Sheriff of Kent, Greeting: Because a great part of the people and especially of workmen and servants, having died in the plague, many seeing the great necessity of masters and scarcity of servants, will not serve unless they may receive excessive wages ... we ... upon deliberation and in consul with nobles and learned men assisting us, declare that every man and woman of our realm of England of what condition he be, free or bound, able in body and within sixty years of age, having no craft or land to occupy himself and not serving any other ... he shall be bound to serve him who shall require him and take only the wages or salary which were accustomed in England five or six years before.

If any workman or servant retained in any man's service, do depart from the said service without reasonable cause or license, he shall have pain of imprisonment and no one, upon the same penalty, shall receive such a person in his service.

No one, moreover, shall pay or promise to pay to any one more wages or salary than was accustomed as is said before.

—King Edward III of England's Statute on Laborers, 1351.

104. Which of the following changes are behind the statute above?
    (A) The switch of a system to wage labor from coerced labor
    (B) The introduction of New World crops like wheat and potatoes
    (C) The end of labor contract disputes between employers and employees
    (D) The influx of Asian spices and silk, which disrupted the economy

105. Which of the following historical developments caused the change in working relationships as shown in King Edward III of England's Statute on Laborers?
    (A) The European Crusades
    (B) The Hanseatic League
    (C) The Reformation
    (D) The bubonic plague

106. Which of the following was the result of the process described in the reading above?
    (A) The end of European feudalism
    (B) The spread of Islam into Europe
    (C) A split in the Eastern Orthodox Church
    (D) The end of persecution of Jews

(1) That the Roman [Catholic] Church was founded by God alone.

(2) That the pope alone can with right be called universal.

(3) That he alone can depose or reinstate bishops ... .

(10) That [the pope's] name alone shall be spoken in the churches.

(11) That his name is the only name in the world.

(12) That it may be permitted to him to depose emperors ... .

(13) No council may be regarded as general (official) without his consent

(19) That he himself may be judged by no one ... .

(22) That the Roman Church has never erred; nor will it err to all eternity, the Scripture bearing witness.

—In 1075, Pope Gregory VII issued the following decrees: Select Historical Documents of the Middle Ages, Ernest F. Henderson, ed., 1892.

107. The text above demonstrates a historical continuity in Western European politics over

(A) The power of the monarchs over the Roman Catholic Church

(B) The power of the Roman Catholic Church over the monarchs

(C) The conflict between the monarchs and the Roman Catholic Church

(D) The conflict between the Roman Catholic Church and the Byzantine emperors

108. The lay investiture controversies did damage to the authority of the Catholic Church and helped bring about what following change in the centuries that followed?

(A) The increased use of the Latin language for daily use

(B) The use of an Eastern Orthodox Christian calendar

(C) The end of crusading warfare in the Middle East

(D) The split in Christianity with the Protestant Reformation

—The mosaic of Emperor Justinian and his retinue.

109. The above image shows the Byzantine emperor flanked by military and ecclesiastical figures. This plus the halo around his head shows that Justinian and his successors till 1453 justified his rule through the principle of

(A) Hagia Sophia
(B) Pater familias
(C) Senatorial privilege
(D) Caesaropapism

110. Which of the following European regions felt the influence of Byzantine civilization in the postclassical era?

(A) Russia
(B) Iberian peninsula
(C) Scandinavia
(D) British isles

The circumference of the city of Constantinople is eighteen miles; half of it is surrounded by the sea, and half by land, and it is situated upon two arms of the sea, one turning from the sea of Russia [the Black Sea], and one from the sea of Sepharad [the Mediterranean].

All sorts of merchants come here from the land of Babylon, from the land of Shinar [Mesopotamia], from Persia, Media [western Iran], and all the sovereignty of the land of Egypt, from the land of Canaan [Palestine], and the empire of Russia, from Hungary, Patzinakia [Ukraine], Khazaria [southern Russia], and the land of Lombardy [northern Italy] and Sepharad [Spain].

Constantinople is a busy city, and merchants come to it from every country by sea or land, and there is none like it in the world except Baghdad, the great city of Islam. In Constantinople is the church of Hagia Sophia, and the seat of the pope of the Greeks, since Greeks do not obey the pope of Rome. There are also as many churches as there are days of the year … . And in this church [Hagia Sophia] there are pillars of gold and silver, and lamps of silver and gold more than a man can count.

From every part of the Byzantine Empire tribute is brought here every year, and they fill strongholds with garments of silk, purple, and gold. Like unto these storehouses and this wealth there is nothing in the whole world to be found. It is said that the tribute of the city amounts every year to 20,000 gold pieces, derived both from the rents of shops and markets and from the tribute of merchants who enter by sea or land.

—The Itinerary of Rabbi Benjamin Tudela, twelfth century
Medieval Jewish traveler.

111. According to Rabbi Tudela in the above reading, which of the following was true of the city of Constantinople?

   (A) It was at the crossroads of trade and cultural exchange.
   (B) It was impressive but still not an equal to London.
   (C) It was a counterpoint to the city of Rome.
   (D) It was dominated by the Persian minority.

112. Which historical event is Rabbi Benjamin Tudela referring to when he writes that the Greeks "do not obey the pope of Rome"?

   (A) The Protestant Reformation
   (B) The Great Schism
   (C) The Magyar invasions
   (D) The feudal order

113. The Byzantine Empire flourished as a crossroads of trade from which regions?
    (A) Sub-Saharan Africa, India, and the Middle East
    (B) India, Mediterranean, and the Americas
    (C) Mediterranean, the Middle East, and Asia
    (D) The Middle East, Asia, and Scandinavia

114. As seen in the reading, one continuity of the city under both Byzantine and Ottoman rule in its relationship with Jews is its
    (A) Diversity and tolerance
    (B) Continuing violence
    (C) Poverty and desperation
    (D) Distrust of merchants

115. By the 1200s the era of Crusading in the Middle East was coming to an end due to which of the following conditions?
    (A) The decline of the Silk Road
    (B) Strong Islamic control over the region
    (C) The end of European Christianity
    (D) The expansion into the Americas

BALDWIN SEIZES EDESSA.

—Crusader Baldwin Seizes the City of Edessa.
A History of the Crusades: Their Rise, Progress and Results.

116. The image above best represents which of the following major changes?

   (A) The building of strong walls and towers to defend against enemy sieges
   (B) The increase of land-based trade from Eastern Asia to Western Europe
   (C) The weakening of the Byzantine Empire, which will lead to Ottoman control
   (D) The continuing use of wooden ladders to scale siege walls and towers

117. Which of the following historical events contributed most to the situation shown in the image above?

   (A) The Great Schism between the Eastern Orthodox and Western Roman Catholic sects of Christianity
   (B) The fall of the Frankish Carolingian Empire in Western Europe
   (C) Cultural influence from the Byzantine Empire to the early Russian state in Moscow
   (D) The nailing of Martin Luther's 95 theses to the door of the Wittenberg church

—Mongol attack on Suzdal, Russia in 1238.

118. Which of the following best describes Russia's status after the historical event in the image above?

(A) Colonial possession

(B) Trade network

(C) Fiefdom

(D) Tributary state

119. Which of the following historical arguments can be made about the impact of Mongol control over Russia?

(A) Russia was held back by being cut off from Western Europe.

(B) Russia was integrated into the long-distance Chinese trade.

(C) Russia has never been defeated due to its weather and size.

(D) Serfdom in Russia was established on orders from the Mongols.

—The Lewis chessmen were made from walrus ivory from the Arctic circle, carved in Trondheim, Norway, and later found in the Hebrides islands north of Scotland but thought to have been on their way to the Viking port city of Dublin in Ireland.

Photo by Sean McManamon.

120. Which of the following provides some context for the Lewis chessmen and the board game of chess in general?

(A) Economic links between the Aztecs of Mesoamerica and the Viking world of northern Europe

(B) A wider cultural connection with India via the Middle East since chess originated in India

(C) A religious connection with the nonviolent tenants of Chinese Buddhism

(D) The syncretic nature of Scandinavian Christianity and Shamanic Siberian peoples

121. The method of movement of the Lewis chessmen shows a similarity to which of the following trade networks?

(A) Silk Road

(B) Arabian Peninsula

(C) Trans-Saharan

(D) Indian Ocean

122. Which of the following is true of the ivory Lewis chessmen as a trade item?

    (A) It was a staple food and a manufactured good.
    (B) It was a luxury item but also a raw material.
    (C) It was a manufactured good and a luxury item.
    (D) It was a raw material but banned at the time.

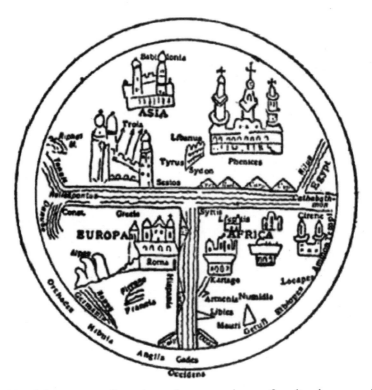

—T and O maps are a figurative and conceptual type of medieval cartography that represents only the top half of a spherical Earth, circa 1200.

123. The medieval T-O map with Jerusalem in the center is best understood in the context of

    (A) The Latin language
    (B) A Christian worldview
    (C) Judaic teachings
    (D) Trade winds

124. One change that can be inferred from the map that took place in the next century was which of the following developments?

(A) European knowledge of the world slowly increased.

(B) Europeans discovered that Africa was smaller than thought.

(C) Europeans saw the city of Rome as a more accurate center of the world.

(D) Europeans relied more on East Asian conceptions of the world.

125. Which of the following is true based on the evidence shown in the T-O map?

(A) It did not show a division between Asia and Europe.

(B) It displays the world as a round sphere.

(C) It is incomplete in its number of continents shown.

(D) It does not include bodies of water.

CHAPTER 2

The Early Modern Era: 1450 to 1750

Controlling Idea: The First Global Age

In this unit the big news, so to speak, is that the North and South American continents are integrated into global long-distance trade networks for the first time. While all civilizations are in ever-closer contact, it is the West that works its way to the center of the world trading network, serving as intermediaries in the ever-greater volumes of trade that wash across the globe between 1450 and 1750. This integration also sees waves of migration across the world, with settlers spreading out from the Old World to the New World. This includes unwilling migrants in Africa being forcibly transported to the Americas as slaves for the benefits of the West. While not dominant by 1750 (except over the Americas), the West nonetheless is becoming positioned to capitalize off its emergent role at the "core" of a new world economy, and the slow integration of the world into a single economic unit begins in this period and has accelerated down to today.

I want to go further,
But my legs are bruised and scratched.
The bony rocks appear chiseled,
The pines look as if they had been dyed.
Sitting down, I feel like a small bird,
As I look out at the crowd of peaks gathered before me.
Having ascended the heights to the brink of the abyss,
I hold fast and ponder the need to sincerely face criticism.
Wherever a road ends, I will set myself down,
Wherever a source opens, I will build a temple.
All this suffices to nourish my eyes,
And rest my feet.

—*Wooded Mountains at Dusk* by Kuncan, 1666.

126. The Chinese poem and painting above best shows the influence of which belief system?

(A) Daoism
(B) Islam
(C) Confucianism
(D) Christianity

127. Which of the following was true of the three Chinese arts shown above: painting, poetry, and calligraphy?

(A) These arts were dismissed by the emperor's court as frivolous.
(B) These arts were officially banned for merchants.
(C) These arts were not tested by the civil service exams.
(D) These arts were largely the domain of the scholar-gentry class.

When the Portgualls come to ... China, to traffic they must remain there but certain days. And when they come in at the gate of the city they must enter their names in a book and when they go out at night they put out their names. They must not lie in the town all night but lie in their boats without the town. The Chinese are very suspicious and does not trust strangers.

—Ralph Fitch's journal in the late sixteenth century describing the Portuguese arrival in China.

128. Based on the reading above, which of the following represents a change in East Asia in the Early Modern Era (1450–1750)?

(A) The Mongols conquered Japan in a series of naval invasions.

(B) Europeans arrived in Asia in search of direct trade.

(C) Merchants were looked down upon in Chinese society.

(D) Trade winds helped Europeans sail across the Indian Ocean.

129. Based on the reading above, which of the following represents a continuity in East Asia?

(A) China maintained a strong xenophobic attitude toward outsiders.

(B) China built boats that had multiple sleeping berths in them.

(C) The Portuguese spread Buddhism to China from Europe.

(D) The Chinese were fully open to outsiders and foreign traders.

—Delftware, fine porcelain made in sixteenth-century Netherlands imitates or copies Ming Chinese designs using white glaze and the distinctive blue color, which in China was called "Mohammedan Blue."

130. Which of the following statements is true based on the image and note above?

    (A) Chinese porcelain was inferior to that of the Dutch/Netherlands.
    (B) China had economic and cultural contacts with the Islamic world.
    (C) China only created porcelain in the color Ming Blue.
    (D) There was no contact between the Netherlands and the Islamic world.

131. Which of the following acts as context for the image and note above?

    (A) The fall of the Ming dynasty in 1644
    (B) The spread of Islam to South Asia
    (C) The strong desire for Asian trade goods
    (D) The Catholic Counter-Reformation

132. The existence of Dutch copies of Chinese luxury goods demonstrates which of the following statements as true?

    (A) The difficulty in obtaining actual Chinese products
    (B) The lax laws in Europe regulating Mohammedan wares
    (C) The extensive Dutch contacts in New Amsterdam
    (D) An increase in the volume of world trade after 1350

Our Confucian teaching is based on the Five Relationships (between parent and child, ruler and minister, husband and wife, older and younger brothers, and friends), whilst the Lord of Heaven Jesus was crucified because he plotted against his own country, showing that he did not recognize the relationship between ruler and subject. Mary, the mother of Jesus, had a husband named Joseph, but she said Jesus was not conceived by him.

Those who follow this teaching [Christianity] are not allowed to worship their ancestors and ancestral tablets. They do not recognize the relationship of parent and child. Their teachers oppose the Buddhists and Daoists, who do recognize the relationship between ruler and subject and father and son. Jesus did not recognize the relationship between ruler and subject and parent and child, and yet the Christians speak of him as recognizing these relationships. What [arrogant] nonsense! ...

—Yang Guangxian between 1659 and 1665.

133. The attitudes above are best understood in the context of which of the following?
    (A) Pro-Buddhist and Daoist sentiments
    (B) Anti-Christian and xenophobic attitudes
    (C) Chinese tribute and trade systems
    (D) Chinese abandonment of Confucianism

134. Which of the following was a long-term result of the introduction of Christianity into China in the sixteenth century?
    (A) Christianity became the new official state religion of the Qing dynasty in 1644.
    (B) Christianity did not become popular with the vast majority of Chinese people.
    (C) Christianity was spread by central Asian nomads along the Silk Road.
    (D) Christianity was adopted by the merchants but rejected by the warrior caste.

—Frontispiece for Athanasius Kircher's *China Illustrated*, published at Amsterdam, 1667. The figures depicted are Jesuits such as missionaries Adam Schall and Matteo Ricci holding a map of China and St. Francis Xavier and Ignatius Loyola venerating an IHS representing Jesus Christ surrounded by angels.

135. The push to spread Roman Catholic Christianity by the Jesuits needs to be understood in the European context of which of the following?

(A) The Spanish Inquisition

(B) The Peasants' Revolt

(C) The Anglican Compromise

(D) The Counter-Reformation

136. The depiction of the missionary Adam Schall in Chinese dress was evidence of which of the following practices of the Jesuits in China?
    (A) The plan to disguise their identity from the Chinese authorities
    (B) The attempt to dress as native scholars so as to appear less foreign
    (C) The difficulty in obtaining European clerical clothing in Asia
    (D) The trade in silk along a network of roads from Asia to Europe

137. This method of Christian Jesuit missionaries adapting to local conditions in China was sharply contrasted with the efforts in which of the following regions?
    (A) The Americas
    (B) The Netherlands
    (C) Southern Africa
    (D) India

> 1. Strengthen filial piety and brotherly affection to emphasize human relations.
> 2. Strengthen clan relations to illustrate harmony.
> 3. Pacify relations between local groups to put an end to quarrels and litigation.
> 4. Stress agriculture and sericulture so that there may be sufficient food and clothing.
> 5. Prize frugality so as to make careful use of wealth.
> 6. Promote education to improve the habits of scholars.
> 7. Extirpate heresy to exalt orthodoxy.
> 8. Speak of the law to give warning to the stupid and stubborn.
> 9. Clarify rites and manners to improve customs.
> 10. Let each work at his own occupation so that the people's minds will be settled.
> 11. Instruct young people to prevent them from doing wrong.
> 12. Prevent false accusations to shield the law-abiding.
> 13. Prohibit sheltering of runaways to avoid being implicated in their crime.
> 14. Pay taxes to avoid being pressed for payment.
> 15. Unite the baojia system to eliminate theft and armed robbery.
> 16. Resolve hatred and quarrels to respect life.
>
> —The Sacred Edict of the Kangxi Emperor, 1670.

138. The promotion of "filial piety" and "brotherly affection" in the first edict are clear references to which philosophy in traditional China?
    (A) Buddhism
    (B) Daoism
    (C) Legalism
    (D) Confucianism

139. Which of the following was a historical argument on the motivations behind Kangxi's Sacred Edict?

(A) The Qing rulers were non-Han Chinese and had to appear to be following traditional Chinese governing precepts to avoid revolts.

(B) The Qing dynasty had overthrown the Mongol Yuan dynasty and wanted to restore Mongol rule and traditional practices.

(C) Having won the Opium War over the French, the Qing sought to reestablish their control over the waterways along the Eastern coast.

(D) The Qing state was decentralizing their power and left much of the country to govern themselves under traditional precepts.

140. Which of the following provides some context for Kangxi's Sacred Edict?

(A) Emperor Kangxi was promoting good governance and stability

(B) Emperor Kangxi was interested in education and learning

(C) Emperor Kangxi led many military campaigns during his reign

(D) Emperor Kangxi, a Daoist, took a passive view of political events

141. Compared to the rule of the Qing dynasty, the Yuan dynasty or Mongols

(A) Discontinued regional trade and the persecuted merchants

(B) Lasted longer than most Chinese dynasties by 200 years

(C) Made little effort to assimilate or follow Chinese methods

(D) Restored the civil service exam and utilized Chinese scholars

Document-Based Question

Please work separately from the book on loose-leaf paper to flush out your ideas before committing your answer to space below.

142. To what extent were the Chinese open to interaction with foreigners and the outside world?

Document 1

Source: Ralph Fitch's journal in the late sixteenth century describes the restrictions placed on the Portuguese.

When the Portgualls come to ... China, to traffic they must remain there but certain days. And when they come in at the gate of the city they must enter their names in a book and when they go out at night they put out their names. They must not lie in the town all night but lie in their boats without the town. The Chinese are very suspicious and does not trust strangers

Document 2

Source: An image shows foreign ambassadors paying tribute and performing the kowtow, ritualistic bowing done the required nine times, to the emperor's officials in China. Ming dynasty text, 1609.

Document 3

Source: One Chinese view of Matteo Ricci and Europeans, late Ming dynasty, early 1600s.

Tianzhu guo (Italy) lies further to the west from the Buddhist state (India). Their people understand literature and are as scholarly and elegant as the Chinese. A certain Li Mateo (Matteo Ricci) came from the said state and after four years reached the boundary of Guangdong by way of India. Their religion worships the Lord in Heaven just as the Confucianists worship Confucius and the Buddhists Buddha. [Ricci's message] explains the truth by comparison with Confucianism but sharply criticizes the theories of nothingness and emptiness of Buddhism and Daosim … . I am very much delighted with his ideas, which are close to Confucianism but more earnest in exhorting society not to resemble the Buddhist, who always like to obscure, incoherent worlds to fool and frighten the populace … . He is very polite when he talks to people and his arguments, if challenged, can be inexhaustible. Thus in foreign countries there are also real gentlemen.

Document 4

Source: Jesuit Johann Schreck in his book, *Diagrams and Explanations of the Wonderful Machines of the Far West*, 1627.

[The Jesuits] made efforts to translate western mathematical and astronomical works into Chinese and aroused the interest of Chinese scholars in these sciences. They made very extensive astronomical observation and carried out the first modern cartographic work in China. They also learned to appreciate the scientific achievements of this ancient culture and made them known in Europe. Through their correspondence European scientists first learned about the Chinese science and culture.

Document 5

Source: Wei Chün, "On Ricci's Fallacies to Deceive the World," late Ming/ early Qing dynasty.

Lately Matteo Ricci utilized some false teachings to fool people, and scholars unanimously believed him … take for example the position of China on the map. He puts it not in the center but slightly to the West and inclined to the north. This is altogether far from the truth, for China should be in the center of the world, which we can prove by the single fact that we can see the North Star resting at the zenith of the heaven at midnight. How can China be treated like a small unimportant country, and placed slightly to the north as in this map?

Document 6

Source: The following document concerning Christianity was written by the scholar and official Yang Guangxian and is part of a series of essays denouncing Christianity written between 1659 and 1665.

Our Confucian teaching is based on the Five Relationships (between parent and child, ruler and minister, husband and wife, older and younger brothers, and friends), whilst the Lord of Heaven Jesus was crucified because he plotted against his own country, showing that he did not recognize the relationship between ruler and subject. Mary, the mother of Jesus, had a husband named Joseph, but she said Jesus was not conceived by him. Those who follow this teaching [Christianity] are not allowed to worship their ancestors and ancestral tablets. They do not recognize the relationship of parent and child. Their teachers oppose the Buddhists and Daoists, who do recognize the relationship between ruler and subject and father and son. Jesus did not recognize the relationship between ruler and subject and parent and child, and yet the Christians speak of him as recognizing these relationships. What [arrogant] nonsense! …

Document 7

Source: He Qiaoyuan, Ming dynasty court official, reports to the emperor on the possibility of repealing the 1626 ban on foreign trade, 1630. Note: The ban was ineffectual and massive amounts of smuggling occurred.

The Spanish have silver mountains, which they mint into silver coins. When Chinese merchants trade in Southeast Asia and the Indian Ocean, they trade the goods we produce for the goods of others. But when they go to Luzon (Philippines) they only return with silver coins. Chinese silk yarn worth 100 bars of silver can be sold in the Philippines at a price of 200 to 300 bars of silver there. Moreover, porcelain from the official pottery works as well as sugar and fruit from my native province, are currently desired by the foreigners.

—Woodblock print showing Samurai Selling Armor to a Scrap Metal Merchant. 1797.

143. Which of the following acts as context for the situation in the image on the woodblock print?

(A) The Tokugawa shogunate drafted merchants into their military.

(B) The Tokugawa era was one of cultural homogeneity.

(C) The Pax Tokugawa made most of the samurai warriors obsolete.

(D) The Tokugawa era was largely one of economic depression.

144. In comparison to Japan, in Europe which of the following is true concerning the warrior classes?

(A) Many took religious vows and left politics.

(B) They adapted to gunpowder weapons.

(C) They were defeated during the Crusades.

(D) They stopped using horses by 1500.

145. In Tokugawa Japan, merchants ranked lower than samurai according to Confucian principles. Which of the following reflects a conflicting idea behind the image above?

(A) The metal in the swords was worth less money than their clothes.

(B) Samurai swords were no longer valued compared to guns.

(C) Merchants and trade were banished to Japan's outlying islands.

(D) Many samurai were economically struggling compared to the merchants.

1. *Japanese ships are strictly forbidden to leave for foreign countries.*

2. *No Japanese is permitted to go abroad. If there is anyone who attempts to do so secretly, he must be executed. The ship so involved must be impounded and its owner arrested and the matter must be reported to the higher authority.*

3. *If any Japanese returns from overseas after residing there, he must be put to death.*

4. *If there is any place where the teachings of padres (Christianity) is practiced, the two of you must order a thorough investigation …*

7. *If there are any Southern Barbarians (Westerners) who propagate the teachings of padres, or otherwise commit crimes, they may be incarcerated in the prison maintained by the Omura domain, as previously …*

10. *Samurai are not permitted to purchase any goods originating from foreign ships directly from Chinese merchants in Nagasaki.*

—The Edicts of the Tokugawa Shogunate in Japan, 1615.

146. The shogun's policies regarding foreign trade as described in the excerpt had which purpose?

    (A) To limit foreign ideas and prevent threats to the shogun's power

    (B) To become dominant in East Asian trading networks

    (C) To stop Japanese merchants from evading taxation on trade goods

    (D) To prevent individual ports from monopolizing trade

147. Which of the following was an effect of the Japanese seclusion policies described in the excerpts?

    (A) The Tokugawa shogunate faced rebellions as a result of economic decline.

    (B) Japan had limited knowledge of foreign technology and culture.

    (C) The Tokugawa shogunate was overthrown by Japanese merchants.

    (D) Japan was completely isolated from regional trade networks.

148. Which of the following changes in Japanese policy concerning interactions occurred under the Tokugawa shogunate?

    (A) Japan increased its overseas trade in raw materials with Ming China and Korea.

    (B) Japan saw a decrease in the populace's practice of Chinese Daoism and shamanism.

    (C) Japan adopted a policy of almost total isolation with the exception of limited trade at Nagasaki.

    (D) Japan promoted the use of diplomacy with China and European nations rather than warfare.

1. *Live an honest and sincere life. Respect your parents, your brothers, and your relatives, and try to live harmoniously with the m all. Honor and treat with respect everyone you meet, even those you see only occasionally. Never behave discourteously or selfishly … .*

2. *… Not one person in ten understands the things of this life nor of the next … If even Buddha himself is said to have known nothing, nothing of the world to come, how can any ordinary mortal know such things? Until you reach fifty, therefore, do not worry about the future life …*

4. *Until you are forty, avoid every luxury, and never act or think like one above your station in life. In matters of business and money making, however, work harder than anyone else … Until you turn fifty, be temperate in all things, and avoid all ostentation and finery, anything, in fact, that might call attention to yourself. Do not cultivate expensive tastes, for you should ignore such things as the tea ceremony, swords, daggers, and fine clothes.*

13. *Those with even a small fortune must remember that their duty in life is to devote themselves to their house and its business. They must not become careless, for if they buy what they want, do as they please, and, in general, live sumptuously, they will soon spend that fortune … Although a samurai can draw on the produce of his tenured lands to earn his livelihood, a merchant must rely on the profit from his business, for without that profit, the money in his bags would soon disappear. No matter how much profit he makes and packs into his bags, however, if he continually wastes that money, he may as well pack it into bags full of holes. Remember this … . These seventeen articles were written not for Sōshitsu's sake but for yours. They are his testament, and you should follow them closely. They should be as important to you as the Great Constitution of Prince Shōtoku. Read them every day, or even twice a day, and be careful to forget nothing.*

—Codes of Merchant Houses: Excerpts from
The Testament of Shimai Sōshitsu.

149. Which of the following was a direct cause of the historical situation described above?

(A) A period of peace and stability
(B) A time of war and conflict
(C) The arrival of the European traders
(D) The importation of Buddhism into Japan

150. Which of the following was a similar type of era in world history?

(A) Mongol Empire invasions
(B) Northern European renaissance
(C) Conquest of the Americas
(D) Islamic expansion

Being a retainer is nothing other than being a supporter of one's lord, entrusting matters of good and evil to him, and renouncing self-interest. If there are but two or three men of this type, the fief will be secure.

> —Tsuramoto Tashiro, a young samurai, from his work *Hagakure*, one of the best known classics on the samurai code, 1716.

151. Which of the following was the Japanese term for a feudal lord?

(A) Ronin

(B) Daimyo

(C) Shogun

(D) Ninja

152. The warrior code above with its emphasis on "being a supporter of one's lord" and "renouncing self-interest" was able to align itself with which belief system that was practiced in Japan?

(A) Shinto

(B) Hinduism

(C) Buddhism

(D) Confucianism

What Heaven imparts to man is called human nature,

To follow our nature is called the Way.

It is rooted in the Mind and lodged in the Teachings

The forms through which it has been bequeathed to us are full of dignity

Eternal and age less as Heaven

> —Excerpts from sixteenth-century Vietnamese poet Nguyễn Bỉnh Khiêm's Inscription for "Three Belief" Temple.

153. Which of the following Asian belief systems shows a clear influence on the Vietnamese reading above?

(A) Confucianism

(B) Daoism

(C) Hinduism

(D) Christianity

154. Which of the following groups in early modern Vietnam would have been educated in the above belief systems?

(A) Peasants

(B) Merchants

(C) Scholars

(D) Samurai

Long before Europeans arrived, maritime Southeast Asia (including present day Malaysia, Indonesia and the Philippines) carried on a substantial long distance trade. Many of the merchants were women—in some cases because commerce was thought too base an occupation for upper-class men, but too lucrative for elite families to abstain from completely ...

the Portuguese, the first Europeans to establish themselves in this world, had found intermarrying with such women to be an indispensable part of creating profitable and defensible colonies. When the VOC gave up on importing Dutch women—having sometimes found "willing" candidates only in the orphanages or even brothels of Holland, and facing discontent among the intended husbands of these women—it turned to the daughters of these earlier Portuguese-Asian unions: they at least spoke a Western language and were at least nominally Christian. Many had also learned from their mothers how useful a European husband could be for protecting their business interests in an increasingly multinational and often violent trading world ...

The VOC's principal goal, of course, was profit, and profit was best secured by monopolizing the export of all sorts of Asian goods—from pepper to porcelain— back to Europe. In theory, the company also claimed—at least intermittently— the right to license and tax (or sink) all the ships participating in the much larger intra-Asian trade, including those of Southeast Asia's women traders. But the realities of huge oceans and numerous rivals made enforcing such a system impossible, and the VOC also faced powerful enemies within. Most company servants soon discovered that while smuggling goods back to Holland was risky and difficult, they could earn sums by trading illegally (or semi-legally) within Asia that dwarfed their official salaries. Here their wives were a perfect vehicle for making a fortune: they were well connected in and knowledgeable about local markets, often possessed considerable capital and able to manage the family business continuously without being susceptible to sudden transfer by the company.

—Kenneth Pomeranz and Steven Topik, historians, *The World That Trade Created: Society, Culture and World Economy 1400 to the Present,* 2006.

155. Which of the following enabled the Dutch to establish and enforce a monopoly on the Southeast Asian spice trade in the seventeenth century?

(A) The establishment of powerful joint-stock companies
(B) The development of exclusive inventions for navigation
(C) Increased scientific knowledge leading to medicines to treat malaria
(D) Population growth as a result of the Columbian Exchange

156. Which of the following acts as context for the relationship between male European merchants and local Southeast Asian women merchants?

(A) Southeast Asia was primarily influenced by Chinese culture and beliefs.
(B) Southeast Asia was ruled by an all-powerful monarch in northern India.
(C) Southeast Asia was not affected by seasonal monsoon or trade winds.
(D) Southeast Asia was not a strict patriarchy and women had some autonomy.

Sweet potato, found in Luzon,*
Grows all over, trouble-free
Foreign devils love to eat it
Propagates so easily.

We just made a single cutting
Boxed it up and brought it home
Ten years later, Fujian's saviour.
If it dies, just make a clone.

Take your cutting, then re-plant it
Wait a week and see it grow
This is how we cultivate it
In our homeland, reap and sow.

*location in the Philippines

—Excerpt from He Qiaoyuan's "Ode to the Sweet Potato," circa 1594.

157. The poem above is clear evidence of which of the following?

(A) China's military conquest of the Philippine islands, including Luzon

(B) Extensive trade contacts between China and outlying regions in Asia

(C) Chinese borrowing of all European trade items and belief systems

(D) Japan's use of terrace farming and rice agriculture from China

158. Which of the following was a direct result of the movement of the sweet potato and other New World food items into China?

(A) Population migration

(B) Population increase

(C) Population decrease

(D) Population stagnation

159. The movement of the sweet potato and other potatoes from their Amerindian origin to China are the context for which historical process?

(A) The Little Ice Age

(B) Triangle trade network

(C) Columbian Exchange

(D) Encomienda system

Lord of the East and West! King whom the kings of earth obey!
Prince of the Epoch! Sultan Suleiman! Triumphant Aye!
Meet 'tis before the steed of yonder Monarch of the realms
Of right and equity, should march earth's rulers' bright array.
Rebelled one 'gainst his word, secure he'd bind him in his bonds,
E'en like the dappled pard, the sky, chained with the Milky Way.
Lord of the land of graciousness and bounty, on whose board
Of favors, spread is all the wealth that sea and mine display;
Longs the perfumer, Early Spring, for th' odor of his grace;
Need hath the merchant, Autumn, of his bounteous hand alway.
Through tyrant's hard oppression no one groaneth in his reign,
And though may wail the flute and lute, the law they disobey.

Beside thy justice, tyranny's the code of Rey-Qubad;
Beside thy wrath, but mildness Qahraman's most deadly fray.
Thy scimitar's the gleaming guide empires to overthrow,
No foe of Islam can abide before thy saber's ray.
Saw it thy wrath, through dread of thee would trembling seize the pine;
The falling stars a chain around the heaven's neck would lay ... .

—Poem by the Turkish poet Baqi in *A Qaisda On Sultan Suleiman.*

160. The poem above is best understood in the context of which of the following?
   (A) The long tradition of laudable verse to promote and legitimize the monarch
   (B) Suleiman's military losses at the hands of the Europeans and Chinese
   (C) The use of awe-inducing architecture to instill fear in one's enemies
   (D) The deadly schism between Sufi and Sunni sects of Islam

161. Which of the following was a basis for the legitimacy of an Ottoman Sultan?
   (A) The ability to write beautiful poetry and song lyrics
   (B) Military success against the enemies of Islam
   (C) The promotion of trade within the Ottoman empire
   (D) Producing numerous sons in order to succeed him

—Photos from the Hagia Sophia in Istanbul, Turkey, showing minarets and large decorative shields with calligraphy inscriptions from the Koran.

162. The addition of Islamic minarets and the shields to the Hagia Sophia church after the Ottoman conquest of the Byzantine Empire and its capital city Constantinople is a result of all of the following EXCEPT

    (A) Appropriation by a triumphalist Islam over Christianity
    (B) Conquest of Constantinople by the Ottoman Turks
    (C) Cultural blending of Islamic and Christian design
    (D) The welcoming of Muslims to the Byzantine church

163. The Hagia Sophia is now a national museum in Turkey's capital of Istanbul. This is best understood in the context of which of the following?

    (A) Mustapha Kemal Ataturk's secularization program
    (B) The military domination of government in postwar Turkey
    (C) The adoption of atheistic communism by Turkey
    (D) The success of Turkey in World War battlefields

Empire	Land Area	Approximate Population	Religious Composition	Estimated Size of Military	Source of Cannons & Firearms
Ottoman Empire c. 1566	c. 1,200,000 square miles	20–35 million	Large majority Sunni; a significant Christian and small Jewish minorities	Largest army recorded: 200,000 cavalry, infantry, artillery + 90 warships	Produced locally
Safavid Empire c. 1600	c. 750,000 square miles	10–15 million	Majority Shia Muslim; small Sunni, Jewish, and Christian minorities	40,000–50,000 cavalry, infantry, artillery; no navy	Imported cannons not widely used, except by European mercenaries
Mughal Empire c. 1600	c. 1 million square miles	105–110 million	Ruling Muslim minority with great Hindu majority plus Sikh, Buddhist, Jain, and Christian minorities	200,000+ cavalry, infantry, artillery; no navy	Imported and produced locally

164. Which of the following conclusions is best supported by the data in the chart above?

(A) The spread of gunpowder weaponry helped these states dominate and retain power.

(B) The importation of gunpowder weaponry limited the reach of these states to Asia.

(C) Gunpowder eliminated forever the use of cavalry on Eurasian battlefields.

(D) The spread of gunpowder weaponry was initiated by Christian and Jewish minorities.

165. Based on a study of the chart, a historian of Muslim rule in the Early Modern World (1450–1750) would most likely support which of the following historical arguments?

(A) The military might of Jewish minorities in the Middle East was a challenge for the Ottomans.

(B) The Safavid Empire easily dominated its Muslim neighbors, the Ottomans and Mughals.

(C) Mughal rulers had a more difficult task of ruling over a large non-Muslim population.

(D) With no Mughal navy, Mughals traders did little business with the outside world.

> *No distinction is attached to birth among the Turks; the deference to be paid to a man is measured by the position he holds in the public service. There is no fighting for precedence; a man's place is marked out by the duties he discharges. In making his appointments the Sultan pays no regard to any pretensions on the score of wealth or rank, nor does he take into consideration recommendations or popularity, he considers each case on its own merits, and examines carefully into the character, ability, and disposition of the man whose promotion is in question. It is by merit that men rise in the service, a system which ensures that posts should only be assigned to the competent . . . .*
>
> *This is the reason that they are successful in their undertakings, that they lord it over others, and are daily extending the bounds of their empire. These are not our ideas, with us there is no opening left for merit; birth is the standard for everything; the prestige of birth is the sole key to advancement in the public service.*
>
> —Ogier Ghiselin de Busbecq, the Holy Roman Empire's ambassador to the Ottoman Court, in his *The Turkish Letters*, 1555–1562.

166. Which of the following is an underlying context for the legal status of the Janissaries described in the excerpt above?

(A) The Janissaries were free agents who sold their services to the highest bidder.

(B) The Janissaries were tied to the land and landowners but had some rights.

(C) The Janissaries were chattel slaves who were bought and sold to landowners.

(D) The Janissaries were the elite forces of the sultan but still under a form of servitude.

167. The formation of the Janissaries was part of a larger system of "collecting" young boys to serve the Ottoman state. Which of the following is the Turkish term for this system?
    (A) Jizya
    (B) Devshirme
    (C) Jihad
    (D) Mamluk

168. Stories exist of Christian families offering their sons to the Ottoman state in the hopes that they might become Janissaries. This was done primarily due to which of the following expectations?
    (A) Social mobility
    (B) Local famines
    (C) Wars of conquest
    (D) Monetary bribes

Nevertheless, there is no cause for improper words: indeed, those vain, heretical amputations are the mere fabrications of the opium-clouded minds of certain secretaries and scribes ... .

At this writing we were engaged upon the hunt near Isfahan; we now prepare provisions and our troops for the coming campaign. In all friendship we say do what you will. Bitter experience has taught that in this world of trial He who falls upon the house of Ali always falls. Kindly give our ambassador leave to travel unmolested. "No soul laden bears the load of another." [Quran 6:164; 53:38] When war becomes inevitable, hesitation and delay must be set aside, and one must think on that which is to come. Farewell.

—Safavid Shah Ismail in a letter to the Ottoman Sultan Selim, 1514.

169. Which is the most distinguishing characteristic of the Safavid dynasty when compared to its Ottoman and Mughal Empires?
    (A) Its high level of literacy and education
    (B) Its official religion of Shia/Shiite Islam
    (C) Its long-distance trade with Japan
    (D) Its use of gunpowder weapons

170. The use of the terms "heretical" and "house of Ali" refers to the dismissive and insulting tone of the document most likely due to which of the following?
    (A) The Sunni/Shia religious divisions in Islam
    (B) The fact that the Safavid had gunpowder weapons
    (C) The vast differences in types of government
    (D) The Protestant Reformations that spread to the Middle East

—Map of Eurasia showing three empires from left: Ottoman, Safavid and Mughal. Courtesy of Pinupbettu.

171. Which of the following brought about the slow decline and undermining of the three empires' economies?

(A) The Catholic Counter-Reformation
(B) The discovery of an all-water route to Asia
(C) The invention of gunpowder and gun technology
(D) The conquest of the Aztec and Incan empires

172. How did rulers of the Ottoman, Safavid, and Mughal Empires respond to the rising influence of the West in world affairs after 1500?

(A) Adoption of firearms and artillery enabled coordinated assaults on the homelands of the Western merchants.
(B) Highly centralized drives to confront the West on the high seas thwarted Western encroachment on trade routes and port cities.
(C) They pursued increased diplomatic and military dependence on Ming and Qing dynasties in China to organize resistance to Western domination.
(D) A tendency to underestimate Western capacities led to failure to adopt Western military, technological, and scientific advances.

—Akbar greets two Jesuit priests in black robes in the meeting house in his capital at Fatehpur Sikri in 1603.

173. Based on the Persian miniature above, which of the following best shows the attitude of the Mughal emperor Akbar towards his non-Muslim subjects?

(A) He imposed the jizya on his Hindu subjects.
(B) He was interested in all religious faiths.
(C) He destroyed their temples and taxed them.
(D) He helped spread Hinduism to Southeast Asia.

174. In comparison to Akbar, his descendant Aurangzeb followed which religious policy in Mughal India?
    (A) He reimposed the jizya and religious intolerance.
    (B) He created a new religion that blended other faiths.
    (C) He added new innovations from Shia Islam.
    (D) He gradually drifted away from strict Islamic doctrine.

175. Mughal attitudes toward religion are best understood in the context of which of the following continuities of India?
    (A) The Mughals were visited by Christian missionaries.
    (B) The Mughal era saw the formation of the Sikh religion.
    (C) The Mughal entered India as seafaring merchants.
    (D) The Mughals ruled over a majority of non-Muslims.

—Early Indian matchlocks as illustrated in the "Baburnama" in the sixteenth century.

176. Which of the following represents a major change in South Asian
governments ability to expand and dominate their empires in the Early
Modern Era (1450–1750)?
    (A) The use of stirrups and saddles
    (B) The use of horses and chariots
    (C) The use of gunpowder weapons
    (D) The use of caravels and lateen sails

177. Which of the following represents a similarity among the nomadic Turkish tribes who later developed into the empires of the Ottomans, Mughals, and Safavids?

(A) Rule by a warrior class
(B) Adoption of Shia Islam
(C) Use of Jewish mercenaries
(D) Trade in tobacco products

When we arrived (at Calicut) they took us to a large church, and this is what we saw: The body of the church is as large as a monastery, all built of hewn stone and covered with tiles. At the main entrance rises a pillar of bronze as high as a mast, on the top of which was perched a bird, ... In the centre of the body of the church rose a chapel, ... Within this sanctuary stood a small image which they said represented Our Lady. Along the walls, by the main entrance, hung seven small bells. In this church the captain-major said his prayers, and we with him. We did not go within the chapel, for it is the custom that only certain servants of the church, called quasees, should enter. These quasees wore some threads passing over the left shoulder and under the right arm, in the same manner as our deacons wear the stole. They threw holy water over us, and gave us some white earth, which the Christians of this country are in the habit of putting on their foreheads, breasts, around the neck, and on the forearms ... . Many other saints are painted on the walls of the church, wearing crowns. They were painted variously, with teeth protruding an inch from the mouth, and four or five arms.

—"Roteiro," a journal of Vasco da Gama's voyage written by an unknown member of the expedition.

178. From the excerpt above, which of the following is true?

(A) DeGama and his men were overwhelmed by the exotic differences of India and Indians.
(B) DeGama and his party mistook Hindus for Christians and a statue of an Indian deity for Mary.
(C) DeGama and his force were attacked upon arrival and nearly wiped out.
(D) DeGama naval fleet never made it past the port of Oran on the Arabian peninsula.

179. Which of the following acts best as a direct cause of the event described above?

(A) The long-held European desire to reach India by an all-water route
(B) The Iberian Christian reconquista against Andalusian Moors
(C) The publication of Ibn Battuta's book in Northern European cities
(D) The desire for new staple crops and tobacco from the Americas

180. The reference that "only certain servants of the church, called quasees, should enter" is referring to which privileged group in Indian society?
    (A) Shudras
    (B) Kshatriyas
    (C) Brahmins
    (D) Vaishiyas

181. In contrast to the Portuguese arrival in India, the Spanish arrival in Americas was
    (A) Marked by cultural misunderstandings
    (B) Caused by a desire for trade with Asia
    (C) Done by long distance oceanic voyages
    (D) Resulted in conquest and settlement

O servant, where does thou seek Me? Lo! I am beside thee.

I am neither in temple nor in mosque: I am neither in Kaaba nor in Kailash. Neither am I in rites and ceremonies … . If thou are a true seeker, thou shalt at once see Me.

"It is needless to ask of a saint the caste to which he belongs … . The barber has sought God, the washerwoman, and the carpenter … .

Hindus and Muslims alike have achieved that End,

Where remains no mark of distinction.

—Fifteenth-century Indian poet and mystic, Kabir.

182. Which of the following is true of the Bhakti movement based on the poem above?
    (A) It was strongly influenced by the new Sikh religion.
    (B) It was a Hindu attempt at accommodation with Islam.
    (C) It blended Chinese Confucianism with Indian Daoism.
    (D) It was the Indian version of the Wahhabi form of Islam.

183. Which of the following belief systems was a new religion from the Early Modern Era in South Asia that sought to navigate the differences between the Muslim rulers and the overwhelmingly Hindu majority?
    (A) Sikhism
    (B) Daoism
    (C) Wahabi
    (D) Jihad

—Frontal shot and detail of the Taj Mahal which was built during the Mughal era between 1631 and 1653.

184. Which of the following statements about the Taj Mahal is best supported by the images above?

(A) It is a classic example of Islamic architecture.

(B) It was used to house the royal Mughal family.

(C) It acted as the Grand Bazaar for merchants.

(D) It was built as a defensive fort against Hindus.

185. Similarly to the Palace of Versailles in France, the Taj Mahal

(A) Was later used to host numerous peace conferences

(B) Was used to demonstrate the power of the monarchs

(C) Was meant to be used as a royal mausoleum

(D) Was famed for its numerous bedrooms and galleries

—Men praying inside the Kok Gumbaz mosque in Central Asia.

—Madrassa of Hodja Akrar, Samarkand in Central Asia.

186. The images of the tombs show a clear influence of what civilization?

(A) Byzantine
(B) Russian
(C) Islamic
(D) Chinese

187. Which of the following took place in Central Asia by the 1700s?

(A) This region will be carved up by large land empires.
(B) The Silk Road trade network will be revived.
(C) Buddhism will spread westward from China.
(D) Rice agriculture will dominate trade and local cuisine.

—World map showing trade-winds by Edmond Halley, 1686.

188. The wind currents shown in the map above were used to great effect during which period of long-distance trade and interaction in world history?

(A) The Crusades
(B) The Age of Exploration
(C) The Peopling of Oceania
(D) The Mongol Expansion

189. The trade winds in the Indian Ocean contributed most directly to which of the following

(A) The spread of Buddhism to the East African coast in the tenth century
(B) The existence of steam technology in navigation during the eighteenth century
(C) The monsoon winds that provided needed water for South Asian agriculture
(D) The use of irrigation canals in ancient Egypt to create surplus crops

—A manuscript page from the African city of Timbuktu showing a table of astronomical information. Early Modern Era (1450–1750).

190. Which of the following explains the importance of astronomy in the Islamic world?

(A) Horoscopes are needed for the pilgrimage to Medina.
(B) Knowledge of astronomy is important for daily prayer.
(C) There is great respect for medical knowledge.
(D) Celestial wonders are considered good luck for trade.

191. By 1200, Baghdad's House of Wisdom, European universities and Timbuktu were similar for being important centers of which of the following?

(A) Trade
(B) Learning
(C) Transportation
(D) Islam

The inhabitants of this country are tawny-colored. Their food is confined to the flesh of seals, whales and gazelles, and the roots of herbs. They are dressed in skins, and wear sheaths over their virile members. They are armed with poles of olive wood to which a horn, browned in the fire, is attached. Their numerous dogs resemble those of Portugal, and bark like them. The birds of the country, likewise, are the same as in Portugal, and include cormorants, gulls, turtle doves, crested larks, and many others. The climate is healthy and temperate, and produces good herbage. On the day after we had cast anchor, that is to say on Thursday (November 9), we landed with the captain-major, and made captive one of the natives, who was small of stature … . He was taken on board the captain-major's ship, and being placed at table he ate of all we ate. On the following day the captain-major had him well dressed and sent ashore.

On the following day (November 10) fourteen or fifteen natives came to where our ship lay. The captain-major landed and showed them a variety of merchandise, with the view of finding out whether such things were to be found in their country. This merchandise included cinnamon, cloves, seed-pearls, gold, and many other things, but it was evident that they had no knowledge whatever of such articles, and they were consequently given round bells and tin rings. This happened on Friday, and the like took place on Saturday.

—An account of Vasco da Gama along the shore of Africa,
1497–1498.

192. The account of Vasco da Gama in Africa is similar to Europeans' experiences in the Americas in that?

(A) They both used Swahili language translators to conduct negotiations.
(B) They both show societies that were governed by democratic principles.
(C) They both had no domesticated animals that could be used for labor.
(D) They both show the relative isolation from the larger interconnected world.

193. Which of the following explains why the African natives were asked about cinnamon, cloves, and gold?

(A) Europeans were primarily interested in commercial opportunities.
(B) Europeans were motivated by religious motives to spread Christianity.
(C) Europeans were conducting scientific surveys of the flora and fauna.
(D) Europeans were interested in feeding the hungry Africans.

—Sketch from *The last journals of David Livingstone in Central Africa, from 1865 to his death.* London, 1874. The encryption reads "Slavers revenging their losses."

194. Images like this showing the cruelty of Arab traders killing some captives were used to
    (A) Help justify the Atlantic Slave trade
    (B) Show that Chinese were active slave raiders in Africa
    (C) Show that farming was unknown in sub-Saharan Africa
    (D) Sell slaves at auction house advertisements in print media

195. The image above shows which part of the journey from point of capture to point of forced labor?
    (A) Middle Passage
    (B) Slave auction
    (C) Journey to the coast
    (D) Indentured servitude

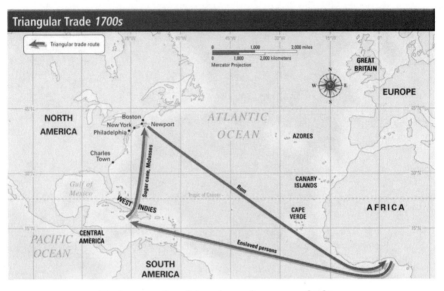

—Trade routes involving the enslavement of Africans.

196. A historian would most likely use the map above in studying which of the following?
    (A) Immigration patterns around the world
    (B) Triangular trade network across the Atlantic
    (C) Industrialization across the Americas
    (D) The market for luxury goods in Asia

197. Which is most true of the Middle Passage?
    (A) It was generally a pleasant voyage and the slaves were well cared for.
    (B) Mortality on the ships was high so slaves were overpacked to offset losses.
    (C) It generally lasted a year or more depending on the monsoon winds.
    (D) African naval expertise was key to guiding vessels across the Atlantic.

198. Compared to the Indian Ocean slave trade, the Atlantic slave trade differed in that
    (A) Slaves were not exchanged for trade goods but tribute
    (B) It offered little social advancement for slaves
    (C) It was larger in scale and greater in profit and mortality
    (D) It was of shorter duration but longer in distance

—Illustration of Inca farmers using a *chakitaqlla* (Andean foot plow).

199. The farming techniques shown above is labor intensive. One continuity in the labor system used by both the Incas and the Spanish conquistadors is which of the following?

(A) slave labor
(B) *mita* labor
(C) indentured servitude
(D) wage labor

—Drawing showing Cortez and La Malinche meeting Moctezuma II, 1519, from the "Lienzo de Tlaxcala," which was created by the Tlaxcalans to remind the Spanish of their loyalty to Castile and the importance of Tlaxcala during the Conquest, ca. 1550.

200. The image above shows evidence of which continuity in Latin American diplomatic relations?

(A) Tribute from conquered peoples
(B) Legalese diplomatic language
(C) Female translators
(D) Ritual bowing

201. The presence of Malinche, as a Tlaxcalan translator for the Spanish, is a reminder of which essential fact in the success of the conquistadores in the early 1500s?

(A) The Aztecs and the Spanish had a patriarchal society.
(B) Lack of immunity in Amerindians played a key role.
(C) Native American allies were vital in the Spanish victory.
(D) The use of wind currents in sea battles against the Aztecs.

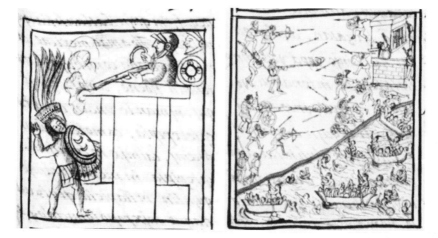

—Images from *The General History of the Things of New Spain* by Fray Bernardino de Sahagún: The Florentine Codex. Book XII: The Conquest of Mexico, 1577].

202. Which of the following can be argued about the Aztec defeat at the hands of the Spanish and their Native American allies?

(A) It was inevitable given the uneven distribution of military technology available to the two sides.

(B) If the Aztecs had used their own gun technology more effectively they could have prevailed.

(C) It was destined by the gods to happen due to the savagery of the Aztecs as shown in human sacrifices.

(D) It followed a long series of conquests by Europeans in the Americas starting with the Vikings.

203. What explains the difficulty of Europeans in conquering Asia when we compare the ease in which they succeeded in conquering the Americas during the Early Modern Era (1500–1800)?

(A) Asia was farther away from Europe than the Americas.

(B) Monsoon winds damaged European ships and troops.

(C) China and Japan also had gunpowder and gun technology.

(D) Europeans outnumbered Native Americans by a large ratio.

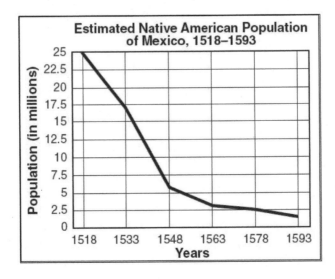

204. Which of the following best explains the changes in Mexico's population from the years in the sixteenth century?

    (A) The introduction of Old World foods to the Americas
    (B) The introduction of Old World diseases to the Americas
    (C) The decline of traditional handicrafts in Mexico
    (D) The introduction of Old World culture into the Americas

205. The demographic situation in Mexico/Central America seen above was vastly different to which part of the world?

    (A) Asian mainland
    (B) Andean America
    (C) North America
    (D) West Indies/Caribbean

A short while ago … we gave, … assigned forever to you and your heirs and successors, kings of Castile and Leon (Spain), all islands and mainlands whatsoever, discovered and to be discovered, toward the west and south, that were not under the actual temporal dominion of any Christian lords. Moreover, we invested therewith you … as lords of them with full and free power, authority, and jurisdiction of every kind, … But since it may happen that your envoys and captains, or vassals, while voyaging toward the west or south, might bring their ships to land in eastern regions and there discover islands and mainlands that belonged or belong to India, … found and to be found, discovered and to be discovered, … We grant to you and your aforesaid heirs and successors full and free power through your own authority, freely to take corporal possession of the said islands and countries and to hold them forever, and to defend them against whosoever may oppose.

Gratis by order of our most holy lord the Pope, September 26th, 1493.

—A papal bill issued by Pope Alexander VI. This decree later had a strong influence on the Treaty of Tordesillas, which divided the world into Spanish and Portuguese spheres of influence in the Early Modern Era.

206. Which two nations were involved in the Treaty of Tordesillas?

(A) England and France
(B) Spain and Portugal
(C) Spain and Italy
(D) Russia and Germany

207. Which of the following shows a continuity with the text above?

(A) The spread of indigenous religions
(B) The slow decline of trade along the Silk Road
(C) Europeans claiming non-European land
(D) The absence of Australia on the map

—Virgin Mary of the Rich Mountain (Potosi) "Bolivia" (seventeenth to eighteenth century).

208. The image of Christianity's Virgin Mary imposed onto the mountain in Potosi in Bolivia is an example of which historical process?

(A) Syncretism
(B) Assimilation
(C) Conquest
(D) Trade

209. The expression in Spanish "vale un Potosí," meaning "to be of great value" refers to the mountain in Bolivia that was famous in the Early Modern Era for which resource?

(A) Gold
(B) Silver
(C) Copper
(D) Tin

—Casta painting showing a mixed race man "Mestizo" with an Indigenous Native American "Indian" woman with mixed race children who were referred to as "coyote."

210. The image above can be best understood in the context of which cultural process throughout history?

(A) The Spanish and Portuguese conquest of the Americas

(B) The capture of slaves in the interior of the African continent

(C) The nineteenth-century Latin American independence movements

(D) The Reconquista in the Iberian Peninsula by Christian forces

211. The image above best demonstrates which of the following conclusions about colonial Latin America in the 1500s to 1800s?

(A) A strong industrial base and infrastructure

(B) A predominantly Christian populace

(C) A decline in agriculture and trade

(D) Sharp racial and class divisions

212. The Casta painting is the result of which historical process?

(A) The feudal conditions of peasants in the Iberian Peninsula

(B) The rejection of Enlightenment principles in the Americas

(C) The Ottoman Empire's Devshirme and Janissary system

(D) The intermarriage between Europeans and Native Americans

The Caribbean was the first region in the Americas to receive African slaves via the transatlantic trade. The Spanish crown subsidized the slave traffic to the island settlements in Cuba, Puerto Rico and Santo Domingo in the early sixteenth century, seeking to stimulate a sugar plantation economy much like those that the Iberians had implanted in the eastern Atlantic islands in the late Middle Ages. The Spanish experiment with slaving and sugar planting was short-lived, even though sugar and slavery never completely disappeared from those islands. None the less, it was not until the mid-seventeenth century when English colonists in Barbados made the transition from tobacco and cotton to sugar planting that the Caribbean became a major site in the Atlantic plantation complex and, along with Brazil, the chief American destination for enslaved African workers. Over the next 200 years, the fortunes of different islands and empires waxed and waned in the Caribbean but slavery and slave trading persisted.

—*Caribbean Emancipation* by Christopher Schmidt-Nowara, 2011.

213. Which of the following provides the historical context for the use of African labor, European markets, and a New World crop as discussed in the secondary source above?

(A) The Scientific Revolution

(B) The Commercial Revolution

(C) The Green Revolution

(D) The French Revolution

214. Which economic system was in place when the exchange of goods discussed in the excerpt above arose?

(A) European mercantilist laws

(B) Laissez-faire principles

(C) Renaissance guild bylaws

(D) Medieval manorialism

215. To which location was the greatest number of enslaved Africans transported?

(A) Spanish Mexico

(B) Portuguese Brazil

(C) British North America

(D) Dutch Indonesia

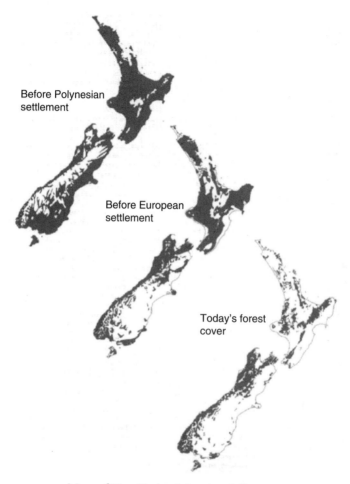

Before Polynesian
settlement

Before European
settlement

Today's forest
cover

—Maps of New Zealand showing deforestation.

216. The image above shows clear evidence of which of the following?

(A) The harmful impact of human settlement
(B) The effect of trade winds on seashores
(C) The damage done by seagull nesting
(D) Rainfall levels between the islands

217. Which of the following peoples first settled in New Zealand starting in 1200?

(A) Europeans
(B) Swahili
(C) Polynesians
(D) Aborigines

—*School of Athens* by the artist Raphael, circa 1509 to 1511.

218. Which of the following breakthrough artistic techniques is utilized in the painting?

(A) Pyramid configuration
(B) Vanishing lines of perspective
(C) Egg yolks as a base for paints
(D) Painting on wet plaster or frescoes

219. Which of the following is a philosophical change during this time that acts as context for the painting?

(A) The increased use of secular and nonreligious themes
(B) The decline of preclassical thought
(C) The rise of a courtier class that espoused chivalric ideals
(D) A decrease in Egyptian and Mesopotamian deities

220. The painting above shows evidence of which of the following?

(A) Medieval figures who helped usher in the Early Modern Era
(B) Individuals from classical and Early Modern Eras
(C) Religious clergy who built up the Roman Catholic Church
(D) People from the Islamic, Jewish, and Christian world

221. One historical argument for the artist Raphael's vision of his era was that

(A) The Islamic world had a huge influence on the Italian and Northern Renaissance.
(B) The classical era and not the Medieval period was the main influence on the Renaissance.
(C) The Byzantine Christian heritage impacted the Renaissance as much as did the Islamic influence.
(D) The Byzantines influenced Renaissance Italy as much as they did early Russia.

I disagree very much with those who are unwilling that Holy Scripture, translated into the vulgar tongue, be read by the uneducated, as if Christ himself taught such intricate doctrines that they could scarcely be understood by very few theologians, or as if the strength of the Christian religion consisted in men's ignorance of it ... . I would that even the lowliest women read the Gospels and the Pauline Epistles. And I would that they were translated into all languages so that they could be read and understood not only by Scots and Irish but also by Turks and Saracens ... . Would that, as a result, the farmer sing some portion of them at the plow, the weaver hum some parts of them to the movement of his shuttle, the traveler lighten the weariness of the journey with stories of this kind!

—Erasmus of Rotterdam, 1529.

222. The above passage clearly shows the influence of which of the following upon Christian theological trends?

   (A) Renaissance humanism
   (B) Enlightenment ideas about rationality
   (C) Catholic dogmatic traditions
   (D) Medieval scholasticism

223. Which of the following best demonstrates the cause for the historical situation in the reading above?

   (A) An increase in spoken languages
   (B) An increase in literacy and printing
   (C) A decrease in Medieval scholarship
   (D) A slow decline in the use of English

224. Based on the evidence in the excerpt above, Renaissance scholars promoted the use of which of the following?

   (A) The Classical languages Greek and Hebrew to best understand Scripture
   (B) The religious conversion of Irish and Turks to Christianity in order to tame their barbarous natures
   (C) The printing of scripture into vernacular languages such as German and English
   (D) The harsh limits put on women to access scriptural and secular literature

225. Which invention in Europe had a profound impact on the increase of literacy?

   (A) Double-entry bookkeeping
   (B) Movable type printing press
   (C) Lateen sails and movable rudders
   (D) Oil-based paints and canvas backings

—"Peasant Dance" by Pieter Bruegel.

226. The painting above is typical of the Northern Renaissance in that

(A) It supported the papacy during the Reformation

(B) It focused on everyday issues and secular concerns

(C) It had bright colors and was painted on canvas

(D) It celebrated religious festivals and ceremonies

227. Which of the following is true of most peasants in Western European societies?

(A) They suffered under harsh conditions since the postclassical era.

(B) They rose in the social structure above merchants and traders.

(C) Their lives began to improve with the end of the Black Death.

(D) They were subject to conscription into the czarist armed forces.

228. Which of the following best defines the legal status of a peasant in Western Europe?

(A) A person who was the property of another and could be bought and sold at will often at auctions.

(B) An industrial worker who was paid hourly wages, or by the piece for his services.

(C) An agricultural worker who was obliged to perform services for a landlord and give their landlord a percentage of their crops.

(D) A person who invests in a risky venture in the hopes of turning a quick profit.

229. In comparison to Russian peasants, Western European peasants by the Early Modern Era differed in that they had which of the following freedoms?

(A) They enjoyed freedom of movement.

(B) They could hunt on their feudal lord's land.

(C) They relied on themselves for protection.

(D) They didn't have to pay tithes to the church.

—*Luther Before the Diet of Worms*, 1521, painted by Anton von Werner.

230. The image depicts Martin Luther answering to Holy Roman Emperor Charles V. Which relationship between church and state best describes Catholic Western Europe in the Early Modern Era?

(A) Rulers created new religions to unify conquered peoples.

(B) Popes asserted that royal laws were superior to divine laws.

(C) Rulers deferred to secular authorities in regulating heresy.

(D) Rulers had mutually supportive relationships with religious authorities.

231. Martin Luther's popularity and survival was due in large part to which of the following factors?

(A) Printing press technology

(B) Black Death/bubonic plague

(C) Gold imports from the Americas

(D) Roman Catholic reforms

—1668 painting of Versailles showing the palace, gardens, and fountains.

The visits of Louis XIV becoming more frequent, he enlarged the château by degrees till its immense buildings afforded better accommodation for the Court than was to be found at St. Germain, where most of the courtiers had to put up with uncomfortable lodgings in the town. The Court was therefore removed to Versailles in 1682, not long before the Queen's death. The new building contained an infinite number of rooms for courtiers, and the King liked the grant of these rooms to be regarded as a coveted privilege. He availed himself of the frequent festivities at Versailles, and his excursions to other places, as a means of making the courtiers assiduous in their attendance and anxious to please him; for he nominated beforehand those who were to take part in them, and could thus gratify some and inflict a snub on others.

—Courtier San Simon on life at Versailles.

232. Which of the following best explains why rulers continue to use monumental architecture during the period from 1450 to 1750?

(A) To celebrate their coronations

(B) To create a gathering places for worship

(C) To legitimize their rule and authority

(D) To provide jobs for the masses

233. Which of the following terms best describes the form of government practiced by the French King Louis XIV?

(A) Constitutional monarchy

(B) Absolute monarchy

(C) Totalitarian dictatorship

(D) Parliamentary mandate

—Print showing the French King Louis XIV visiting the Academy of the Sciences in 1671.

234. Based on the image above, which of the following was a cause of the Scientific Revolution in Europe during the seventeenth and eighteenth centuries?

(A) Royal patronage and support
(B) The trial of Galileo Galilei
(C) The backing of the Pope
(D) The spread of gunpowder

235. Compared to the result depicted in the image, a scientific revolution did NOT come to Asia because of which of the following?
    (A) Asia was completely isolated from the West and refrained from trade and contact.
    (B) Asia had little experience with literacy and lacked an educated scholar class.
    (C) Asian monarchs were primarily interested in conquest and less in art and science.
    (D) Intellectual curiosity was being stifled by a strict adherence to belief systems.

Nine Principles of National Economy

First: to inspect the country's soil with the greatest care and not to leave the agricultural possibilities ... unconsidered. Above all no trouble or expense should be spared to discover gold and silver

Fourth, Gold and silver once in the country, where from its own mines or obtained by industry from foreign countries, are under no circumstances to be taken out for any purposes ... but must always remain in circulation

Fifth, the inhabitants of the country should make every effort to get along with their domestic products ... and to do without foreign products as far a possible (except where great need leaves no alternative ... which Indian spices are an example)

Seventh, such foreign commodities should in this case be imported in unfinished form and worked up within the country, thus earning the wages of manufacturing [here].

Eight, opportunities should be sought night and day for selling the country's ... goods to these foreigners in manufactured form ... .

—*Austria Over All, If She Only Will,* by Philip Von Hornick, 1684.
Hornick was a Prussian civil servant.

236. Which of the following economic policies is reflected in the reading above?
    (A) Socialism
    (B) Trade guilds
    (C) Mercantilism
    (D) Capitalism

237. The economic philosophy highlighted above was an aspect of what political system?
    (A) Totalitarian dictatorship
    (B) Islamic theocracy
    (C) Liberal democracy
    (D) Absolute monarchy

Formerly the earth produced all sorts
of fruit, plants and roots.
But now almost nothing grows ... .
Then the floods, the lakes and the blue waves
Brought abundant fish.
But now hardly one can be seen.
The misery increases more.
The same applies to other goods ... .
Frost and cold torment people
The good years are rare.
If everything should be put in a verse
Only a few take care of the miserables ... .

—Olafur Einarsson (1573–1659),
a pastor in eastern Iceland in the North Atlantic.

238. According to a popular historical argument, which of the following is described above?

(A) The Columbian Exchange
(B) The bubonic plague
(C) The Big Wind
(D) The Little Ice Age

239. Which of the following resulted from the condition described above?

(A) Iceland's population increased.
(B) Iceland's population declined.
(C) Iceland's population stayed the same.
(D) Iceland's population migrated to Greenland.

—"Standing on the Ugra River," 1480. Miniature in Russian chronicle, sixteenth century. "And our men had beaten many foes with arrows and muskets, and their arrows had fallen between our men, and had nobody hurting, and had repelling them off the shore."

240. Which of the following acts as context for the image above of Russia in the Early Modern Era (1450–1750)?

   (A) The extension of the Silk Road into Russia
   (B) The rise of the Russian csars and state
   (C) The decline of serfdom in European Russia
   (D) The use of the rivers as conduits for trade

241. Based on the image and the brief text, which technology had diffused into the Russian state by the fifteenth century?

(A) Navigational

(B) Bow and arrow

(C) Gunpowder

(D) Steam power

In the year 1497, in the month of September, the Grand Prince of all Rus' Ivan Vasilievic, with his children and boyars, compiled a code of law on how boyars and major-domos (okolnichii) are to administer justice.

Article 8. And if evidence is brought against anyone of theft, brigandage, murder, false accusation, or any other such evil deed, and he is a notorious criminal, then the boyar is to order him executed and the sum at issue paid from his property, and whatever remains of this property shall be taken by the boyar and his secretary for themselves.

Article 57. And peasants may leave a canton [to go to another canton], or [go] from village to village, once a year, for a week before and a week after St. George's Day in the autumn.

—The Sudebnik was the legal code of Russia passed in 1497.

242. The code of laws above show a large degree of autonomy for Russian nobles, the boyars. This was probably due to which factor?

(A) Russia's tradition of liberal light-handed government

(B) Russia's trust in its tradition and religions

(C) Russia's lack of warm water ports and harbors

(D) Russia's immense size and difficulty of governing

243. What is one theory for the continuation of serfdom in Russia whereas it had largely died out in Western Europe?

(A) Its vast size yet relatively small population led to a need to control serfs as a source of labor.

(B) Serfs were originally from southern Europe and the popularity of scientific racism hardened attitudes towards them.

(C) The end of the Silk Road trade made agriculture more important and serfs were now being sold for money.

(D) Russia borrowed many Mongol ideas and the Mongols convinced peasants to become serfs.

—Woodcut of Czar Peter the Great shearing off the beard of a noble.

244. Czar Peter was opposed to nobles having beards. He felt they were in opposition to which of the following changes, he trying to institute in Russia?

(A) Technology
(B) Modernization
(C) Centralization
(D) Expansion

245. Which of the following items of clothing or appearance was NOT seen by various governments in world history as oppositional to change?

(A) Shaved heads and pigtails during the Qing dynasty
(B) Brimmed hats during Ataturk's reign in Turkey
(C) Powdered wigs during the French Revolution
(D) Wearing samurai swords in Meiji Japan

246. How did Russia tend to fit into the emerging global economy in the period 1450–1750?

(A) As a source of serf labor transported to till the soils of Western Europe

(B) As a market for grain grown in the New World

(C) As the primary Old World destination of the silver being taken out of the New World

(D) As a supplier of grain, timber, fur, and other raw materials to the West

In October 1679, Frederick Philipse shipped the following ship cargo from Manhattan to Amsterdam on board *The Charles*.	In May 1680, *The Charles* returned to Manhattan with a ship cargo to New York that included the following items.
2345 beaver skins	55 coils of heavy rope
2694 small furs	538 pair of Wadmoll stockings
14 cat skins	1494 rolls of Holland cloth
104 black bear skins	20 dozen pewter spoons
1355 fox skins	209 gun barrels
438 otter skins	18 cases of window glass
1382 raccoon skins	725 drinking glasses
512 cow skins (in the hair)	18 dozen spectacles
181 hogsheads (large barrels) of Maryland tobacco	290 iron pots
166 sticks of Honduras logwood	503 gross of tobacco pipes
	200 cases of nails
	22 shovels
	10 pieces of colored calico cloth

—Ship ledgers of the Dutch ship *The Charles*.

247. The goods listed above are best described as which of the following pairs?

(A) Raw materials/manufactured goods

(B) Animals products/metal products

(C) Of American origin/of Asian origin

(D) Factory goods/unfinished goods

248. The goods listed to and from the colony of Manhattan and Amsterdam above demonstrate which of the following economic practices/theories?

(A) Communism

(B) The guild system

(C) Capitalism

(D) Mercantilism

—Sketch of a Caravel ship.

249. Ships such as the one in the image were most likely to be financed or backed by

(A) Wealthy individual investors

(B) Joint-stock companies

(C) Piracy and theft

(D) Letters of marque

250. Which of the following was NOT a technological innovation in the Iberian ship development in the fifteenth and sixteenth centuries?

(A) Sternpost rudder

(B) Lateen sails

(C) Deep water hulls

(D) Multiple ranks of oars

Short-Answer Question

One cannot claim that Europe indeed discovered America in 1492, when its actual image of it at the time was that of a few islands off the shores of China. In order for Europeans fully to discover America, they first had to realize that what Columbus had in fact discovered beyond the Atlantic was a previously unknown fourth continent that was absolutely distinct and separate from other three, a "New World," so to speak.

That such a continent did not appear all of a sudden full-blown on October 12, 1492, is quite evident from the way it is actually portrayed on European maps from the early sixteenth to late eighteenth century. As one observer of the sixteenth-century cartographic [the science of drawing maps] scene put it, Europe's image of the New World "seems to have developed through a process of slow and painful accretion [gathering] with many maps representing abortive [unsuccessful] efforts to synthesize [combine] logical configurations out of fragmentary and confusing information."

—Eviatar Zerubavel in *Terra Cognita:*
The Mental Discovery of America (1992).

251. (a) Explain ONE way in which this document challenges the idea of a "European discovery" of the Americas?

252. (b) Give ONE piece of evidence from the reading above that supports the author's claim above?

253. (c) Give ONE piece of evidence NOT from the reading that supports the author's claim?

CHAPTER 3

The Modern Era: 1750 to 1900

Controlling Idea: The Long Nineteenth Century

Historians have written of the *Long nineteenth century* from 1750 to 1914 but recently cut down to 1900. This dynamic period has seen two major revolutions: economic in the industrial revolution and political in a series of revolutions. Originally limited to a core in the Western world, revolutions soon spread out to all corners of the globe that were first exposed in the previous era. In 1750 the Industrial Revolution was in its infancy and did not shape life in a significant way outside the West and its New World colonies. By 1900 there was not a corner of the globe that had not been impacted by the growth of this dynamic new economic force. This era also saw an unprecedented amount of migration both willingly and with the continuation of the slave trade, unwilling. This change was most visible in the new technology and transformed societies. Industrialization was symbiotic with the rise of capitalism. This era also saw challenges to capitalism in socialism, communism, and even in artistic and literary forms. The political corollary of these economic changes was that the old feudal and monarchical systems of rulers were overthrown and undermined in a series of events that took off on a global scale in the wake of the French Revolution. The long nineteenth century continued with the increase of more widespread beliefs, or "isms," such as nationalism and feminism.

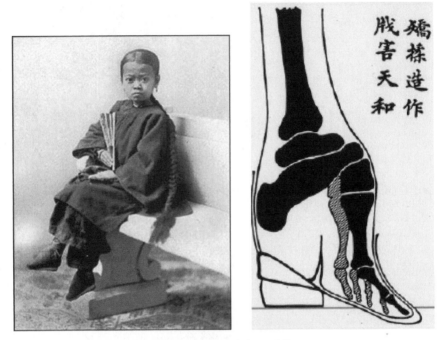

—Chinese girl with bound feet.

254. Which of the following conclusions is best supported by the two images above?
    (A) Chinese society supported female empowerment.
    (B) Chinese society was heavily influenced by Vietnam.
    (C) Chinese society was a strict patriarchy.
    (D) Chinese society practiced social Darwinism.

255. The practice of footbinding diminished in China during the late nineteenth and early twentieth centuries. Which of the following had the greatest impact on its ending?
    (A) Japanese imperialists
    (B) American merchants
    (C) Daoist monks
    (D) Western missionaries

When Chinese civilization encounters a barbarian people, those barbarians are transformed by Chinese ways into a civilized people. Barbarians look up to China and are delighted to receive its civilizing influence. This is the way things are in the natural order of things. This is the way human beings ought to feel. China is like the roots of a plant supplying nourishment for the branches and leaves. It is like the hands and feet that protect the belly and chest of the human body. This should never change ... .

These Europeans come from a land far away from China, so it is only natural that their customs are quite different from Chinese customs ... .

However, unfortunately the world is such a big place that Europe had no contact with China for quite a long time ... . That meant that, regrettably, Europe was not introduced to the basic principles of the Great Way, and Europeans were not turned into more virtuous people by its civilizing power. Europe has instead been saturated with a lot of misleading notions, and Europeans as a result tend to spout a bunch of nonsense, criticizing the teachings of the earlier Confucian sages and condemning the teachings of later NeoConfucian philosophers. It appears to be next to impossible to awaken those men to their true inner nature and get them to change their mistaken practices. Europeans do have a remarkable talent for technology. They easily surpass the Chinese in that area. But that achievement makes them arrogant, and they think that they can convert the whole world to their way of thinking. They need to think again!

—Korean scholar Yi Hangno (1792–1868),
"Sinifying the Western Barbarians."

256. Which of the following explains why Yi Hangno held such attitudes?

(A) Korea was a country with a long Chinese influence.
(B) Confucianism, like China's writing system, was rejected.
(C) Korea was colonized by Japan in the sixteenth century.
(D) Korea sent educational missions to Germany and France.

257. According to the text, the cause of the lack of interaction between Europe and China is due to

(A) Warfare
(B) Geography
(C) Philosophy
(D) Belief systems

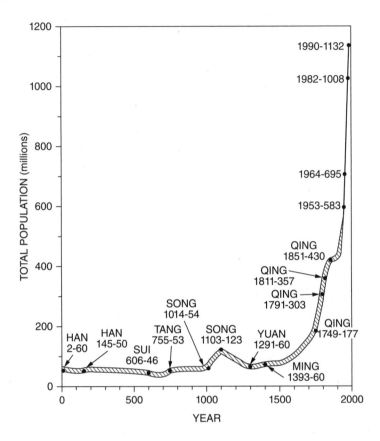

258. Which of the following best supports a historical argument for the huge population growth illustrated in the chart during the Qing dynasty from 1644 to 1911?

(A) New World crops
(B) Gunpowder technology
(C) Domestication of animals
(D) Silk Road trade

259. Which of the following resulted from the big jump in China's population during the Qing dynasty (1644–1911)?

(A) A strict ban on polygamy as a way to increase the number of available brides
(B) A steady migration from China to areas like the Americas and South East Asia
(C) A one-child policy for each married couple in the People's Republic of China
(D) The formation of state education for each child born in China before 1911

You, O King from afar, have yearned after the blessings of our civilization, and in your eagerness to come into touch with our converting influence have sent an Embassy across the sea bearing a memorial. I have already taken note of your respectful spirit of submission, have treated your mission with extreme favor and loaded it with gifts, ... honoring you with the bestowal of valuable presents.

... Hitherto, all European nations, including your own country's barbarian merchants, have carried on their trade with Our Celestial Empire at Canton. Such has been the procedure for many years, although Our Celestial Empire possesses all things in prolific abundance and lacks no product within its borders. There was therefore no need to import the manufactures of outside barbarians in exchange for our own produce. But as the tea, silk, and porcelain which the Celestial Empire produces are absolute necessities to European nations and to yourselves, we have permitted, as a signal mark of favor, that foreign hongs should be established at Canton, so that your wants might be supplied and your country thus participate in our beneficence. But your Ambassador has now put forward new requests which completely fail to recognize the Throne's principle to "treat strangers from afar with indulgence," and to exercise a pacifying control over barbarian tribes, the world over ... .

Your Ambassador requests facilities for ships of your nation to call at Ningpo, Chusan, Tientsin and other places for purposes of trade. Until now trade with European nations has always been conducted at Macao, where the foreign hongs are established to store and sell foreign merchandise. Your nation has obediently complied with this regulation for years past without raising any objection. Furthermore, no interpreters are available, so you would have no means of explaining your wants, and nothing but general inconvenience would result. For the future, as in the past, I decree that your request is refused and that the trade shall be limited to Macao.

—Letter to Queen Victoria of England from
Chinese Commissioner Lin ZeXu, 1839.

260. The letter above is best understood in the context of

(A) The Taiping Rebellion

(B) The Macartney mission

(C) The Meiji Restoration

(D) The Opium War

261. Which was a direct result of the historical events referred to above?

(A) The island of Hong Kong became a British colony.

(B) The port of Yokohama was opened to trade.

(C) The Russians were forced to pay an indemnity.

(D) Korea was put under Japanese protection.

British Trade in Hongkong and other Chinese ports

Average Annual Value	1854–63 in thousands	1864–73 in thousands	1874–83 in thousands
Imports	£9,796	£11,941	£13,302
Exports	£3,242	£8,193	£8,432

British Economic Interests In The Far East by E. M. Gull, 1943.

262. Which of the following best represents an economic development in the period 1750 to 1900 that led to the situation represented in the chart?
    (A) China's trade with the outside world increased.
    (B) China's trade with the outside world decreased.
    (C) China's trade with the outside world stayed the same.
    (D) China's currency was based on gold and platinum.

263. Which of the following best represents a political development in the period 1750 to 1900 that led to the situation represented in the chart?
    (A) China suffered a devastating civil war called the Taiping Rebellion.
    (B) China lost the Opium War, which had its origins in trade relations
    (C) The succession of the Qing Emperor Tongzhi from Qing Emperor Xianfeng
    (D) The opening of Japan by US gunboats under Commodore Matthew Perry

—*China: The Cake of Kings ... and Emperors*, in Le Petit Journal, 1898.

264. Which of the following contributed most directly to the condition depicted in the cartoon above?

(A) China's total isolation from the rest of the world

(B) China's military weakness compared to the West

(C) China's dynastic cycle guaranteed transition to a ruling elite capable of halting Western imperial designs on China

(D) China's trade imbalance with Japan and the West

265. China's condition in the cartoon is best compared to the situation in which of the following areas of the world in the late nineteenth and early twentieth century?

(A) Africa
(B) Western Europe
(C) United States of America
(D) Eastern Europe

266. Based on the image, why is Japan seated at the table instead of being a victim itself of being cut into pieces?

(A) Japan modernized and strengthened itself through the Meiji reforms.
(B) Western nations were not interested in Japan due to its small size.
(C) Japan had not opened itself to outside influences yet by 1898.
(D) By 1898 Japan had already defeated Britain and France in war.

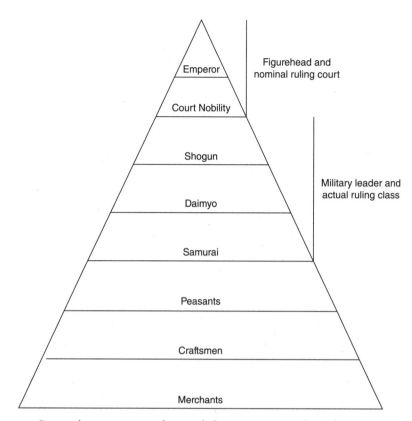

—Image above represents the social classes in Japan under Tokugawa shogunate, (1600–1868).

267. Which of the following shows a strong continuity in Japanese society?

(A) Craftsmen above peasants in the social pyramid
(B) The daimyo or land-owning nobles ruling over domains
(C) A scholar-elite staffing government positions
(D) Merchants at the bottom of the social pyramid

268. One key difference in the social pyramid of Tokugawa Japan compared to China is that

(A) The samurai were in China and also acted as a scholar-gentry class.
(B) Peasants in China had a higher status than in Japan during the Qing dynasty.
(C) The Japanese emperor had no real power and was a symbolic figurehead.
(D) The merchants were at the bottom of the social pyramid.

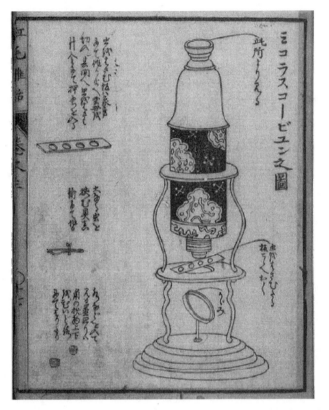

—Illustration of a microscope in a 1787 book, *Various Accounts from the Dutch.*

269. The image above is proof of which of the following truths of Japanese isolation?

(A) It was absolute with zero contact between Japan and the outside world.

(B) It was never total isolation and a small but important stream of information came through Nagasaki.

(C) The Japanese learned more from China during the Tokugawa era than earlier eras.

(D) The Japanese were only interested in religious and other cultural Western influences.

270. Which types of information from the outside world were Japan and China most interested in attaining?

(A) Religious and cultural

(B) Linguistic and social

(C) Scientific and technical

(D) Governmental and diplomatic

GREAT AND GOOD FRIEND: I send you this public letter by Commodore Matthew C. Perry, an officer of the highest rank in the navy of the United States, and commander of the squadron now visiting your imperial majesty's dominions.

I have directed Commodore Perry to assure your imperial majesty that I entertain the kindest feelings toward your majesty's person and government, and that I have no other object in sending him to Japan but to propose to your imperial majesty that the United States and Japan should live in friendship and have commercial intercourse with each other.

The Constitution and laws of the United States forbid all interference with the religious or political concerns of other nations. I have particularly charged Commodore Perry to abstain from every act which could possibly disturb the tranquility of your imperial majesty's dominions.

The United States of America reach from ocean to ocean, and our Territory of Oregon and State of California lie directly opposite to the dominions of your imperial majesty. Our steamships can go from California to Japan in eighteen days … .

I am desirous that our two countries should trade with each other, for the benefit both of Japan and the United States. We know that the ancient laws of your imperial majesty's government do not allow of foreign trade, except with the Chinese and the Dutch; but as the state of the world changes and new governments are formed, it seems to be wise, from time to time, to make new laws. There was a time when the ancient laws of your imperial majesty's government were first made.

…

I have sent Commodore Perry, with a powerful squadron, to pay a visit to your imperial majesty's renowned city of Yedo: friendship, commerce, a supply of coal and provisions, and protection for our shipwrecked people. May the Almighty have your imperial majesty in His great and holy keeping!

… Your good friend, MILLARD FILLMORE

—Website Asia for Educators.

271. This letter by US president Fillmore is addressed to "his imperial majesty" in Japan. This indicates which of the following statements about US knowledge of Japan in the 1850s?

(A) They were very respectful and tried to adhere to Confucian notions of propriety and diplomacy.

(B) They failed to understand that Japan was a tributary nation to China, similar to how Korea and Vietnam were tribute states.

(C) They were unaware that the Japanese emperor was a figurehead and that the shogun actually rules the nation.

(D) They believed that the Japanese emperor was a direct descendant of the sungoddess Amaterasu.

272. Which of the following was a direct result of the visit of US commodore Matthew Perry to Japan in 1854?

(A) Japan opened up and soon sent diplomatic missions to Western nations.

(B) Japan reverted to its samurai tradition and fought losing battles to stay isolated.

(C) Japan chose to only open up to the Russians and signed a treaty in Hokkaido.

(D) Japan increased some trade but resisted US efforts at diplomatic relations.

—*Steam train between Tokyo and Yokohama* by HIroshige, 1875.

273. Which of the following events was most important in creating the economic conditions illustrated in the image above?

(A) The Tokugawa shogun's decision to isolate itself from the world in 1613

(B) U.S. Navy commodore Matthew Perry's visit to Tokyo Bay in 1853

(C) The Chinese acceptance of the Treaty of Nanking in 1842 to open more trade ports

(D) The Japanese seizure of Korea and Taiwan in the Sino-Japanese War in 1895

274. Compared to the changes in Japan shown in the image, by the late nineteenth century China

    (A) largely did not reform its society and economy

    (B) surpassed Japan in reforming its society and economy

    (C) had still not opened its nation to foreign trade and influence

    (D) had only reformed its economy but not its politics or society

275. The Japanese woodblock print was produced in a domestic system with specialized labor with a breakdown of labor tasks. This was part of a Japanese tradition that stretched back to before the Tokugawa era. Which of the following therefore is true?

    (A) Japan's belief system had switched to the monotheistic faith of Christianity.

    (B) Japan's artistic tradition had long surpassed the West in its use of colors and detail.

    (C) Japan's society held merchants and craftsmen in the highest regard and status.

    (D) Japan's modernization had some antecedents before the encounter with the West in 1853.

Timeline

—1871, Meiji government had already issued the (Cropped Hair Edict), encouraging samurai to cut their distinctive chonmage top-knot.

—1873, The samurai were replaced by a modern, Western-style, conscripted army. This new army consisted largely of peasants.

—1873, Samurai retained some of their salaries, paid for by the new Meiji government, but these were so low that many samurai were forced to find new employment.

—1876 (Sword Abolishment Edict), samurai lost their right to wear swords.

—1876, Meiji government stipends to samurai and daimyo were permanently suspended, and samurai were required to convert them into interest-bearing government bonds.

276. Which of the following changes can be discerned from a close analysis of the text above?

(A) The samurai were increasingly becoming the ruling class of Japan.
(B) Young samurai were slowly adopting Western style of dress and hairstyle.
(C) Color photography was available to all Japanese, even the peasant class.
(D) Women could also become samurai if they passed the civil service exams.

277. Based on the timeline above, which of the following changes will take place soon?

(A) Samurai numbers will increase by opening the status to peasants.
(B) Samurai will be required to carry two swords to show status.
(C) Samurai status will be determined by civil service exams.
(D) Samurai status will eventually be eliminated.

The money that a factory girl earned was often more than a farmer's income for the entire year. For these rural families, the girls were an invaluable source of income. The poor peasants during this period had to turn over 60 percent of their crops to the landlord. Thus the poor peasants had only bits of rice mixed with weeds for food. The peasants' only salvation was the girls who went to work in the factories.

—Buddhist priest from a rural area on textile workers in Japan, circa 1900.

278. Compared to the situation in the excerpt, mechanization of the cotton textile industry in Western nations was similar in that they

(A) Relied exclusively on believers in Buddhism
(B) Relied on generous government financing
(C) Relied on a rice-based diet for workers
(D) Relied heavily on female labor from rural areas

279. A historian studying Japanese industrialization would most likely find this account useful as a source of information because?

(A) Buddhism has been a popular religion in Japan for centuries.
(B) The priest was from an area that recruited these workers.
(C) The landlords and factory owners were often the same individuals.
(D) The Buddhist clergy encouraged the monastic lifestyle for women.

—The port of Hanoi in Indochina in 1891 from French newspaper *Le Monde* illustrated.

280. In the French newspaper image above, which of the following demonstrates continuity in Southeast Asia in the era of 1750–1900?

(A) The use of conical straw hats, carrying poles, and rickshaws

(B) The use of steam-powered riverboats and rickshaws

(C) The importation of European manufactured goods

(D) The building of French government buildings

281. The image is similar to other Asian port cities such as Shanghai, Kobe, and Manilla in which of the following areas?

(A) These port cities were all part of French colonies since the eighteenth century.
(B) These areas of the world were intensely connected to the world commerce.
(C) These ports all used sail boats and other older means of transportation.
(D) The local people were opposed to trade and interaction with Europe.

The peoples we will be living alongside are Muslims; their first article of faith is "There is no other god but God, and Mahomet is his prophet." Do not contradict them; treat them as you treated the Jews, the Italians; respect their muftis and their imams, as you respected their rabbis and bishops. Have the same tolerance for the ceremonies prescribed by the Quran, for their mosques, as you had for the convents, for the synagogues, for the religion of Moses and that of Jesus Christ. The Roman legions used to protect all religions. You will here find different customs to those of Europe, you must get accustomed to them. The people among whom we are going treat women differently to us; but in every country whoever violates one is a monster. Pillaging only enriches a small number of men; it dishonors us, it destroys our resources; it makes enemies of the people who it is in our interest to have as our friends. The first city we will encounter was built by Alexander [the Great]. We shall find at every step great remains worthy of exciting French emulation.

—Napoleon to his troops just before disembarking at
Alexandria, Egypt in 1798.

282. Based on the reading above, what attitude did Napoleon seem to want to impart to his troops toward the Egyptians?

(A) Hatred
(B) Acceptance
(C) Indifference
(D) Piety

283. The French invasion of Egypt signals the beginning of what era in the Middle East periodization?

(A) Ancient
(B) Postclassical
(C) Modern
(D) Postmodern

284. Napoleon's military venture in Egypt resulted in which discovery in an unrelated field?

(A) Gold deposits were found in the Nile Delta region by French sailors.
(B) New trade routes were opened to the Red Sea and Indian Ocean.
(C) The Rosetta Stone was found, which enabled translation of hieroglyphics.
(D) Egyptian-built steam engines were quickly adopted by France.

—Hilye, a calligraphy panel that describes the physical appearance of the Prophet Muhammad by Kazasker Mustafa İzzet Efendi (1801–1876).

285. The above image from the nineteenth century about the Muslim prophet Muhammad represents a continuity in Sunni Islamic tradition in that

(A) It adheres to a mystical and less doctrinaire form of Islam

(B) It shows an image that borrows heavily from Buddhist influences

(C) It refrains from depicting any human image especially the prophet

(D) It uses phrases and words from both the Old and New Testaments

286. Which of the following changes were introduced into the Middle East in the early 1800s and would later challenge the image?

(A) Gunpowder weapons

(B) Printing press

(C) Radio technology

(D) Cameras

287. The reason for the elimination of the Mamluks of Egypt and Janissaries in the Ottoman Empire was which of the following?

(A) New technology such as tanks and planes made foot soldiers obsolete.

(B) Confucian teachings did not value military skills on the battlefield.

(C) The Mamluks and Janissaries had non-Islamic origins and were suspect.

(D) They were rebellious and refused to modernize their weapons and tactics.

Short-Answer Question

[Ottoman Pasha Muhammad] Ali understood the potential of this new export crop and ordered it grown throughout the country. Coercion was integral to this project from the beginning. Peasants were forced to cultivate cotton on state-owned lands for their yearly corvée duty, a forced-labor tax. On their own lands they were also forced to plant cotton in specific ways, to sell their crop to the state, and to work without pay. The government set prices for the cotton and controlled all aspects of its transport and sale to foreign merchants in Alexandria, who were explicitly disallowed to directly purchase cotton from Egyptian growers. Workers were also forced to dig canals to water the crop and to build roads that crisscrossed Lower Egypt to move it to market. As Merchants' Magazine and Commercial Review observed in New York in 1843, "Cotton is not willingly cultivated by the fellah [peasant], and would probably be scarcely produced at all but through the despotic interference of the pasha."

—Sven Beckert, Empire of Cotton: A Global History, 2014.

288. Identify ONE similarity of crop production with another part of the world in the nineteenth century.

289. Identify ONE difference of crop production with another part of the world in the nineteenth century.

290. Identify ONE similarity or difference of crop production with a different time period (up to 2001).

Hatt-ı Hümayun granted that all forms of religion freely worshiped, no subject hindered in the exercise of the religion, nor be in any way annoyed. No one shall be compelled to change their religion.

Hatt-ı Hümayun granted that all the subjects, without distinction, shall be received into the Civil and Military Schools. Every community is authorized to establish Public Schools of Science, Art, and Industry. However, in these public schools the methods of instruction and the choice of professors in schools of this class shall be under the control of a "Mixed Council of Public Instruction (Council of Public Instruction)" (Education ministry).

Hatt-ı Hümayun granted that there will be formulation of the new Codes; penal, correctional, and commercial laws, and rules of procedure and they were translated and published in all the languages

—Excerpt from the Tanzimat Reforms.

291. Which group in Ottoman society would be most upset by the changes described above?

(A) Turkish Muslims
(B) Armenian Christians
(C) Ottoman Jews
(D) Arab Muslims

292. The Tanzimat reforms represented which of the following changes in the Ottoman Empire?

(A) Imperialism
(B) Modernization
(C) Mechanization
(D) Nationalism

293. Which of the following historical events prompted the Ottomans to begin the Tanzimat reforms?

(A) Russo-Japanese War
(B) The Auspicious Event
(C) Battle of the Pyramids
(D) The Crimean War

Figures on Nationalities within the Ottoman Empire

Ethnic Group (Total Population) Percentage of Empire	Subgroup	Subgroup Population
Turkish group (14,020,000) 49.1%	Ottoman Turks	13,500,000
	Turkomans	300,000
	Tatars	220,000
Greco-Latin group (3,520,000) 12.3%	Greeks	2,100,000
	Kutzo-Vlachs	220,000
	Albanians	1,200,000
Slavic group (4,550,000) 15.9%	Serbo-Croatians	1,500,000
	Bulgarians	3,000,000
	Cossacks	32,000
	Lipovans	18,000
Georgian group (1,020,000) 3.6%	Circassians	1,000,000
	Lazes	20,000
Indian group (212,000) .7%	Gypsies	212,000
Persian group (3,620,000) 12.7%	Armenians	2,500,000
	Kurds	1,000,000
	Druze, Mutawalis, Nusayris, and Yazidis	120,000
Semites (1,611,000) 5.6%	Jews	158,000
	Arabs	1,000,000
	Syrian-Chaldaeans	160,000
	Maronites	293,000

Total Population of the Ottoman Empire, 1876: 28,553,000

294. The series of reforms around the mid-nineteenth century that put all Ottomans, regardless of religion or ethnicity, on an equal footing legally was called

(A) The 100 Days of Reform
(B) The Tanzimat Reforms
(C) The Meiji Reforms
(D) The Dhimmi Reforms

295. By the end of the nineteenth century, which of the following was a result of the Ottoman division of its subjects by ethnicity and region?

(A) A rise in nationalism among the empire's ethnicities

(B) Calls for the creation of a worker-led state

(C) A migration of peoples to the Americas from Eurasia

(D) The expansion of the Ottoman Empire in Asia

"SAVE ME FROM MY FRIENDS!"

—Political cartoon depicting the Afghan Emir Sher Ali with his "friends," the Russian Bear and British Lion (1878).

296. The cartoon above is best understood in the context of which of the following?

(A) Hundred Days of Reform in Western China

(B) Janissary Revolt or Auspicious Incident

(C) Power rivalries or "The Great Game" in Central Asia

(D) Sunni and Shiite divide over the caliphate

297. Which of the following mirrors the situation that the peoples of central Asia found themselves in dealing with outside powers?

(A) Scramble for Africa

(B) Sepoy Rebellion

(C) Treaty of Kanagawa

(D) Suez Crisis

Reading 1

The tobacco concession granted a monopoly on both the purchase and sale of tobacco within Persia to an English company, headed by Major Gerald Talbot, for a period of fifty 108 years. During this period the Qajar rulers would annually receive 15,000 pounds and 25 percent of the profit generated by the concession arrangement. The agreement stated all producers were required to inform the concessionaires of the amount of crop that they produced annually and then sell their entire crop to the British company. All tobacco merchants were required to seek permits from the concessionaires and immediately pay, in cash, for all tobacco they obtained. The plan was, basically, to interject the company into the traditional relationships between individual producers and regional sellers.

—Secondary sources by SC Poulson,
on the British tobacco concession in Persia/Iran.

Reading 2

In the name of God the Merciful, the Forgiving. Today the use of tunbaku and tobacco, in whatever fashion, is reckoned as war against the Imam of the Age (may God hasten his glad advent)

—Fatwa or Islamic decree.

298. The share of the Imperial Tobacco Corporation was part of the concession forced on Perisa by Britain in the late 1800s. This demonstrates which of the following conclusions?

(A) Tobacco was the main export from Britain, where it originated.
(B) Persia was a major player in the big power rivalry in central Asia.
(C) Europeans could dominate a nation despite not militarily conquering it.
(D) Britain was concerned about Italian influence in central Asia.

299. The fatwa against tobacco was very effective and tobacco use dropped significantly in Persia from the 1890s to the early 1900s. This is in part explained by which of the following?

(A) Christian authorities took a dim view of tobacco use.
(B) The surgeon general issued a warning against tobacco.
(C) It was seen as a favor to opium merchants and users.
(D) Persians were increasingly upset with Europeans influence.

—Robert Clive and Mir Jafar after the Battle of Plassey, 1757.

300. In the painting above, which of the following changes in Indian political life occurs?

(A) Elephants are now being traded by the British to China and Southeast Asia.

(B) The East India Company rises to become a major power on the subcontinent.

(C) The Islamic empires like the Mughals now start using gunpowder weapons.

(D) The Dutch and Portuguese go to war over control over Sri Lanka.

301. Which rival European power did the British defeat in the eighteenth century in its drive to control the Indian subcontinent?

(A) Netherlands

(B) France

(C) Italy

(D) Portugal

We desire no extension of our present territorial possessions; and, while we will permit no aggression upon our dominions or our rights to be attempted with impunity, we shall sanction no encroachment on those of others. We shall respect the rights, dignity, and honor of native princes as our own and we desire that they, as well as our own subjects, should enjoy that prosperity and that social advancement which can only be secured by internal peace and by good government ... .

Firmly relying ourselves on the truth of Christianity, and acknowledging with gratitude; the solace of religion, we disclaim alike the right and the desire to impose our convictions on any of our subjects. We declare it to be our royal will and pleasure that none be in anywise favored, none molested or disquieted, by reason of their religious faith or observances, but that all shall alike enjoy the equal and impartial protection of the law ... . Our clemency will be extended to all offenders, save and except those who have been or shall be convicted of having directly taken part in the murder of British subjects. With regard to such, the demands of justice forbid mercy. To all others in arms against the government we hereby promise unconditional pardon, amnesty ... of all offenses against ourselves, our crown and dignity, on the return to their homes and peaceful pursuits.

—Queen Victoria, in 1858. Victoria proclaims the principles
by which India will henceforth be ruled. Edited excerpt.

302. Which of the following continuities can be seen in Queen Victoria's proclamation in 1858?

(A) The British self-confidence of the superiority of the Christian religion
(B) The British desire to not extend their present territorial possessions
(C) The British respect for the rights of the native princes or maharajahs
(D) The British level of control over the Indian economy and taxation

303. What would provide context on why Queen Victoria sought to include the phrase "We declare it to be our royal will and pleasure that none be in anywise favored, none molested or disquieted, by reason of their religious faith or observances" in her proclamation?

(A) It was hoped that many Indians would convert to Christianity.
(B) Victoria is knowledgeable that Muslims were the majority of the Indian population.
(C) It was a lack of religious sensibilities that caused the Sepoy Rebellion.
(D) The East India Company was not interested in promoting the Hindu religion.

One industrial initiative in India developed around Calcutta, where British colonial rule had centered since the East India Company founded the city in 1690. A Hindu Brahman family, the Tagores, established close ties with many British administrators. Without becoming British, they sponsored a number of efforts to revivify India, including new colleges and research centers. Dwarkanath Tagore controlled tax collection in part of Bengal, and early in the 19th century he used part of his profit to found a bank. He also bought up a variety of commercial landholdings and traditional manufacturing operations. In 1834 he joined with British capitalists to establish a diversified company that boasted holdings in mines (including the first Indian coal mine), sugar refineries, and some new textile factories; the equipment was imported from Britain. Tagore's dominant idea was a British-Indian economic and cultural collaboration that would revitalize his country. He enjoyed a high reputation in Europe and for a short time made a success of his economic initiatives. Tagore died on a trip abroad, and his financial empire declined soon after. This first taste of Indian industrialization was significant, but it brought few immediate results. The big news in India, even as Tagore launched his companies, was the rapid decline of traditional textiles under the bombardment of British factory competition; millions of Indian villagers were thrown out of work. Furthermore, relations between Britain and the Indian elite worsened after the mid-1830s as British officials sought a more active economic role and became more intolerant of Indian culture. One British official, admitting no knowledge of Indian scholarship, wrote that "all the historical information" and science available in Sanskrit was "less valuable than what may be found in the most paltry abridgements used at preparatory schools in England." With these attitudes, the kind of collaboration that might have aided Indian appropriation of British industry became impossible.

—Peter Stearns, historian,
The Industrial Revolution in World History, 1993.

304. The British view of Indian culture discussed in the passage is best understood in the context of which of the following?

(A) Changes in Indian government as a result of the Enlightenment

(B) Emerging racial ideologies that were used to justify imperialism

(C) The rise of Marxist ideas regarding the working class

(D) The migration of Indian laborers overseas for plantation labor

305. Which of the following was an effect of the decline in Indian industries discussed in the passage?

(A) India's economy became dependent on Britain for natural resources and raw materials.

(B) India's participation in the world economy declined significantly.

(C) India's economy shifted from producing manufactured goods like cotton textiles to exporting raw materials like cotton.

(D) India's economy relied on the import of British food supplies and culinary expertise.

To sum up the whole, the British rule has been: morally, a great blessing; politically, peace and order on one hand, blunders on the other; materially, impoverishment, relieved as far as the railway and other loans go. The natives call the British system "Sakar ki Churi," the knife of sugar. That is to say, there is no oppression, it is all smooth and sweet, but it is the knife, notwithstanding. I mention this that you should know these feelings. Our great misfortune is that you do not know our wants. When you will know our real wishes, I have not the least doubt that you would do justice. The genius and spirit of the British people is fair play and justice.

—Dadabhai Naoroji in a speech to a London audience in 1871.

306. A historian studying the Raj period of India would find this account most useful for understanding the views of which group of Indians towards British rule?

(A) Hindu peasants
(B) Muslim merchants
(C) Colonial elites
(D) British civil servants

307. Which of the following is generally true of indigenous individuals promoted to assist Western imperialists in their rule of the colony?

(A) When possible, Christians were chosen.
(B) They tended to be from minority ethnic groups.
(C) They were given some Western education and technical training.
(D) All of the above

—Magazine sketch called Christmas in India, in *The Graphic*, 1881.

308. Which of the following changes in migration patterns for the British in India is reflected in the image above?

(A) Family units were becoming more common among British settlers.

(B) British settlers brought their family servants with them to India.

(C) British settlers practiced polygamy to assimilate to Muslim India.

(D) British settlers were now being housed in tents rather than houses.

309. Which of the following acts as a major cause for the scene in the British newspaper, *The Graphic*, in 1881?

(A) The use of Indian servants by expatriate families

(B) The use of sepoy troops in British armed forces

(C) Improved transportation and health services

(D) An increase in available food for British settlers

—Diagram of a slave ship from the Atlantic slave trade. From evidence delivered before the British House of Commons in 1790 and 1791.

310. The image above, which gave a glimpse into the horrors of the Atlantic Slave trade, helped popularize which social movement?

(A) Suffrage

(B) Right to unionize

(C) Religious toleration

(D) Abolition

311. The image above helped bring about which important change in world history?

(A) The ban on torture in the British law system

(B) The end of slavery in the Atlantic world

(C) The refitting of ocean-going passenger ships

(D) The addition of lifeboats in case of storms

We have the power in our hands, moral, physical, and mechanical; the first, based on the Bible; the second, upon the wonderful adaptation of the Anglo-Saxon race to all climates, situations, and circumstances ... the third, bequeathed [given] to us by the immortal James Watt. By his invention [of the steam engine] every river is laid open to us, time and distance are shortened. If his spirit is allowed to witness the success of his invention here on earth, I can conceive no application of it that would meet his approbation [approval] more than seeing the mighty streams of the Mississippi and the Amazon, the Niger and the Nile, the Indus and the Ganges, stemmed by hundreds of steam-vessels, carrying the glad tidings of "peace and good will towards men" into the dark places of the earth which are now filled with cruelty. This power, which has only been in existence for a quarter of a century, has rendered rivers truly "the highway of nations," and made easy what it would have been difficult if not impossible, to accomplish without it ... .

—Macgregor Laird, Scottish explorer and shipbuilder,
wrote this narrative after traveling by steamship up the
Niger River in West Africa between 1832 and 1834.

312. Which of the following best explains the historical circumstances that led to British exploration in West Africa in the 1830s?

   (A) British industrial power
   (B) British moral superiority
   (C) British desire for tea
   (D) British limited monarchy

313. Which of the following best describes his attitudes toward European and non-Western cultures?

   (A) Socialist
   (B) Social Darwinist
   (C) Misogynist
   (D) Indifference

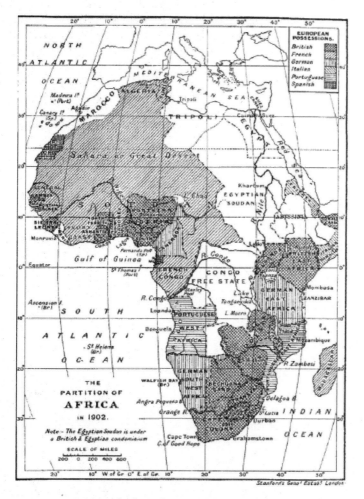

—Map of Africa showing political divisions.

314. Many of the political divisions shown on this map were directly related to the

(A) Slave trade
(B) Boer War
(C) Opium Wars
(D) Berlin Conference

315. The political divisions in Africa were based primarily on which of the following factors?

(A) Geographic and topographic features
(B) Linguistic and cultural differences
(C) European desires and claims
(D) The location of manufacturing centers

The first large-scale production [of cocoa] was in the 1880s from Portuguese plantations on the islands of São Tomé and Principe. These plantations became notorious for using workers who were slaves in all but name, despite slavery having been officially abolished in 1875. Between 1888 and 1908 over 67,000 people from the African mainland were shipped to the two islands, mostly from Angola. In 1905 William Cadbury, concerned about reports of slavery, joined with Frys, Rowntrees and the Stollwerck chocolate firm of Cologne, and together sent Dr. Joseph Burtt to investigate conditions on the islands and in Angola. Burtt reported that Angolan people were taken to the islands "against their will, and often under conditions of great cruelty", and that it was almost unknown for them to return to their homeland. Death rates were extremely high, an average 11% per year for adults for those estates on Principe. In 1909 the four companies announced that they would boycott cocoa from São Tomé and Principe in future, but forced labor in the Portuguese colonies continued.

—An account from cocoa production from the *Cocoa Industry in West Africa, a history of exploitation.*

316. Which of the following cash crop also often involved forced labor or slavery?

(A) Potatoes
(B) Sugar
(C) Peppers
(D) Bananas

317. Which of the following is true based on the account above of cocoa production in West Africa?

(A) Slavery or forced labor was completely wiped out in the world by the mid-1800s
(B) Slavery as a form of labor was not used for the production of cocoa
(C) The Portuguese were not interested in cocoa production
(D) The abolition of slavery was difficult to enforce in some areas of Africa

—French Senagalese soldiers.

318. How does the image above show how Europeans were in part able to conquer or subdue large territories in Africa during the Age of Imperialism?

(A) The ethnic/linguistic or tribal differences among Africans
(B) Military superiority such as rifles, gunboats, and telegraphs
(C) The use of native troops who knew the land and languages
(D) Strict military and educational standards for students

319. The image above shows a strong similarity to what other historical situation in world history?

(A) Sepoy soldiers in India
(B) Kansu Braves in China
(C) Creole officers in the Americas
(D) Samurai warriors in Japan

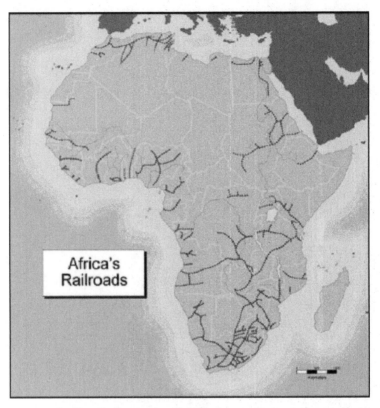

—Map of Africa showing railroads built during the Age of Imperialism.

320. Based on the image above of Africa during the late nineteenth century and early twentieth century, one effect of European imperialism on Africa was

(A) The improvement of working conditions in Africa

(B) That African economies became dependent on the exportation of raw materials

(C) Africans' acceptance of the doctrine of the "White Man's Burden"

(D) Widespread Western education and literacy of African peoples

321. Many of the nations colonized were rich in natural resources. How did social Darwinists view the mining of natural resources in these colonized lands?

(A) It was their right to take what they wanted.

(B) It was a necessity for their colonies to survive.

(C) It was a way to preserve traditional economies.

(D) It was a way to protect Africans from the Industrial Revolution.

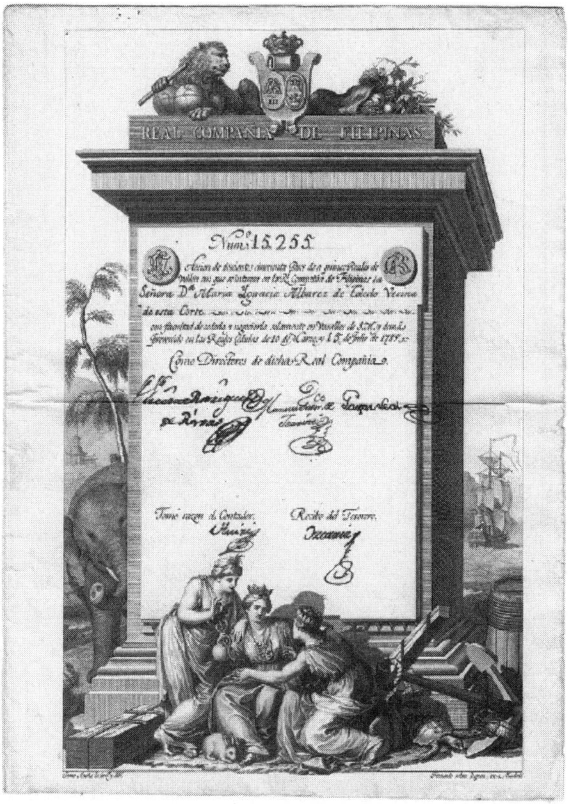

—Corporate share of the Real Compañia de Filipinas (Royal Philippine Company), which had a monopoly on trade in the Americas for Spanish monarchy, issued 1785.

322. Which economic system determined the regulations that governed the Royal Philippine Company in the Spanish empire?

(A) European mercantilist laws
(B) Laissez-faire principles
(C) Renaissance guild bylaws
(D) Medieval manorialism

323. The rules regulating joint-stock companies, like the Royal Philippine Company, gave them a monopoly on colonial trade and colonial critics claimed that they impeded local businesses. Which of the following regions were also upset at the economic rules that governed the use of monopoly over colonial trade?

(A) The Low Countries
(B) Russian empire
(C) American colonies
(D) Siberian steppe

By the late eighteenth century the French colony at San-Domingue had become the largest producer of arguably the New World's most important commodity—sugar. Loss of this colony to the "excesses of liberty" that the French Revolution had inspired among the enslaved population on that island was intolerable to the ruling classes that emerged in France by the turn of the nineteenth century. In May 1802, Napoleon's force tried to reestablish slavery in Haiti. Toussaint L'Ouverture, leader of the Haitian Revolution, was kidnapped and deported back to France. The effect was to enrage the black majority and provoke even greater rebellion. By now black soldiers had gained experience in organizing an army. The French were at a disadvantage, they were more susceptible to disease (particularly yellow fever) than their opponents and reinforcements were difficult to obtain from France. The French troops were also demoralized by fighting against enemies who sang La Marseillaise and invoked revolutionary ideas. One officer, Lacroix, asked, "Have our barbarous enemies justice on their side? Are we no longer the soldiers of Republican France? And have we become the crude instruments of Policy.

—Mark Almond, historian.

324. The secondary source above supports which of the following conclusions?

(A) French soldiers sent to Haiti had more immunity to disease than Haitians fighting for their homeland.

(B) Napoleon's soldiers sent Toussaint L'Ouverture back to Haiti, where he died of yellow fever.

(C) British and French soldiers fought together to end slavery in the Americas as a whole.

(D) Some French soldiers in Haiti questioned the incompatibility of their mission with Republican values.

325. Which factor had the LEAST impact on creating the conditions that gave rise to the situation described in the passage?

(A) The French island colony of Haiti was extremely valuable for France because of its sugar crop.

(B) Slavery was first established in Santo Domingue/Haiti in the early 1700s by French traders and settlers.

(C) French revolutionary ideas such as equality and democracy began to spread to Haiti by 1790.

(D) The British antislavery movement was established by the Quaker and Evangelical Christian community.

[To] Mr. URBAN,

THE scheme for the abolition of the slave-trade is, in every view of it, absurd and impolitic. It is founded on a mistaken notion of humanity, or rather on ignorance, folly, and enthusiasm. The Negroes of Africa, in their native country, are apparently useless in the great scale of human society; they are totally incapable of refinement, arts, or sciences. The only way to promote their civilization, to make them service-able in their generation, and happy in themselves is to introduce them into a state of activity and industry. Man was not designed for a life of idleness. An idle man is a wretched creature. A Negro, removed to the West Indies, is placed in a climate much more agreeable to a laborer than the burning plains of Africa. His work in the Plantations is not harder, or more oppressive, than that of our common laborers in England, such as miners, blacksmiths, founders ... and many others, whose situation is viewed, by those very humane and compassionate people who are advocates for their African brethren, without the least concern. Yet most of these drudges in this country have been compelled by necessity to leave the place of their nativity.

—A planter's letter to a newspaper, early 1800s.

326. Which of the following best explains the use of the phrase "mistaken notion of humanity" as a reaction against a growing movement?
   (A) Abolition
   (B) Industrialization
   (C) Feminism
   (D) Consumerism

327. Which of the following conclusions can be argued about the above reading?
   (A) Europeans were interested in bringing industrialization to sub-Saharan Africa.
   (B) Europeans were genuinely concerned about the welfare of Africans.
   (C) Europeans were very knowledgeable about conditions in sub-Saharan Africa.
   (D) Europeans had very little accurate knowledge about sub-Saharan Africa.

Politics doesn't interest me, but as a good citizen I feel free to express my opinions and to censure the government. Democracy, which is so loudly proclaimed by the deluded, is an absurdity in our countries, flooded as they are with vices and with their citizens lacking all sense of civic virtue, the prerequisite to establishing a real republic. But monarchy is not the American ideal either; if we get out of one terrible government just to jump headlong into another, what will we have gained? The republican system is the one we must adopt a strong central government whose representatives will be men of virtue and patriotism, who thus can direct the citizens along the path or order and progress

—Letter by Bernardo O'Higgins, Chilean general, 1822.

328. Which of the following provides context for the passage above?
    (A) Latin American governments were indigenous chieftains.
    (B) Latin American governments were still monarchies.
    (C) Latin American governments were always democracies.
    (D) Latin American governments were often dictatorships.

329. The great difference between the type of governments in Latin America and the United States in their postindependence periods is often argued to be due to
    (A) The strong sense of unity among Latin Americans
    (B) The sharp racial and class divisions in the Americas
    (C) The prevailing influence of the Roman Catholic Church
    (D) Geographic barriers and distance in Latin America

Military Rule in Latin America to 1900

Country	Date of Independence	Periods of Military Rule	Total Years of Military Rule
Columbia	1831		0
El Salvador	1830		0
Costa Rica	1830		0
Nicaragua	1830	1855–1857	2
Brazil	1821	1889–1894	5
Uruguay	1830	1876–1886	10
Honduras	1830	1830–1847	17
Peru	1825	1846–1854 1884–1895	19
Ecuador	1830	1851–1856 1861–1875 1878–1882 1892–1895	28
Guatemala	1830	1840–1865 1871–1885	39
Bolivia	1825	1848–1870 1876–1880	26
Chile	1818	1818–1851	33
Haiti	1804	1804–1843 1847–1859	47
Venezuela	1830	1831–1835 1839–1843 1846–1858 1861–1868	49
Paraguay	1815	1815–1869 1894–1898	57
Mexico	1821	1823–1843 1846–1855 1863–1867	33

330. Which of the following acts as context for the chart?

(A) The lack of economic development in Latin America

(B) The political instability in many Latin American nations

(C) The political dominance of the Catholic church

(D) The migration of French revolutionaries to the Americas

331. Causation for the political process in the chart is due to which of the following?

(A) Enlightenment writings and ideas

(B) The abolition of slavery

(C) The Industrial Revolution

(D) Sharp racial and class divisions

—Photograph of guano mining in the Islands off Peru, ca. 1860.

—Advertisement for guano, which is bird droppings and found on islands off South America.

332. Which of the following least explains causation for the use of almost exclusively Chinese labor in the guano fields of the islands off Peru?
(A) The ending of the slave trade of Africans
(B) Overpopulation in China during the nineteenth century
(C) The attitude of the Qing that such laborers were disloyal
(D) Improved methods of transportation and communication

333. The sale of guano fertilizer by nations like Peru and Chile shows a strong continuity in the period before and after political independence, in terms of which of the following?
(A) The export of American raw materials to wealthier nations
(B) The import of Chinese to make up for labor shortages
(C) The use of advertisements to reach a new and larger market
(D) The influence of European revolutionary ideas

334. The combination of a cheap raw material, a labor force that is mobile, advertising, and transportation to wealthy markets indicate which fact about the world's economy by the 1900?
(A) Interdependence
(B) Importation
(C) Disconnection
(D) Socialism

—Photograph of Mexico City, 1890.

335. Which examples of modernity from the Porfirio Diaz regime in Mexico can be seen in the photograph?

(A) Market stalls
(B) Electrical lines
(C) Horse and carriages
(D) Tree-lined streets

336. The image above shows a street in Mexico City in 1890 as an example of the success of the Porfirio Diaz regime. Which of the following was NOT an aspect of the regime?

(A) Foreign investment
(B) Crony capitalism
(C) Persistent poverty
(D) Democratic rights

Population of the Hawaiian Islands in the Pacific, 1778–1878

Year	Population
1778	242,000
1823	135,000
1831–32	124,000
1835–36	107,000
1850	84,000
1853*	73,000
1860	70,000
1866	63,000
1872	57,000
1878**	58,000

*1853: 97.5% of the population born in Hawaii

**1878: 83.6% of the population born in Hawaii

337. Which of the following explains the changes in the Hawaiian population?
   (A) Gunpowder weapons such as breech-loading rifles
   (B) Deadly hurricanes, tsunamis, and volcanoes
   (C) Disease-related deaths due to lack of Hawaiian's immunity
   (D) Changes in Hawaiian marriage customs and birth control

338. Which of the following was a similarity that Hawaii shared with the people of the Americas, Siberia, Australia, and other indigenous peoples in their interaction with Europeans?
   (A) Conversion to Roman Catholic Christianity
   (B) Long-standing geographic isolation
   (C) Adoption of the English language
   (D) Acceptance of Dutch learning

Document-Based Question

Please work separately from the book on loose-leaf paper to flush out your ideas before committing your answer to space below.

339. Develop an argument on the extent to which the Lisbon earthquake of 1755 impacted Portugal and the world.

Document 1

Source: Radio interview with Mark Molesky, in his book, *This Gulf of Fire: The Destruction of Lisbon, or Apocalypse in the Age of Science and Reason,* recorded on November 2, 2015.

It was one of the largest earthquakes in history, estimated measurement between 8.5 and perhaps 9.2 on the Richter scale. It was the largest earthquake to affect Europe in the last 10,000 years, and its tremors and reverberations were felt as far away as Sweden, Northern Italy, and the Azores in the Central Atlantic.

SIEGEL: In Lisbon, churches collapsed. Of course, it's a great feast day. Many are inside. Buildings fall down. There are many six- and seven-story buildings that people live in. They fall to the ground. And that's only the beginning of what's happening.

MOLESKY: Yeah, absolutely. An enormous cloud of dust is thrown into the air, and as that dust settles, this new Lisbon is revealed. Tens of thousands of people have died. The fascinating thing about the Lisbon earthquake is that, as a mega-thrust earthquake in the Atlantic Ocean, it caused a very rare Atlantic Ocean tsunami. And about a half hour after the earthquake, this tsunami smashed into the Iberian Peninsula, went up the Tagus river and hit the riverbank in Lisbon where thousands of survivors and eyewitnesses to the earthquake had gathered, pulling many into the Tagus and out into the Atlantic ... .

SIEGEL: If this weren't enough, in the 18th century, of course, people lit their homes with candles and lamps. As the buildings came down, the city erupted into fire.

MOLESKY: Yeah. It was the middle of the 9 o'clock mass. And hundreds of little fires started across the city. Within a few hours, they coalesced in what I believe to be a firestorm, which is a fire that becomes so hot and so intense that it produces its own wind system. It actually pulls oxygen into itself, becoming hotter and asphyxiating people who were perhaps a hundred feet away. And this killed thousands more who were trapped or couldn't escape from the rubble and, in fact, did more physical damage to Lisbon than the earthquake had. It essentially gutted the heart of this great world empire.

Document 2

Source: Jesuit Priest Gabriel Malagrida, *An Opinion on the True Cause of the Earthquake*, 1756.

Learn, O Lisbon, that the destroyers of our houses, palaces, churches, and convents, the cause of the death of so many people and of the flames that devoured such vast treasures, are your abominable sins, and not comets, stars, vapours and exhalations, and similar natural phenomena ... . It is scandalous to pretend the earthquake was just a natural event, for if that be true, there is no need to repent and to try to avert the wrath of God, and not even the Devil himself could invent a false idea more likely to lead us all to irreparable ruin. Holy people had prophesied the earthquake was coming, yet the city continued in its sinful ways without a care for the future. Now, indeed, the case of Lisbon is desperate. It is necessary to devote all our strength and purpose to the task of repentance ... .

Document 3

Source: Excerpt from the novel *Candide* from the French author Voltaire, 1756.

Will you say, in seeing this mass of victims: "God is revenged, their death is the price for their crimes?" What crime, what error did these children, Crushed and bloody on their mothers' breasts, commit? Did Lisbon, which is no more, have more vices Than London and Paris immersed in their pleasures? Lisbon is destroyed, and they dance in Paris! ... . When the earth gapes my body to entomb, I justly may complain of such a doom ... . We rise in thought to the heavenly throne, But our own nature still remains unknown.

Document 4

Source: Questionnaire given to every church parish in Portugal in 1758 on the orders of the prime minister, the marquis of Pombal.

1. At what time did the earthquake begin, and how long did the earthquake last?

2. Did you perceive the shock to be greater from one direction than another? Example: from north to south?

3. Did buildings seem to fall more to one side than the other?

4. How many people died and were any of them distinguished?

5. Did the sea rise or fall first, and how many hands did it rise above the normal?

6. If fire broke out, how long did it last and what damage did it cause?

Document 5

Source: Immanuel Kant, German philosopher, in one of three texts attempting to explain the causes of earthquakes, 1756.

... even though earthquakes occur in this country fairly often and at all seasons, the most terrible and most frequent ones are felt in the months of autumn towards the end of the year. This observation is confirmed not only by numerous cases in America, for apart from the destruction of the city of Lima ten years ago, and that of another equally populous city in the previous century, very many examples have been noted, but also in our part of the world we find, apart from the latest earthquake, many other historical instances of earthquakes and volcanic eruptions that have occurred more frequently in autumn than at any other time of the year.

Document 6

Source: Jean-Jacques Rousseau in a letter to Voltaire, 1756.

I do not see how one can search for the source of moral evil anywhere but in man ... . Moreover ... the majority of our physical misfortunes are also our work. Without leaving your Lisbon subject, concede, for example, that it was hardly nature that there brought together twenty-thousand houses of six or seven stories. If the residents of this large city had been more evenly dispersed and less densely housed, the losses would have been fewer or perhaps none at all.

Document 7

Source: Map of Lisbon, 1786, showing its reconstruction plan that was uses a grid system, supposed to help in any future disaster situation.

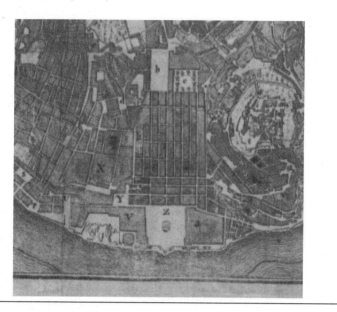

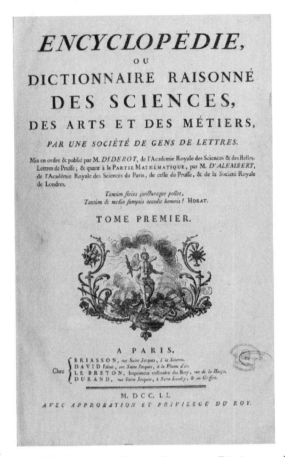

—Cover page of the Encyclopedia or a Systematic Dictionary of the Sciences, Arts and Crafts, edited by Denis Diderot and printed in 1751.

340. The printing of the Encyclopedia in 1751, whose front page above is titled "Encyclopedia: A Systematic Dictionary of the Sciences, Arts, and Crafts," is best seen in the context of which of the following?

(A) The Glorious Revolution
(B) The Enlightenment
(C) The Copernican Revolution
(D) The Inquisition

341. The Enlightenment was followed by and helped bring about which historical processes in world history?

(A) Political revolutions
(B) Scientific revolutions
(C) Columbian Exchange
(D) The Thirty Years' War

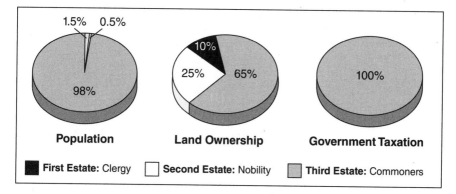

Source: Jackson J. Spielvogel, *World History*. New York: Glencoe/McGraw-Hill, 2003 (adapted).

342. The pie charts above are best understood in the context of

(A) Conditions that led to the French Revolution

(B) European practice of slavery in France

(C) Industrial Revolution effects on workers

(D) Patriarchy in prerevolutionary France

343. As seen in the pie charts above, compared to the American Revolution, the French Revolution

(A) Had less impact on the world's supply of cotton and tobacco

(B) Was also brought about by the poor conditions of the bourgeoisie

(C) Was a social upheaval as well as a political revolution

(D) Led to the rise of a military general who ruled as dictator

From this date to the end of the Terror, twenty-three months later, the story of the relations between the Revolution and the Church, though wild and terrible, is simple: it is a story of mere persecution culminating in extremes of cruelty and in the supposed uprooting of Christianity in France. The orthodox clergy were everywhere regarded by this time as the typical enemies of the revolutionary movement; they themselves regarded the revolutionary movement, by this time, as being principally an attempt to destroy the Catholic Church. There followed immediately a general attack upon religion ... . The attempt at mere "de-christianisation," as it was called, failed, but the months of terror and cruelty, the vast number of martyrdoms (for they were no less) and the incredible sufferings and indignities to which the priests who attempted to remain in the country were subjected ... . Conversely, the picture of the priest, ... as the fatal and necessary opponent of the revolutionary theory, became so fixed in the mind of the Republican that two generations did nothing to eliminate it, and that even in our time the older men, in spite of pure theory, cannot rid themselves of an imagined connection between the Catholic Church and an international conspiracy against democracy. Nor does this non-rational but very real feeling lack support from the utterances of those who, in opposing the political theory of the French Revolution, consistently quote the Catholic Church as its necessary and holy antagonist.

—Hilaire Belloc, *The French Revolution*, 1911.

344. The reading above can be understood best in the context of which of the following statements about the French Revolution?
   (A) The Catholic Church was seen as one of the pillars of the Old Regime and a natural enemy of political change.
   (B) The Catholic Church was an all-powerful institution in Europe and had retained all of its power since the Middle Ages.
   (C) The revolutionaries tried to ally themselves with the Catholic Church due to its belief in social justice and antihierarchal stance.
   (D) The French Revolution opposed the spreading of the Catholic faith as foreign to its native Jewish belief system.

345. The reading above is written from the historical perspective of which of the following authors?
   (A) An American sailor
   (B) An Italian anarchist
   (C) A French revolutionary
   (D) A French Catholic

This great increase in the quantity of work, which, in consequence of the division of labour, the same number of people are capable of performing, is owing to three different circumstances; first, to the increase of dexterity in every particular workman; secondly, to the saving of the time which is commonly lost in passing from one species of work to another; and, lastly, to the invention of a great number of machines which facilitate and abridge labor, and enable one man to do the work of many.

—Adam Smith, *The Wealth of Nations*, 1776.

346. According to Adam Smith in his seminal work, *The Wealth of Nations*, 1776, which of the following is true?

(A) The division of labor leads to greater output of production.

(B) The dexterity of workers increased through industrialization.

(C) Productivity of machines decreased due to lack of resources.

(D) The world's population decreased because of mechanization.

347. The principle outlined above by Adam Smith was key to the success of which historical process?

(A) Western Imperialism

(B) Industrial Revolution

(C) Scientific Revolution

(D) Growth of Democracy

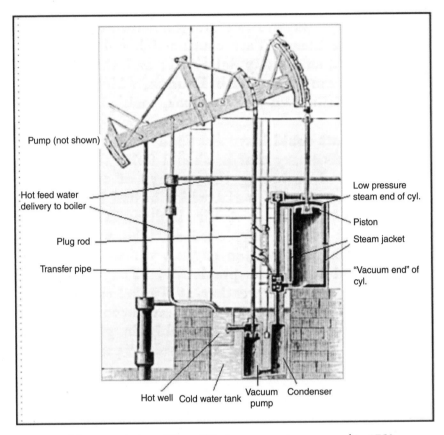

—Schematic design of James Watt's steam engine, patented in 1750.

348. James Watt's steam engine patented in 1750 was a result of which of the following historical events and processes?

(A) The practical application of science in technology

(B) The Enlightenment thought on natural rights

(C) The development of iron and bronze technology

(D) The Colombian Exchange of plants and animals

349. All of the following are historical factors that help explain Britain's role as a leader of industrialization EXCEPT

(A) The government's support of patents that protected innovation

(B) The rich deposits of iron and coal lying close together in the British Isles

(C) The lack of an educated middle class with an entrepreneurial attitude

(D) The building of transportation infrastructure

I think I may fairly make two postulata. First, that food is necessary to the existence of man. Secondly, That the passion between the sexes is necessary, and will remain nearly in its present state ... . Assuming then my postulata as granted, I say, that the power of population is indefinitely greater than the power in the earth to produce subsistence for man. Population, when unchecked, increases in a geometrical ratio. Subsistence increases only in an arithmetical ratio. A slight acquaintance with numbers will shew the immensity of the first power in comparison of the second. By that law of our nature which makes food necessary to the life of man, the effects of these two unequal powers must be kept equal. This implies a strong and constantly operating check on population from the difficulty of subsistence. This difficulty must fall somewhere; and must necessarily be severely felt by a large portion of mankind.

—Thomas Malthus, *An Essay on the Principle of Population*, 1798.

350. Based on the reading above, Thomas Malthus in his famous piece is warning of which problem?

(A) Depopulation
(B) War and conflict
(C) Overpopulation
(D) Sexually transmitted disease

351. Which of the following historical processes most closely bears out the thesis Malthus put forward?

(A) The Green Revolution
(B) The Irish potato famine
(C) The American Civil War
(D) The trans-Atlantic migration

—Print showing a nineteenth-century factory in the British Midlands.

352. The image above is best explained by which of the following processes during the Industrial Revolution?

(A) Domestic system to factory system
(B) Rural population to urban populations
(C) Luddite activity to union creation
(D) Market Revolution to Russian Revolution

353. What other mid-eighteenth and early nineteenth-century development came alongside improvements in productivity?

(A) Urban poverty became less visible and declined.
(B) The social standing of working women to men was equal.
(C) The growth of existing large cities expanded rapidly.
(D) Sanitation and availability of fresh water improved.

"Heaven helps those who help themselves" is a well-tried maxim, embodying in a small compass the results of vast human experience. The spirit of self-help is the root of all genuine growth in the individual; and, exhibited in the lives of many, it constitutes the true source of national vigor and strength. Help from without is often enfeebling in its effects, but help from within invariably invigorates. Whatever is done for men or classes, to a certain extent takes away the stimulus and necessity of doing for themselves; and where men are subjected to over-guidance and over-government, the inevitable tendency is to render them comparatively helpless. Even the best institutions can give a man no active help. Perhaps the most they can do is, to leave him free to develop himself and improve his individual condition. But in all times men have been prone to believe that their happiness and well-being were to be secured by means of institutions rather than by their own conduct. Hence the value of legislation as an agent in human advancement has usually been much over-estimated.

—Samuel Smiles, Scottish author, in *Self-Help*, 1859.

354. Smiles's argument is best understood in the context of which of the following?

(A) Discontent among the owners of transnational business over trade regulation

(B) Disputes among factory workers over wages and working hours

(C) Conflicting visions of Marxists and union members in addressing working conditions

(D) Debates over the role of government in implementing social and urban reforms

355. Smiles's view regarding legislation would most likely be supported by which of the following groups?

(A) Factory workers

(B) Marxist socialists

(C) Laissez-faire capitalists

(D) The merchant class

Population of Ireland Since 1500

Year	Millions	Year	Millions
1500	1	1870	5.5
1670	1	1890	4.8
1750	2.9	1910	4.5
1780	3.5	1930	4
1810	5.1	1950	4.3
1840	8.2	1970	4.2
1850	7	1990	5

356. The situation shown in the map above is a long-term effect on Europe of

(A) The religious divide between Catholics and Protestants
(B) The invention of the printing press and literacy
(C) The durability of the nuclear family in Ireland
(D) The introduction of New World crops to Europe

357. The blight (a disease termed *Phytophthora infestans*) that struck Ireland's potatoes was thought to have been due to the use of guano (bird droppings) from islands off Peru as a manure/fertilizer. This demonstrates which of the following conclusions?

(A) The use of chemical fertilizers in Ireland and Europe was decreasing.
(B) The spread of disease was through human-to-human contact.
(C) Peru and Ireland's involvement in the world economy was intensifying.
(D) The disease caused people to begin to quarantine Peruvian food products.

358. The lack of adequate response from the ruling British government to the crisis in Ireland was due in large part to

(A) The high costs of maintaining the British Army in China and Japan
(B) The belief in the capitalist/laissez-faire model to meet any shortcomings
(C) The economic recession in Britain due to the Industrial Revolution
(D) The fear that the French would take advantage of the rebellion in Ireland

—Newspaper drawing of Luddittes smashing a power loom in 1812.

359. The Luddite movement of early nineteenth-century England is best seen as

(A) A reaction to the Industrial Revolution
(B) A reaction to Communist ideology
(C) Supporters of social Darwinism
(D) A reaction to population increases

360. How did Karl Marx suggest the workers ought to resolve their conflict with their employers?

(A) Return to life as a rural peasant and take up subsistence farming similar to life before industrialization
(B) Continue his efforts to smash the machines and return the economy to the era of small-scale handicraft production
(C) Take up arms, establish rule of the proletariat and institute public ownership of the means of production
(D) Cooperate with industrial capitalists to boost efficiency and output for the benefit of the state

In spite of the fact that we have no such fleet as we should have, we have conquered for ourselves a place in the sun. It will now be my task to see to it that this place in the sun shall remain our undisputed possession, in order that the sun's rays may fall fruitfully upon our activity and trade in foreign parts, that our industry and agriculture may develop within the state and our sailing sports upon the water, for our future lies upon the water. The more Germans go out upon the waters, whether it be in races or regattas, whether it be in journeys across the ocean, or in the service of the battle flag, so much the better it will be for us ... . As head of the Empire I therefore rejoice over every citizen, whether from Hamburg, Bremen, or Lübeck, who goes forth with this large outlook and seeks new points where we can drive in the nail on which to hang our armor ... .

—Kaiser Wilhelm II of Germany in a speech to the North German
Regatta Association, 1901.

361. The speech by Wilhelm II best illustrates which of the following patterns of the period 1750–1900?

(A) The growing demand for settler colonists to alleviate population pressures

(B) The establishment of transoceanic empires by industrial powers

(C) The rise of resistance movements opposing imperialism

(D) The use of religious ideologies to justify the imperial expansion

362. The speech by the German Kaiser Wilhelm II aligns most strongly with which of the following beliefs?

(A) Social Darwinism

(B) Marxism

(C) Appeasement

(D) Industrialization

A few steps from the road I noticed a peasant who was ploughing his field ... . It was Sunday then ... . The peasant was ploughing with great care. "Have you not any time to work during the week, that you work on a Sunday, and at that in a great heat?" "In the week, sir, there are six days, and we have to work for the manor six times a week, and in the evening we haul the hay from the meadows, if the weather is good; and on holidays the women and girls go to the woods to gather mushrooms and berries ... ." Do you work the same way for your master? "No, sir! It would be sinful to work the same way; he has in his fields one hundred hands for one mouth, and I have but two hands for seven mouths, if you count it up. If you were to work yourself to death at your master's work, he would not thank you for it. The master will not pay the capitation tax; he will let you have no mutton, no hempen cloth, no chicken, no butter ... . The conversation with this agriculturist awakened a multitude of thoughts in me. Above all, I thought of the inequality of the peasant's condition. I compared the crown peasants with those of the proprietors. Both live in villages, but while the first pay a stated tax, the others have to be ready to pay whatever the master wishes. The first are judged by their peers; the others are dead to the laws, except in criminal matters. A member of society only then is taken cognizance of by the Government that protects him when he violates the social bond, when he becomes a criminal! That thought made all my blood boil. Beware, cruel proprietor! On the brow of every one of your peasants I see your condemnation! ..."

—From *Journey from St. Petersburg to Moscow* by
Alexander Nikolaevich Radishchev, 1790.

363. Which of the following provides context for the historical situation described in the reading?

(A) Russian autocracy
(B) Russian serfdom
(C) Russian semi-isolation
(D) Russian transportation

364. Which of the following can be argued is a result of the continuation of serfdom in Russian till the mid-nineteenth century?

(A) Russia's late development of a modern economy
(B) Russia's vast size and large population
(C) Russia's Eastern Orthodox Christian religion
(D) Russia's practice of slavery and indentured servitude

Development of the Extractive Industries

Product	1877	1887	1892	1897
Coal	110	227	424	684
Oil	13	167	299	478
Cast iron	23	36	64	113
Iron	16	22	29	30
Steel	3	14	31	74

Russia in Comparison

Nation Circa 1898	Coal in Puds per Inhabitant	Cotton in Pounds per Inhabitant
Britain	311	53
Germany	143	14
Belgium	204	NA
France	20	11
USA	162	28
Russia	5.8	5

Note: The term "puds" was a measurement at the time in iron and steel manufacturing.

365. Based on the first chart, which term best fits the items Russia was recording for its industrialization program?

(A) Mercantile goods
(B) Agricultural goods
(C) Luxury items
(D) Industrial goods

366. Which of the following can we best conclude from reading the two charts above?

(A) Russia was increasing production internally and overtaking its fellow European nations.
(B) While Russia had increased production internally, it lagged far behind other European nations.
(C) Russia was lagging behind in both domestic production as well as other European states.
(D) Russian industrial output saw no change despite the country undertaking a program of industrialization.

—Cartoon from the American magazine Judge that shows US president Roosevelt saying to the Russian czar, "Stop your cruel oppression of the Jews!"

367. What name was given to late nineteenth-century czarist policies that imposed Russian cultural values across the empire?

(A) Czarification
(B) Slavification
(C) Muscovication
(D) Russification

368. The oppression of Jews in the Russian empire later led to which of the following historical processes?

(A) The formation of guerilla bands to resist czarist police and military
(B) The migration of millions of Jews to the Western Europe and the Americas
(C) The conversion of most Jews to Eastern Orthodox Christianity
(D) The sale of personal items to fund a tribute to the Russian state

—Ceiling painting at the former headquarters of the British East India Company, 1778.

369. Which of the following best represents the context for the painting above?

(A) A sharp decrease in cultural diffusion

(B) The spread of Western technology such as printing

(C) An increase in global economic integration

(D) The introduction of slavery into the Asian landmass

370. Which of the following is an interpretation of the above image?

(A) A grateful Eastern Hemisphere offering up its bounty to Great Britain

(B) Asian peoples being enslaved by the nations of the Americas

(C) Mythical figures from the classical world worshiping Zeus

(D) Trade between animist deities and Christian saints

371. Which of the following famous incidents was the British East India Company NOT involved in?

(A) Boston Tea Party

(B) China's Opium Wars

(C) India's Sepoy Rebellion

(D) Congress of Vienna

The Present Era: 1900–Present

Controlling Idea: An "Age of Extremes"

Numerous terms have been used to describe this era, such as "The Dark Century" and "The Bloody Twentieth Century." Dr. Eric Hobsbawm called it "The Age of Extremes," and this phrase is a useful way to begin to conceptualize the dizzying scope and pace of change we have seen in the years since the opening shots of World War I in 1914. Where before we had wars, now we have world wars. Where before we had powers, now we have seen superpowers. The explosion of technological innovation and productive capacity we saw in the Industrial Revolution has been expanded upon in ways individuals alive in 1914 could scarcely dream of. Yet all too familiar—in point of fact ancient, patterns of poverty still define life for billions of people. It is, then, an "age of extremes" in wealth and poverty and an "age of extremes" for the biosphere where we have reached the situation in which man-made gasses contribute to planetary climate change. As the millennium approached, the global tapestry we see is one of an ever-more connected world or globalization. We see the acceleration of movements of ideas, trade goods, and people. While there have been major disruptions with globalization, we also saw a rise in the standard of living to unprecedented levels.

—Cartoon in *Puck*, an American magazine published in 1900 in the aftermath of the Boxer Rebellion in China.

372. The illustration would be most useful to a historian studying which of the following?

(A) Advances in military technology as a result of industrialization
(B) Chinese Confucian views of economic imperialism
(C) Tactics used by imperial powers to conquer territories
(D) European responses to the weakness of non-European states

373. Which of the following was most directly a result of the events shown in the cartoon?

(A) 1905 Russo-Japanese War
(B) 1905 Russian Revolution
(C) 1899 Boer War
(D) World War II in 1939

—Female students marching in a demonstration as part of the May Fourth Movement, 1919.

374. A similarity between the May Fourth Movement of 1919 and the Tiananmen Square demonstrations in 1989 is the actions of which of the following groups in Chinese society?

(A) Peasants
(B) Workers
(C) Students
(D) Warlords

375. The direct reason for the upsurge in nationalist feeling was which of the following historical events in 1919?

(A) The rise of Fascism
(B) The Versailles treaty
(C) The Boxer Rebellion
(D) The Long March

376. Based on the image above, which of the following can be said about the protesters?

(A) Footbinding was no longer being practiced by many urban elites.
(B) The English language was spoken by most rural women.
(C) China was transitioning to being a matriarchal society.
(D) Communism was discarded as a viable economic theory.

A revolution is not a dinner party .... *A revolution is an insurrection, an act of violence by which one class overthrows another. A rural revolution is a revolution by which the peasantry overthrows the power of the feudal landlord class. Without using the greatest force, the peasants cannot possibly overthrow the deep-rooted authority of the landlords which has lasted for thousands of years. The rural areas need a mighty revolutionary upsurge, for it alone can rouse the people in their millions to become a powerful force. All the actions mentioned here which have been labeled as "going too far" flow from the power of the peasants, which has been called forth by the mighty revolutionary upsurge in the countryside* .... *In this period it was necessary to establish the absolute authority of the peasants. It was necessary to forbid malicious criticism of the peasant associations. It was necessary to overthrow the whole authority of the gentry, to strike them to the ground and keep them there. There is revolutionary significance in all the actions which were labeled as "going too far" in this period. To put it bluntly, it is necessary to create terror for a while in every rural area, or otherwise it would be impossible to suppress the activities of the counter-revolutionaries in the countryside or overthrow the authority of the gentry. Proper limits have to be exceeded in order to right a wrong, or else the wrong cannot be righted.*

—Mao Tse-Tung's *Hunan Peasant Movement Investigation*, 1927.

377. Which of the following historical arguments correctly relates to the reading above?

(A) Mao believed in the ability of capitalist countries to reform themselves to stave off revolution.

(B) Mao wanted to liberate the merchants from the bottom of the Confucian social class structure.

(C) Mao theorized that the rural masses would bow to the demands of the bourgeoisie city dwellers.

(D) In focusing on the peasants' revolutionary potential, Mao deviated from classical Marxist theory.

378. The line "A revolution is not a dinner party" is a clear reference to

(A) Cosmopolitan lifestyles

(B) Political violence

(C) Agrarian innovations

(D) Ideological purity

Grain scattered on the ground, potato leaves withered;
Strong young people have left to make steel;
Only children and old women reap the crops;
How can they pass the coming year?
Allow me to raise my voice for the people!

—Poem by Peng Dehuai, a government official, who wrote it during
his inspection tours through China in the fall of 1958.

379. The famine during the Great Leap Forward (1958–1961) described in the
poem above was caused by which of the following?

(A) A potato blight or disease
(B) Economic mismanagement
(C) A decline in foreign trade
(D) A declining population

380. A key cause of the agricultural problems during the Great Leap Forward
(1958–1961) was the forced collectivization. This was most similar to the
situation in which nation?

(A) France
(B) Ireland
(C) Chile
(D) Russia

—Poster, circa 1960–1976.

381. Based on the image above, which other nation also used a similar artistic style in depicting women and a similar feminist message in its state propaganda?

(A) Fascist Italy

(B) Soviet Union

(C) Weimar Germany

(D) Showa Japan

382. Which of the following conclusions is true about women's rights in Mao's China?

(A) Due to the problems associated with the Great Leap Forward, women had no more rights than under the Qing dynasty.

(B) Women were given full equality by the state and soon achieved many positions in government, including the premiership.

(C) Women were given full reproductive rights with no limits on family size.

(D) Although gains were made by women, the reality never lived up to the state propaganda.

East is Red The east is red, the sun is rising. China has brought forth a Mao Zedong. He amasses fortune for the people, Hurrah, he is the people's great savior. Chairman Mao loves the people, He is our guide, To build a new China, Hurrah, he leads us forward! The Communist Party is like the sun, Wherever it shines, it is bright. Wherever there is a Communist Party, Hurrah, there the people are liberated!

> —Revolutionary song written in 1942 that was the de facto national anthem in the 1960s.

383. Which of the following provides context for the song lyrics above?

(A) Mao Zedong purged the party during the Long March.

(B) A cult of personality built up around Mao Zedong.

(C) It chronicled the fall of the Ming dynastic cycle.

(D) It encouraged the adoption of free-market policies.

384. This Chinese song would most likely have been sung during the

(A) May Fourth Movement

(B) Cultural Revolution

(C) Boxer Rebellion

(D) Tiananmen Square incident

385. The Tiananmen Square demonstrations in 1989 were actually sparked by foreign affairs outside China. Which of the following was the spark?

(A) The economic and political changes taking place in Russia under Mikhail Gorbachev

(B) The Ronald Reagan revolution in American politics in 1980s America

(C) The oil and energy crisis of the 1970s in the Middle East

(D) The dashed hopes for democracy and economic development in Latin America

Source: Associated Press photographer Jeff Widener was in Beijing covering the protest and massacre when he took the famous "Tank Man" photograph on June 5th, 1989.

I heard this noise of tanks coming down the street, and I went out to the balcony and I see the column of tanks coming towards me. And I'm thinking, "This is a nice, compressed shot of the tanks."

All of a sudden this guy with shopping bags walks out in front. I'm looking at it and I get annoyed. I look at Kirk and say, "This guy's going to screw up my composition," and he goes, "They're going to kill that guy! They're going to kill him!" ... You hear gunfire going on everywhere and the guy doesn't flinch .... When I finally got to the balcony, I took one, two, three shots ... .

You could say it's David and Goliath, but I think it goes beyond David and Goliath. Here's this guy who's obviously just out shopping, and finally he's just had enough. He goes out in the street with these oncoming tanks. If he's halfway normal he thinks he's going to die. But he doesn't care; he just doesn't care because—for whatever reason, whether he's lost a loved one or he's just had it with the government—whatever it is, his statement is more important than his own life.

Everybody connects to this that all hope is not lost, that you can make a stand. There is some dignity and that you fight for your rights.

386. Photos of the Tiananmen Square demonstrations are banned in China. This is an example of which of the following?
    (A) Propaganda
    (B) Conscription
    (C) Censorship
    (D) Corvée labor

387. Which of the following provides context for the Tiananmen Square demonstrations?
    (A) China is still ruled by an imperial monarchy system of the Qing dynasty.
    (B) China has experienced economic reforms but no political reforms for decades.
    (C) China has adopted capitalism and democracy since the reign of Deng Xiaopeng.
    (D) China has not changed its economic system but has adopted free elections.

КЪ ВОЙНѢ РОССІИ СЪ ЯПОНІЕЙ.

—Russian image on the upcoming war against Japanese forces in 1904.

388. The image above is best described as an example of

(A) Russian propaganda

(B) Japanese censorship

(C) Russian newspaper editorial

(D) Japanese woodblock print

389. The war between the Russians and Japanese was fought over

(A) Competing ideologies of Russian autocracy versus Japanese democracy

(B) The buffer state of Poland

(C) Territory in China/Manchuria

(D) A disputed election in Russia

—Boy's kimono, 1933, courtesy of Sam Perkins.

390. The kimono shown above shows clear evidence of which of the following political attitudes prevalent among many Japanese people in the 1930s?

(A) Communism
(B) Industrialism
(C) Militarism
(D) Pacifism

391. The sentiment in Japan as shown in the boy's kimono was fostered by which of the following events?

(A) The economic hardships brought about by the Great Depression
(B) The Second Industrial Revolution, which greatly raised living standards
(C) The increased migration of Japanese settlers to the Asian mainland
(D) The spread of pacifist literature and attitudes among college elites

—Photo was taken in 1942–1943 in the Pacific campaign against Japanese forces. This photo was censored until after the war.

392. The above photo of dead US marines and damaged landing craft is best understood in the context of the following?

(A) The Pacific theater involved an "island hopping" campaign in light of the region's geography.

(B) The Pacific theater used a blitzkrieg campaign modeled on its use of tanks in Europe.

(C) The war in the Pacific involved large amounts of US civilian casualties.

(D) The Pacific theater did not use any air power and relied on seagoing forces instead.

393. Similarly to the later US involvement in Vietnam, a difficulty for Allied forces in the Pacific theater of World War II was

(A) The harsh and long winters that are common to the region
(B) The hostility from the local populations to the Allied cause
(C) The difficult terrain that soldiers had to fight in
(D) The lack of support from their fellow citizens at home

394. The censoring of the previous photo and other photos during World War II is best understood in the context of which of the following?

(A) World War II was a series of guerilla insurgencies.
(B) World War II was a total war involving civilians.
(C) World War II was a war of ideas such a communism.
(D) World War II was fought for religious reasons.

Aspiring sincerely to an international peace based on justice and order, the Japanese people forever renounce war as a sovereign right of the nation and the threat or use of force as means of settling international disputes. In order to accomplish the aim of the preceding paragraph, land, sea and air forces as well as other war potential will never be maintained. The right of belligerence of the state will not be recognized.

—Article 9 of the Japanese Constitution, 1947.

395. Which of the following is a key factor behind the reasoning for the above document?

(A) Japan's so-called economic miracle after World War II
(B) Japan's desire to stay neutral during the Cold War
(C) Japan's brutal civil war between Communists and non-Communists
(D) Japan's total defeat in World War II at the hands of the Allies

396. Japan's foreign policy in the post–World War II era could be best described as which of the following?

(A) Militarist
(B) Containment
(C) Pacifist
(D) Detente

—Map showing the progress of the Korean War.

397. Based on the map, which of the following was the stated goal of the United States of America in the Korean War?

(A) Contain the spread of communism
(B) To interfere in the Korean Civil War
(C) To conquer and colonize Korean territory
(D) To maintain the occupation of nearby Japan

398. Korea and Germany were similar in the post–World War II era in that they were divided. Which of the following provides some context for that?

(A) Both led to a devastating war and ongoing conflict.
(B) Both required the assistance of the United Nations.
(C) Both divisions were due to wartime agreements.
(D) Both divisions were permanent and remain so.

All men are created equal. They are endowed by their Creator with certain inalienable rights; among these are Life, Liberty, and the pursuit of Happiness. This immortal statement was made in the Declaration of Independence of the United States of America in 1776. In a broader sense, this means: All the peoples on the earth are equal from birth, all the peoples have a right to live, to be happy and free … . we, members of the Provisional Government of the Democratic Republic of Vietnam, solemnly declare to the world that Vietnam has the right to be a free and independent country—and in fact is so already. The entire Vietnamese people are determined to mobilize all their physical and mental strength, to sacrifice their lives and property in order to safeguard their independence and liberty.

—The Vietnamese Declaration of Independence, which was read
by Ho Chi Minh in Hanoi on September 2, 1945.

399. Which of the following statements is a historical argument on the Vietnamese Declaration of Independence shown above that was read out in the city of Hanoi on September 2, 1945?

(A) The intended audience was the Western powers, especially America, as much as it was the Vietnamese people.

(B) The Japanese reacted with fury and began to indiscriminately kill Vietnamese intellectuals and professionals.

(C) The Dutch colonial forces ignored the document and began preparations to regain their former colonial possession.

(D) The American president Harry Truman issued a strong statement of support for the Vietnamese nationalists.

400. The Vietnamese Declaration of Independence shows the clear influence of

(A) The social Darwinist theories that portrayed Asians as inferior to Caucasians

(B) The nonviolent doctrine of ahisma that was used by Mohandas K. Gandhi in India

(C) Enlightenment principles that were similar to the American Declaration of Independence

(D) Fascist ideals encapsulated in Benito Mussolini's 1932 article "What Is Fascism"

Indices of Growth and Change in the Pacific Rim: Gross National Product (GNP), 1965–1996

Nation	% Labor Force in Agriculture		% Population Urban	
	1965	**1996**	**1965**	**1996**
China	78	72	17	31
Indonesia	66	55	41	82
Japan	20	7	71	78
South Korea	49	18	41	82
Malaysia	54	27	34	54
Thailand	80	64	13	20

Source: Adapted from World Bank, World Development Indicators (Washington, D.C., 1998).

401. Which of the following is an economic change in Pacific Rim nations from 1965 to 1996 that can be deduced from the chart above?

(A) Pacific nations began to import more than export.
(B) The financial sector had a difficult time raising capital.
(C) More people moved to the countryside than urban areas.
(D) The industrial sector of the Pacific nation's economies grew.

402. Which of the following best explains the cause of the social and economic changes taking place in Pacific nation's from 1965 to 1996?

(A) These nations adopted Marxist Leninist ideologies and communism as an economic system.
(B) These nations industrialized with the exception of Japan, which had begun industrialization earlier.
(C) These nations practiced forced relocation from the countryside to the cities to act as a cheap labor source.
(D) These nations adopted English as an official language and other westernization methods.

403. Based on the chart, which area of the world began to industrialize only in the decades after World War II?

(A) Northeast Asia
(B) North Africa
(C) Southeast Asia
(D) Oceania

Short-Answer Question

Please work separately from the book on loose-leaf paper to flush out your ideas before committing your answer to space below.

Document 1

> *Article 1. The landownership system of feudal exploitation by the landlord class shall be abolished and the system of peasant landownership shall be introduced in order to set free the rural productive forces, develop agricultural production, and thus pave the way for new China's industrialization.*
>
> *Article 2. The land, draft animals, farm implements, and surplus grain of the landlords and their surplus houses in the countryside shall be confiscated.*
>
> *Article 3. The rural land belonging to ancestral shrines, temples, monasteries, churches, schools, organizations and other land owned by public bodies shall be requisitioned ...*
>
> *Article 10. All land and other means of production thus confiscated and requisitioned ... shall be taken over by the hsiang [peasants' council] for unified, equitable and rational distribution to poverty-stricken peasants who have little or no land and who lack other means of production. Landlords shall be given an equal share so that they can make their living by their own labor and thus reform themselves through labor.*
>
> Source: *Agrarian Reform Law of the People's Republic of China*, 1950.

Document 2

> The American occupation had assumed responsibility for 686,965 acres owned by Japanese landlords during the colonial period. Through the sale of this property beginning in the spring of 1948, 587,974 tenant families, or 24.1 percent of southern Korea's agricultural population, acquired new land. But while these measures improved conditions for some Korean farmers, they represented only a partial solution to the country's land problems … .
>
> Nevertheless, land reform remained at the top of the agenda when the new South Korean government was inaugurated in 1948. After a year of debate between the Department of Agriculture and the National Assembly, the ROK government in June 1949 drafted a law providing for the distribution of all land not cultivated by the owner and all holdings of more than 7.5 acres. The measure stipulated that the government would calculate the land's average annual production and then compensate landlords at 150 percent of this sum. Farmers who bought the land were to repay the government 125 percent of their average annual production over a ten-year period … . Naturally, the KDP [conservative] dominated assembly resisted the legislation because it would deprive landlords of the very source of their social dominance.

Source: Gregg Brazinsky, *Nation Building in South Korea*, 2018.

404. (a) Identify ONE similarity between the Chinese and South Korean land reform programs.

405. (b) Identify ONE difference between the Chinese and South Korean land reform programs.

406. (c) Describe ONE reason for either a similarity or difference between the Chinese and South Korean land reform programs.

Since China's reform and opening up started more than two decades ago, a special social group has come into being. Mostly coming from the countryside, they are mainly doing low paying manual work in the fields of construction, commerce, service and so on. They become the floating population in big cities, called as migrant workers or peasant workers. China's floating population has increased from 70 million of 1993 to 140 million of 2003, exceeding 10 percent of the total population and accounting for about 30 percent of rural labor force. At present [2005], the general floating direction is from the countryside to cities, from underdeveloped regions to developed regions, and from central and western areas to eastern coastal areas ... .

Source: People's Daily Online, July 27, 2005.

407. Which of the following is NOT among the "Four Modernizations" put forward by Deng Xiaoping as key to economic self-reliance and emergence of China as a world power by the early twenty-first century?

(A) Agriculture
(B) Industry
(C) Science and technology
(D) Classless society

"It is no use for you to argue," Talaat answered, "we have already disposed of three quarters of the Armenians; there are none at all left in Bitlis, Van, and Erzeroum. The hatred between the Turks and the Armenians is now so intense that we have got to finish with them. If we don't, they will plan their revenge." "If you are not influenced by humane considerations," I replied, "think of the material loss. These people are your business men. They control many of your industries. They are very large tax-payers. What would become of you commercially without them?" "We care nothing about the commercial loss," replied Talaat. "We have figured all that out and we know that it will not exceed five million pounds. We don't worry about that. I have asked you to come here so as to let you know that our Armenian policy is absolutely fixed and that nothing can change it. We will not have the Armenians any-where in Anatolia. They can live in the desert but nowhere else."

I still attempted to persuade Talaat that the treatment of the Armenians was destroying Turkey in the eyes of the world, and that his country would never be able to recover from this infamy. "You are making a terrible mistake," I said, and I repeated the statement three times. "Yes, we may make mistakes," he replied, "but"—and he firmly closed his lips and shook his head—"we never regret.

—Henry Morgenthau's conversation with Mehmed Talaat, the Turkish Minister of the Interior, in 1915 during World War I, recalled for his book, *Ambassador Morgenthau's Story*, 1918.

408. The situation in the reading above is clear evidence of which of the following conclusions?

(A) Turkish elites were financially supportive of Armenian immigration to South or North America.

(B) Turkish elites were rightly concerned about economic repercussions that would follow their actions.

(C) Turkish elites were motivated by a feeling of scientific superiority that placed the Armenians as subhuman.

(D) Turkish elites knowingly committed acts of genocide against a minority ethnic group within their empire.

409. Which of the following long-term causes most directly led to the actions described in the reading above?

(A) New technology being used to develop deadlier weapons

(B) The formation of the Triple Entente Alliance system

(C) Rising nationalism among various ethnic groups

(D) The European mandate system in the Middle East

410. Compared to the German apologies for the Holocaust after World War II, the current Turkish government

(A) Denies a genocide of Armenians took place at all

(B) Has apologized and paid restitution to survivors

(C) Refuses to pay damages to Jews for the crimes

(D) Has been the subject of controversy over its textbooks

The Middle East Before and After World War I Settlements, 1914–1922

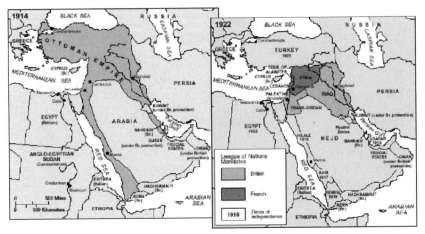

—Map of the Middle East after World War I.

411. Which statement best explains what the map shows?

(A) The impact of the Allied victory in World War I

(B) The rise of nationalist movements in former colonies and territories

(C) The enactment of Wilson's principle of self-determination

(D) The success of the Central Powers at the Paris Peace Conference

412. How does the map reflect the broken promises to Arabs?

(A) The divisions eliminated the possibility of future nationalist movements in the Middle East and North Africa.

(B) They had been promised self-rule, not a mandate system, if they fought with the Allies in the war.

(C) The divisions violated the existing principles of Pan-Arabism, or the unification of all Arab lands.

(D) They had been promised colonies of their own from which to repair their war-torn economies.

Population in British Mandate of Palestine, 1922–1945

Year	Total Population	Muslim	Jewish	Christian	Other
1922	752,048	589,177	83,790	71,464	7,617
1931	1,036,339	761,922	175,138	89,134	10,145
1945	1,764,520	1,061,270	553,600	135,550	14,00
Average compounded growth rate per annum, 1922–1945	3.8%	2.6%	8.6%	2.8%	2.7%

413. Which best explains the vast increase of Jewish migration to the British Mandate of Palestine in the years from 1922 to 1945?

   (A) Improvements in communication and transportation
   (B) The continuation of Ottoman policy of toleration of non-Turks
   (C) The persecution of Jews in Europe by Nazi Germany
   (D) Changes in the intracommunal relations of the Jewish diaspora

414. Based on the low numbers of Jews compared to Arab Muslims, which historical argument can be made?

   (A) The dispossession of the Palestinians was unjust in the eyes of many people in the world today.
   (B) The Jewish population in Palestine had a low birth rate due to traditional family planning methods.
   (C) Jews were still suffering from wars and persecution in the classical and postclassical eras.
   (D) Muslim inheritance rituals encouraged the birth of many children, hence a high birth rate.

Document-Based Question

Please work separately from the book on loose-leaf paper to flush out your ideas before committing your answer to space below.

415. Evaluate the extent to which different national aspirations (desires) clashed with each other in the Middle East during and after World War I?

Document 1

Source: The McMahon–Hussein Correspondence was an exchange of letters (14 July 1915 to 30 January 1916) during World War I, between the Sharif of Mecca, Husayn bin Ali, and Sir Henry McMahon, British High Commissioner in Egypt, concerning the political status of lands under the Ottoman Empire. The Arab side was already looking toward a large revolt against the Ottoman Empire; the British encouraged the Arabs to revolt and thus hamper the Ottoman Empire, which had become a German ally in the war after November 1914.

From Sharif Hussein to McMahon July 1915.

Whereas the whole of the Arab nation without any exception have decided in these last years to live, and to accomplish their freedom, and grasp the reins of their administration both in theory and practice; and whereas they have found and felt that it is to the interest of the Government of Great Britain to support them and aid them to the attainment of their firm and lawful intentions (which are based upon the maintenance of the honor and dignity of their life) without any ulterior motives whatsoever unconnected with this object;

And whereas it is to their (the Arabs') interest also to prefer the assistance of the Government of Great Britain in consideration of their geographical position and economic interests.

From McMahon to Hussein, October 1915.

The districts of Mersina and Alexandretta, and portions of Syria lying to the west of the districts of Damascus, Homs, Hama and Aleppo, cannot be said to be purely Arab, and must on that account be excepted from the proposed limits and boundaries. With the above modification and without prejudice to our existing treaties concluded with Arab Chiefs, we accept these limits and boundaries, and in regard to the territories therein in which Great Britain is free to act without detriment to interests of her ally France, I am empowered in the name of the Government of Great Britain to give the following assurance and make the following reply to your letter: Subject to the above modifications, Great Britain is prepared to recognize and support the independence of the Arabs within the territories in the limits and boundaries proposed by the Sherif of Mecca.

Document 2

Source: US president Woodrow Wilson, excerpt from his *Fourteen Points*, January 1916.

The Turkish portion of the present Ottoman Empire should be assured a secure sovereignty, but the other nationalities which are now under Turkish rule should be assured an undoubted security of life and an absolutely unmolested (bothered) opportunity of autonomous development.

Document 3

Source: *Sykes-Picot Agreement*, May 1916. This secret war-time treaty between two European officials was intended to fulfill a long-standing desire to carve up the Ottoman empire at the conclusion of the war.

.

It is accordingly understood between the French and British governments: That France and Great Britain are prepared to recognize and protect an independent Arab states or a confederation of Arab states. (A) and (B) marked on the annexed map, under the suzerainty of an Arab chief ... That in the blue area (A) France and in the red area (B) great Britain shall be allowed to establish such direct control or indirect administration or control as they desire and as they may think fit to arrange with the Arab state ... That in the brown area there shall be established an international administration, the form of which is to be decided upon after consultation with Russia, an subsequently in consultation with other allies and, the representatives of the sheriff of Mecca.

Document 4

Source: Map based on the Sykes-Picot Agreement, 1916, between Britain and France.

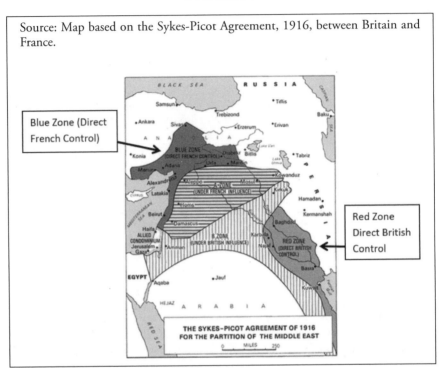

Blue Zone (Direct French Control)

Red Zone Direct British Control

THE SYKES–PICOT AGREEMENT OF 1916 FOR THE PARTITION OF THE MIDDLE EAST

Document 5

Source: Balfour Declaration, November, 1917. This famous document reflected the approval of Britain for Jewish people to return to their ancestral homeland with conditions.

Dear Lord Rothschild,

I have much pleasure in conveying to you, on behalf of His Majesty's Government, the following declaration of sympathy with Jewish <u>Zionist</u> (Jewish nationalist) aspirations which has been submitted to, and approved by, the Cabinet. His Majesty's Government view with favor the establishment in Palestine of a national home for the Jewish people, and will use their best endeavors to facilitate the achievement of the object, it being clearly understood that nothing shall be done which may prejudice the civil and religious' rights of existing non-Jewish communities in Palestine, or the rights and political status enjoyed by Jews in any other country". I should be grateful if you would bring this declaration to the knowledge of the Zionist Federation. Yours sincerely, (Signed) Arthur James Balfour

Document 6

Source: Article 22 of the Covenant of the League of Nations, June 1919.

1. To those colonies and territories which as a consequence of the late war have ceased to be under the sovereignty (authority) of the States which formerly governed them and which are inhabited by peoples not yet able to stand by themselves under the strenuous conditions of the modern world, there should be applied the principle that the well-being and development of such peoples form a sacred trust of civilization and that securities for the performance of this trust should be embodied in this Covenant.

2. The best method of giving practical effect to this principle is that the tutelage (supervision) of such peoples should be entrusted to advanced nations who by reason of their resources, their experience or their geographical position can best undertake this responsibility, and who are willing to accept it, and that this tutelage should be exercised by them as Mandatories on behalf of the League.

3. Certain communities formerly belonging to the Turkish Empire have reached a stage of development where their existence as independent nations can be provisionally recognized subject to the rendering of administrative advice and assistance by a Mandatory until such time as they are able to stand alone. The wishes of these communities must be a principal consideration in the selection of the Mandatory

Document 7

Source: Syrian Congress Memorandum. July, 1919. This document was sent to the commission overseeing the transfer of Ottoman territories to the Mandate Powers of Britain and France.

7. We oppose the pretension (questionable claim) of the Zionists to create a Jewish commonwealth in the southern part of Syria, known as Palestine, and oppose Zionist migration to any part of our country; for we do not acknowledge their title but consider them a grave peril to our people from the national, economical, political points of view. Our Jewish compatriots shall enjoy our common rights and assume the common responsibilities.

9. The fundamental principles laid down by President Wilson in condemnation of secret treaties impels us to protest most emphatically against any treaty that stipulates the partition of our Syrian country and against any private engagement aiming at the establishment of Zionism in the southern part of Syria … .

Among our forefathers were those who maintained that the land of Islam is the fatherland of all Muslims. However, that is a colonialist formula used to advantage by every colonizing nation that seeks to expand its possessions and to extend its influence daily over neighboring countries. Today the [traditional Islamic] formula has no reason to exist. We must replace this formula with the only doctrine that is in accord with every Eastern nation that possesses a clearly defined sense of fatherland. That doctrine is nationalism. Our love of Egypt must be free from all conflicting associations. We must suppress our propensity for anything other than Egypt because patriotism, which is love of fatherland, does not permit such ties. Our Egyptian-ness demands that our fatherland be our qibla and that we not turn our face to any other.
Marks the direction of Mecca, to which a Muslim turns in prayer.

—Ahmad Lutfi as-Sayyid, founder of the Egyptian People's Party in 1907, *Memoirs*, Egypt, 1965.

416. Which of the following was a continuity in the Middle East and can be seen in the account above?

(A) The colonization of Egypt by European powers
(B) A debate on the proper role of Islam in government
(C) The love of fatherland by the citizens of the Middle East
(D) The switch from nationalism to socialism in economics

417. Which shift across the Middle East has been taking place from the 1970s and continues until today?

(A) From socialism to nationalism
(B) From Islamism to nationalism
(C) From nationalism to Islamism
(D) From communism to Islamism

The Security Council,

- *Expressing its continuing concern with the grave situation in the Middle East,*

- *Emphasizing the inadmissibility of the acquisition of territory by war and the need to work for a just and lasting peace in which every State in the area can live in security,*

- *Emphasizing further that all Member States in their acceptance of the Charter of the United Nations have undertaken a commitment to act in accordance with Article 2 of the Charter,*

- *Affirms that the fulfillment of Charter principles requires the establishment of a just and lasting peace in the Middle East which should include the application of both the following principles:*

  1. *Withdrawal of Israeli armed forces from territories occupied in the recent conflict;*

  2. *Termination of all claims or states of belligerency and respect for and acknowledgement of the sovereignty, territorial integrity and political independence of every State in the area and their right to live in peace within secure and recognized boundaries free from threats or acts of force*

—United Nations Resolution 242, November 22, 1967.

418. The resolution above by the United Nations supports which of the following conclusions?

(A) Israel in conjunction with Britain and France seized the Suez Canal from Egypt in 1956.

(B) Nuclear proliferation in the Middle East is of the highest concern and must be approved by the Security Council.

(C) The communal violence between Sunni and Shia Muslims must end and all land seized must be returned.

(D) The lands (West Bank, Gaza Strip, and East Jerusalem) seized by Israel are not accepted by the world community.

419. The Arab-Israeli conflict has changed since United Nations Resolution 242 in all of the following ways EXCEPT

(A) from nationalist divisions to one of religious divisions

(B) from wars between states to one of numerous terrorist acts

(C) from small-scale guerilla war to one of devastating total war

(D) from threats of conventional weapons to threats of nuclear weapons

Nationalization of the oil industry is the primary step to be taken in this direction. The revenue derived from oil, if controlled by the people of Iran can remedy the prevailing disastrous condition of our country. We must ... rid ourselves of foreign domination and take our destiny in our own hands. Hence I declare that struggle to achieve this objective is part of the duty of every Muslim Iranian and the only way to end the poverty and misery of the Iranian nation.

—Abol-Ghasem Kashani, Iranian Member of Parliament, 1951.

420. The nationalization of Iran's oil industry is best understood in the context of which historical process?
   (A) The appeal of Marxism among agricultural workers
   (B) The rise of nationalism in the non-Western world
   (C) Global conflict of the twentieth century
   (D) The decline in technology in the Middle East

421. Which of the following is true about the nationalization of Iran's oil industry?
   (A) It was unique among non-Western nations after World War II
   (B) It was discouraged by the Soviet Union and other Communist nations
   (C) It was similar to what was happening in other newly decolonized countries
   (D) It was encouraged by Great Britain, which was weaker after World War II

—Soviet helicopter-tank operation in Afghanistan.
—Afghan warriors, the Mujahideen, with two captured Soviet field guns, 1984.

422. The Soviet invasion in 1979 led to which of the following conditions in Afghanistan?

    (A) The stabilization of government, economy, and society
    (B) Industrialization under a socialist command economy
    (C) The opening up of trade relations with the outside world
    (D) A protracted conflict and the emergence of a power vacuum

423. This conflict has often been called the Soviet Union's "Vietnam" due to all of the following EXCEPT

    (A) The aspect of a guerilla insurgence versus a modern army
    (B) The defeat and withdrawal of the major superpowers' forces
    (C) The difficulty in fighting in jungle terrain and rice fields
    (D) The lack of support for and disillusionment among Russian soldiers

For the last few decades there has been a rapid decline of the handwoven cloth industry throughout the country on account of the competition of machine manufactures. The machine-made goods imported from abroad are much cheaper and of finer quality .... Though many still wear clothing made from cloth woven on handlooms, large numbers of handloom weavers have been abandoning their looms.

—Radhakamal Mukerjee, Indian economist, 1916.

424. Which of the following was a historical argument made by Indians such as Radhakamal Mukerjee above and Jawaharlal Nehru in general?

(A) Cheap cloth is a benefit for everyone from workers to consumers.

(B) British imperialism led to the "deindustrialization" of India.

(C) Machine-made cloth is of better quality than handmade cloth.

(D) Agricultural-based societies were "purer" than industrial societies.

425. Which of the following acts as context for the changes occurring in the Indian economy as described by Mukerjee?

(A) New taxation policies by the Indian National Congress

(B) The invention of the printing press and caravel ships

(C) The rise of regionalism rather than ethnonationalism

(D) The increased integration of India into the world economy

General Dyer with his troops, giving no warning of any sort or kind, fires indiscriminately into this mass of people until he has practically exhausted the whole of his available ammunition. There has never been such an incident in the whole annals of Anglo-Indian history, nor, I believe, in the history of our Empire, from its very inception down to the present day … . It is for the House of Commons to take upon itself, on behalf of the British Empire as a whole, the responsibility of condoning and adopting one of the worst outrages in the whole of our history.

—British Parliamentary debates on the
Amritsar Massacre in India, 1919.

426. The above account of the incident shows which of the following changes in British imperialism in India?

(A) The economic exploitation of India by Great Britain
(B) The use of violence against anti-imperialist protesters
(C) The decline of the Ottoman Empire in India
(D) The major decisions made in London affecting Indians

427. Which of the following was a natural result of the Amritsar massacre?

(A) Indians began to demand more autonomy or home rule from British rule.
(B) The British left India in 1920, one year after the event.
(C) Japan liberated India from British rule during World War I.
(D) The demand for full independence from Britain became a mass movement.

—Mohandas Gandhi on the Salt March, 1930.

428. The image above shows an example of Gandhi's belief in

(A) The rejection of world opinion

(B) Armed anticolonial rebellion

(C) The practice of civil disobedience

(D) Separate Hindu and Muslim states

429. Which person would probably have most strongly opposed Gandhi's actions shown in the image?

(A) A British military officer stationed in India

(B) The leader of the Indian National Congress

(C) The leader of the Muslim coalition in South Africa

(D) A resident of India seeking independence from Britain

—A refugee special train at Ambala Station during the partition of India.

430. The relocation of Hindus and Sikhs from Pakistan to India and Muslims
from India to Pakistan between 1945 and 1955 reflects which of the
following world historical processes?

(A) The migration of former colonial subjects to imperial capitals

(B) Population resettlement caused by redrawing former colonial borders

(C) The development of ethnic enclaves as these migrants moved for work

(D) The seasonal migration patterns associated with temporary work

431. Which of the following legacies of British colonial rule proved most
disruptive in the immediate aftermath of Indian independence?

(A) Education of diverse Indian elites in a common English language

(B) Hindu-Muslim rivalry fostered by colonial divide and rule practices

(C) Establishment of parliamentary democratic norms in government

(D) Toleration of caste distinctions

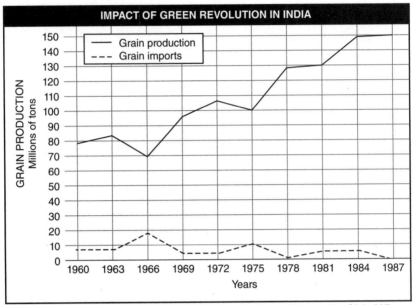

Source: James Killoran et al., *The Key to Understanding Global History,*
Jarrett Publishing Co. (adapted)

432. Based on the chart above, the Green Revolution was

   (A) A major failure in its goal to produce more food
   (B) A boon to Europe at the expense of Asia and Latin America
   (C) A mixed success of larger increases in Mexico than in Pakistan
   (D) A major success in its goal of increasing food supply

433. Which of the following is a historical argument about food and India in the modern era?

   (A) India's success with the Green Revolution has forever ended malnutrition.
   (B) India's food staples are exclusively New World crops of potatoes and corn.
   (C) India's democratic system has been successful in eliminating famine thus far.
   (D) India's nuclear program has come at the expense of its food supply.

1. *The constitution should provide for a Federation of Pakistan in its true sense based on the parliamentary form of government with supremacy of a Legislature directly elected on the basis of universal adult franchise.*

2. *The federal government should deal with only two subjects: Defense and Foreign Affairs, and all other residual subjects should be vested in the federating states.*

3. *Two separate, but freely convertible currencies for two wings should be introduced; or if this is not feasible, there should be one currency for the whole country, but effective constitutional provisions should be introduced to stop the flight of capital from East to West Pakistan. Furthermore, a separate Banking Reserve should be established and separate fiscal and monetary policy be adopted for East Pakistan.*

4. *The power of taxation and revenue collection should be vested in the federating (regional) units and the federal center would have no such power.*

5. *There should be two separate accounts for the foreign exchange earnings of the two wings; the foreign exchange requirements of the federal government should be met by the two wings equally or in a ratio to be fixed; indigenous products should move free of duty between the two wings.*

6. *East Pakistan should have a separate militia or paramilitary force.*

—The Six-Point Program of the Bangladeshi Nationalists, 1966.

434. Which of the following was a short-term result of the six-point program listed above?

(A) The partition of India
(B) The withdrawal of British forces
(C) The partition of Pakistan
(D) The first freely held elections

435. Which of the following historical arguments is proven true by the situation in East Pakistan/Bangladesh?

(A) Pakistan is stronger without Bangladesh as a region.
(B) Islam was not enough to overcome other cultural differences.
(C) Chinese aggression was behind the crisis in 1971.
(D) India intended to absorb Bangladesh as a new state.

—Stamp, circa 1938.

436. Which of the following best provides context for the image above?
(A) The Cold War after World War II
(B) European imperialism in Africa
(C) African colonial troops in World War I
(D) Improved naval technology

437. Which change did the twentieth century see take place in Africa that is reflected in the image?
(A) The demonization of British royalty in African print images
(B) The switch from electronic-based media to paper media
(C) Modern systems of transportation and communication
(D) The draining of Lake Victoria for irrigation purposes

"Five years later a naturalist came to see him and, after passing through his garden, said: 'That bird is an eagle, not a chicken.'" "'Yes,' said its owner, 'but I have trained it to be a chicken. It is no longer an eagle, it is a chicken, even though it measures fifteen feet from tip to tip of its wings.'" "'No,' said the naturalist, 'it is an eagle still: it has the heart of an eagle, and I will make it soar high up to the heavens.'" "'No,' said the owner, 'it is a chicken, and it will never fly.'" They agreed to test it. The naturalist picked up the eagle, held it up, and said with great intensity, 'Eagle, thou art an eagle; thou dost belong to the sky and not to this earth; stretch forth thy wings and fly.'" "The eagle turned this way and that, and then, looking down, saw the chickens eating their food, and down he jumped." "The owner said: 'I told you it was a chicken.'" "'No,' said the naturalist, 'it is an eagle. Give it another chance tomorrow.'" After two more unsuccessful attempts "The eagle looked around and trembled as if new life were coming to it; but it did not fly. The naturalist then made it look straight at the sun. Suddenly it stretched out its wings and, with the screech of an eagle, it mounted higher and higher and never returned. It was an eagle, though it had been kept and tamed as a chicken!" "My people of Africa, we were created in the image of God, but men have made us think that we are chickens, and we still think we are; but we are eagles. Stretch forth your wings and fly! Don't be content with the food of chickens!"

—*The Eagle That Would Not Fly*, a parable by James Aggrey, a Ghanaian, born scholar.

438. This parable is best understood in the context of which concept?

(A) Chickens and eagles were a great resource for the colonial powers.

(B) Colonialism had a negative impact on the psyche of colonial peoples.

(C) Colonialism encouraged non-Westerners to be content with outside rule.

(D) Communism spread widely among newly liberated peoples and nations.

439. *The Eagle That Would Not Fly* parable by James Aggrey was a great inspiration to people in Africa. For what other colonized nation in the twentieth century could it also be an inspiration?

(A) France

(B) Russia

(C) Thailand

(D) Korea

Palm Oil Exports (Tons)

Year	British West Africa	French West Africa	Belgian Congo	Total	Malaya	Sumatra
1929	137,609	33,516	27,768	198,893	2,500	31,960
1930	139,453	38,370	36,670	214,193	3,253	48,552
1931	119,857	28,103	22,595	170,355	5,136	62,260
1932	118,970	22,595	39,332	180,897	7,905	83,484
1933	130,332	22,260	51,628	204,220	12,100	114,348
1934	115,062	26,259	44,332	185,653	15,851	119,271
1935	145,921	87,660	–	233,581	24,598	143,200
Mean	129,420		–	193,149		

—Chart of African and South East Asian Palm Oil exports, 1929–1935.

440. Which colonized area was the most productive area for palm oil in the interwar years?

(A) French West Africa
(B) British West Africa
(C) Sumatra
(D) Malaya

441. Which of the following best describes the relationship between Europe and Africa in the interwar years?

(A) Free enterprise/free trade
(B) Command economy
(C) Mercantilism
(D) Extractive colonialism

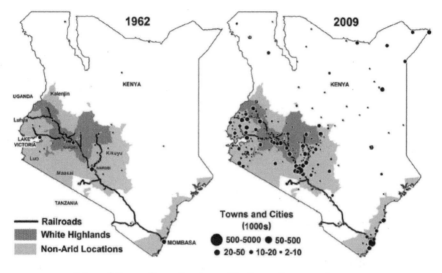

—Map of Kenya from the time of independence to the present.

442. Based on the photograph, the presence of a large number of European settlers in Kenya was most likely due to

(A) a hospitable climate and good farmland

(B) rainforest conditions and abundant animals

(C) a halfway point between England and India

(D) spice and tea plantations in North Kenya

443. Which of the following can be concluded from the image above?

(A) Most Kenyans moved to the coastline for economic opportunities.

(B) European settlement patterns played a large role in later urbanization.

(C) Swahili was the common language of European settlers in Kenya.

(D) The Mau Mau uprising against European rule took place in the North.

444. British rule in Kenya came to an end through a similar historical process as that of French Algeria in that both

(A) Were due to a civil war between Communist and non-Communist forces

(B) Came about peacefully because of United Nations resolutions and mandates

(C) Were achieved when a neighboring African state invaded and liberated them

(D) Followed a brutal guerilla insurgency and colonial attempts at suppression

In the twentieth century, and especially since the end of the war, the processes which gave birth to the nation states of Europe have been repeated all over the world. We have seen the awakening of national consciousness in peoples who have for centuries lived in dependence upon some other power. Fifteen years ago this movement spread through Asia. Many countries there, of different races and civilizations, pressed their claim to an independent national life. Today the same thing is happening in Africa, and the most striking of all the impressions I have formed since I left London a month ago is of the strength of this African national consciousness. In different places it takes different forms, but it is happening everywhere. The wind of change is blowing through this continent, and whether we like it or not, this growth of national consciousness is a political fact. We must all accept it as a fact, and our national policies must take account of it. Well you understand this better than anyone … here in Africa you have yourselves created a free nation. A new nation. Indeed in the history of our times yours will be recorded as the first of the African nationalists. This tide of national consciousness which is now rising in Africa, is a fact, for which both you and we, and the other nations of the western world are ultimately responsible.

—Speech given in 1960 by British prime minister
to the South African Parliament, which had achieved
independence from Britain in 1910.

445. The speech above is best understood in the context of

(A) The aftermath of the Second World War
(B) The Cold War between the US and USSR
(C) South African agricultural policy
(D) The Spanish influenza pandemic

446. The "winds of change" that the prime minister speaks of resulted in which of the following changes?

(A) The growth in Communist ideology amongst Africans
(B) The use of trade winds for the new economies
(C) Many newly independent nations in Africa
(D) The end of the slave trade amongst Islamic nations

447. Although this speech was made in the South Africa parliament, it was ignored by the white settlers since they had a policy of

(A) Containment
(B) Apartheid
(C) Laissez-faire
(D) Assimilation

—Sign in South Africa, circa 1960 to 1990.

448. The sign above indicates which continuity in South Africa from the European colonial period during the end of the twentieth century?

(A) The use of Dutch language by English-speaking Africans
(B) The persistence of racist policies by white-dominated governments
(C) The migration of Dutch settlers to southern Africa
(D) The spread of Communist ideas in West Africa

449. Which of the following was one result of the effort to end apartheid in South Africa?

(A) Apartheid still continues to this day.
(B) It encouraged the spread of apartheid.
(C) It was ineffective in ending apartheid.
(D) Apartheid is no longer practiced in South Africa.

450. Why was South Africa's independence struggle atypical when compared with most other African nations?

(A) Few other African nations gained independence in the 1960s.
(B) South Africa embarked on a program of rapid state-directed industrialization soon after achieving independence.
(C) Independence was negotiated by a South African government that consisted of white settlers only.
(D) South Africa nationalized gold and diamond mines and directed profits from their operation into development projects to lift the standard of living of the black majority there.

February 13 [1905]

DEAR SISTER: … And now I inform you that I have very good work. I have been working for 3 months. I have very good and easy work. I earn $8.00 a week. Brother has work also, And as to Brylska, I don't know how she is getting on, and I don't think about her at all. Inform me what is going on in our country, who has come to America, and who got married, and what is the talk in our country about revolution and war, because I have paid for a newspaper for a whole year and the paper comes to me twice a week, so they write that in our country there is misery. They say that in Warsaw and Petersburg there is a terrible revolution and many people have perished already. As to the money, I cannot help you now, sister. You will excuse me yourself, I did not work for five months … .

ADAM RACZKOWSKI

—"American letter."

—Advertisement from 1908.

451. The so called "American letter" puts forth which viewpoint about immigration to the Americas in the early twentieth century?

(A) The only destination for migrants was America.

(B) "Push-pull" factors were key motivations for migration.

(C) Visas were necessary for entry into nations.

(D) Paper letters were rarely used by the migrants.

452. Based on the image, immigration to the Americas was promoted from which areas of the world?

(A) Other regions within the Americas

(B) European nations, especially ones with cultural ties

(C) East Asian nations, particularly the Philippines

(D) African nations with Portuguese colonial ties

While conditions in Nicaragua and the action of this government pertaining thereto have in general been made public, I think the time has arrived for me officially to inform the Congress more in detail of the events leading up to the present disturbances and conditions which seriously threaten American lives and property, endanger the stability of all Central America, and put in jeopardy the rights granted by Nicaragua to the United States for the construction of a canal. It is well known that in 1912 the United States intervened in Nicaragua with a large force and put down a revolution, and that from that time to 1925 a legation guard of American Marines was, with the consent of the Nicaragua government, kept in Managua to protect American lives and property. In 1923 representatives of the five Central American countries, namely, Costa Rica, Guatemala, Honduras, Nicaragua, and Salvador, at the invitation of the United States, met in Washington and entered into a series of treaties.

—Calvin Coolidge, Intervention in Nicaragua, 1925.

453. Which of the following represents a continuity in Latin America from the post-Independence era till today?

(A) The United States has not been interested in economic investment in Latin America.

(B) US presidents often invited representatives from Cuba and Nicaragua to summits in Washington.

(C) The perception of the United States as a powerful but overbearing neighbor.

(D) Latin American nations were allied closely with their former colonial masters.

454. Which of the following is true regarding US and Latin American relations in the interwar era (1919–1941)?

(A) The United States was nervous about Communist aggression in the Andean nations of Peru and Ecuador.

(B) The policy of isolationism applied more to European affairs than Latin American affairs.

(C) Latin American nations formed a single economic union to compete with the United States.

(D) Nations rallied to Nicaragua's side and declared war on the United States in 1930.

—1930s-era mural in the town hall of the Mexican city of Valladolid.

455. The causes of the Mexican Revolution of 1910 to 1920 were mainly based on which of the following?

(A) The grievances of the poor and vulnerable

(B) The injuries done to the Catholic Church

(C) The spread of Bolshevik ideas from Russia

(D) The rise of Mexican nationalism

456. In comparison to the Chinese Revolution of 1910, the Mexican Revolution also

(A) overthrew a long-ruling monarchical dynasty

(B) was caused by anger over foreign domination

(C) resulted from the sale and use of opium

(D) led to the establishment of communism

—Female volunteers in the British army from the Caribbean, 1944.

457. The image shown above best demonstrates which of the following conclusions?

(A) Suffrage was granted to women for their participation in World War II.

(B) War-related factory jobs were the only employment that women could acquire.

(C) Women were encouraged to take part in frontline combat positions.

(D) Total war requires the active involvement of the civilian population.

458. Which of the following was a direct result of the participation of Caribbean-Americans and other nonwhite colonial peoples in Europe and Canada in World War II?

(A) A nonaligned stance during the Cold War

(B) A push for racial justice and civil rights

(C) Being suspected of Communist sympathies

(D) A call for more environmental protections

The armed forces, with the help of the national police, have assumed con-
trol of Chile. A four-man junta, composed of the chiefs of the armed services
and the carabineros intends to govern with advice from civilians. The junta's
plans for political reform indicate that such civilians will be businessmen and
professional guild leaders responsible for recent anti-government shutdowns,
rather than political leaders who had opposed Allende. The new rulers have
declared Congress to be in recess.

—CIA document about the coup détat in Chile against
President-elect Salvador Allende in 1973.

459. The reading above is best understood as which continuity in Latin
American politics?

- (A) Dominance of the Roman Catholic church
- (B) The popularity of the ideas of Karl Marx
- (C) Unstable democracies and constant coups d'états
- (D) Increasing trade exports to North America

460. The coup d'état in Chile by General Pinochet was supported by the
United States of America at the time. This is best understood in the
context of which of the following developments?

- (A) The spread of communism to the Western Hemisphere with the
  Cuban Revolution in 1959
- (B) The fall of communism in 1989 that was triggered with the USSR's
  reforms under Gorbachev
- (C) The defeat of Nazi Germany and Fascist Italy at the end of the Second
  World War
- (D) The desire of the United States to only support military-led
  governments like their own

The Cuban people hold a special place in the hearts of the people of Africa. The Cuban internationalists have made a contribution to African independence, freedom and justice unparalleled for its principled and selfless character. We in Africa are used to being victims of countries wanting to carve up our territory or subvert our sovereignty. It is unparalleled in African history to have another people rise to the defence of one of us. The defeat of the apartheid army was an inspiration to the struggling people in South Africa! Without the defeat of Cuito Cuanavale our organizations would not have been unbanned! The defeat of the racist army at Cuito Cuanavale has made it possible for me to be here today! Cuito Cuanavale was a milestone in the history of the struggle for southern African liberation!

—Nelson Mandela in a speech in Havana in 1991
praising Cuba for its role in Angola.

461. Which conclusions can be made about the role of Cubans in Africa in the 1960s and 1970s?

(A) Communist states were sympathetic toward conflicts of national liberation.

(B) Cubans saw great economic opportunities for themselves in Africa.

(C) Russia criticized Cubans for their lack of support for African decolonization.

(D) Cubans were still heavily involved in the African slave trade.

462. The Cold War impacted the newly freed states of Africa by all of the following EXCEPT

(A) Attempts by most states to maintain a nonalignment policy during the conflict

(B) Competition by Western powers and the Soviets to draw African nations to their side of the conflict

(C) A series of generally low-level proxy wars between Communist inspired and non-Communist forces

(D) The buildup of nuclear missile bases aimed at America from states in western and central Africa

—Memorial book on the ANZAC forces in World War I. *The Anzac Book,* London, New York: Cassell, 1916.

463. The participation of many Australians and New Zealanders in the ANZAC Corps on the side of Britain in World Wars I and II is best understood in the context of which of the following?

(A) Spheres of influence
(B) British protectorates
(C) Penal colonies
(D) White settler colonies

464. Which of the following was a continuity in Australia and New Zealand's connection to Great Britain in the twentieth century?

(A) Loyalty to the mother country
(B) A strong independence movement
(C) High trade barriers for Great Britain
(D) Increasing immigration barriers to Asians

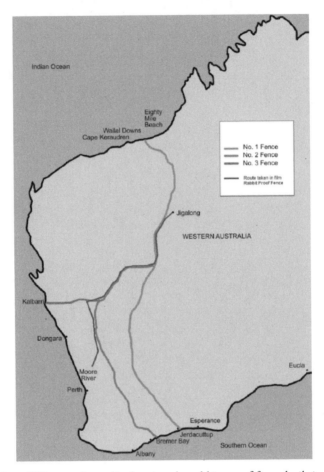

—Map of Western Australia showing the rabbit-proof fence built in 1907 but left to ruin by the 1950s.

465. The map showing Australia's rabbit proof fence demonstrates which of the following conclusions?

(A) Rabbits have long inhabited the continent of Australia.

(B) Mammals can be eradicated through rifles and traps.

(C) The environmental impact of European settlements

(D) Sea walls would also have helped with rabbits and rodents.

466. Which of the following is a continuity of world history that can accurately be stated that is related to Australia's rabbit-proof fence?

(A) In the long run, walls or barriers are often ineffective.

(B) Australia was geographically isolated for centuries.

(C) Rabbits do not breed or reproduce particularly fast.

(D) Human contact has rarely been a driver of history.

—Indian soldiers in the British armed forces in World War I trenches in France, 1915.

467. The image above is best understood in the context of

(A) The global nature of World War I due to imperialism

(B) The division of the world into Muslim and non-Muslim

(C) The spread of nationalist sentiment before World War I

(D) The ending of nonviolent protest among Indians

468. By comparison, World War I differed from World War II in which of the following ways?

(A) World War II was a more limited geographical conflict.

(B) World War II was more mobile in its type of warfare.

(C) World War II was less destructive in terms of civilians.

(D) World War II resulted in a period of stability in China.

—WWI Poster for the Young Women's Christian Association, 1917.

469. The poster above is best understood in the context of
(A) Suffrage movement that demanded votes for women
(B) Total war involving mobilization of the civilian population
(C) New birth control methods that freed mothers from unplanned pregnancies
(D) Germany's Nazi propaganda machine

470. Which of the following events happened partly as a result of the actions portrayed in the poster?
(A) The Bolshevik Revolution in Russia
(B) The Great Depression
(C) Women achieving suffrage after WWI in the United States and Britain
(D) Germany declaring war on Serbia in 1914

Turning and turning in the widening gyre
The falcon cannot hear the falconer;
Things fall apart; the centre cannot hold;
Mere anarchy is loosed upon the world,
The blood-dimmed tide is loosed, and everywhere
The ceremony of innocence is drowned;
The best lack all conviction, while the worst
Are full of passionate intensity.

—"The Second Coming" (first stanza) by William Butler Yeats, 1919.

471. Which of the following best explains the context behind the poem above?

(A) An emotional hardening back to a mythological age of heroes
(B) Feelings of deep anxiety and fear in the post–World War I era
(C) A rational appeal for a more scientific approach to humanity
(D) A classic interpretation of the correct behavior for family members

472. The lines "things fall apart; the centre cannot hold" makes reference to which historical change?

(A) The Great Depression and its devastating unemployment problem
(B) The assassination of the Archduke Ferdinand of Austria-Hungary
(C) The failure of the League of Nations to solve the Ethiopian crisis
(D) The fall of some monarchies and challenges to traditional elites

> *... For Fascism, the growth of empire, that is to say the expansion of the nation, is an essential manifestation of vitality, and its opposite a sign of decadence. Peoples which are rising, or rising again after a period of decadence, are always imperialist; and renunciation is a sign of decay and of death. Fascism is the doctrine best adapted to represent the tendencies and the aspirations of a people, like the people of Italy, who are rising again after many centuries of abasement and foreign servitude. But empire demands discipline, the coordination of all forces and a deeply felt sense of duty and sacrifice: this fact explains many aspects of the practical working of the regime, the character of many forces in the State, and the necessarily severe measures which must be taken against those who would oppose this spontaneous and inevitable movement of Italy in the twentieth century ...*

—What Is Fascism, Benito Mussolini, 1932.

473. Based on the above reading, which of the following actions was justified according to the precepts of Fascism?

(A) The anti-Semitic policies of Fascist Italy

(B) The Italian invasion of Ethiopia

(C) The Axis alliance with Germany and Japan

(D) The surrender of Italy in 1943 when the Allies invaded

474. Which of the following nations followed a similar foreign policy as Fascist Italy in the interwar period?

(A) Soviet Union

(B) France

(C) Japan

(D) Mexico

—German school map of Europe, circa 1930s.

Staat	Heeresstärke	
	im Frieden	voraussichtlich im Kriege
Deutschland . . .	100 000	100 000
Albanien	13 000	30 000
Belgien	71 760	600 000
Bulgarien	20 000	20 000
Dänemark	wechselnd bis 26 000	150 000
Estland	14 000	120 000
Finnland	26 000	300 000
Frankreich	655 490	5 000 000
Griechenland . .	66 136	600 000
Großbritannien .	240 000 □	2 000 000
Irland	14 927	?
Italien	417 000	5 000 000
Jugoslawien . . .	wechselnd bis 140 000	2 000 000
Lettland	23 500	150 000
Litauen	17 800	200 000
Niederlande . . .	35 000	300 000
Norwegen	wechselnd bis 30 000	110 000
Österreich	30 000	30 000
Polen	300 000	3 600 000
Portugal	67 000	870 000
Rumänien	255 000	2 000 000
Rußland	wechselnd bis 1 250 000	7 000 000
Schweden	wechselnd bis 57 000	400 000
Schweiz	wechselnd bis 35 000	400 000
Spanien	175 000	1 800 000
Tschechoslowakei	180 000	1 500 000
Türkei	150 000	1 500 000
Ungarn	35 000	35 000

*) einschl. 61 000 in Indien

—Detail of map above showing size of European nations' armed forces.

Photo by Sean McManamon.

475. Based on the German school map, which of the following comparisons is true?

(A) Germany was allowed to build up its armed forces to levels reached by its former enemies.

(B) Germany was smaller than most of its neighboring countries with the exception of France.

(C) Germany was demilitarized after World War I, while nations like France, Russia, and Poland built up their armed forces.

(D) Germany expanded its territory after World War I at the expense of its neighbors like France.

476. Which historical argument is supported by the map used in German schools in the interwar era (1919–1939)?

(A) Germany surrendered on the battlefield in World War I and formally at the Treaty of Versailles.

(B) Germany was barely affected by the provisions of the Treaty of Versailles.

(C) Germany was able to gain much territory and concessions at the Treaty of Versailles.

(D) Germany was unfairly treated by the Allied powers at the Treaty of Versailles.

Dates of the Great Depression

Country	Depression Began	Recovery Began	Decline in Industrial Production During the Great Depression
United States	mid-1929	mid-1933	47%
Germany	early-1928	mid-1932	42%
Italy	mid-1929	early-1933	33%
France	mid-1930	mid-1932	31%
United Kingdom	early-1930	late-1932	16%
Japan	early-1930	mid-1932	9%

477. Based on the countries in this table, the decline in industrial production during the Great Depression was relatively more severe in countries
   (A) That had industrialized more recently
   (B) That had large overseas colonial empires
   (C) Where the Great Depression began earlier
   (D) Where WWI battles had been fought

478. Which is the most important reason why Germany suffered so severely from the Great Depression?
   (A) The refusal of the Soviets to repay war debt to Germany and Austria.
   (B) The economic disruptions due to the provisions of the Versailles treaty.
   (C) The billions of dollars in war reparations that France owed to Germany.
   (D) The printing of less paper money in Germany, causing deflation.

"It made me feel good because my husband was over there in Europe fighting, and here I was doing my part ... [Plus] I made more money! ... It was work that you were proud of."

—Ruth Wilson, one of the so-called Black Rosies, an African-American female factory worker during World War II.

479. Which of the following was a direct result of the participation of African Americans and other nonwhite colonial peoples in Europe and Canada in World War II?

(A) A nonaligned stance during the Cold War
(B) A push for racial justice and civil rights
(C) Being suspected of Communist sympathies
(D) A call for more environmental protections

480. The introduction of female African American workers in defense factories during World War II best demonstrates which of the following conclusions?

(A) Suffrage was granted to women for their participation in World War II.
(B) War-related factory jobs were the only employment that women could acquire.
(C) Women were encouraged to take part in frontline combat positions.
(D) Total war requires the active involvement of the civilian population.

Source: Walter Stier, the official responsible for the "special trains" that transported millions of Jews and other victims to concentration camps such as Auschwitz, is being questioned after the war.

What's the difference between a special and a regular train?

A regular train may be used by anyone who purchases a ticket ... . A special train has to be ordered. The train is specially put together and people pay group fares ... .

But why were there more special trains during the war than before or after?

I see what you're getting at. You're referring to the so-called resettlement trains ... . Those trains were ordered by the Ministry of Transport of the Reich [the German government].

But mostly, at that time, who was being "resettled"?

No. We didn't know that. Only when we were fleeing from Warsaw ourselves, did we learn that they could have been Jews, or criminals, or similar people.

Special trains for criminals?

No, that was just an expression. You couldn't talk about that. Unless you were tired of life, it was best not to mention that.

But you knew that the trains to Treblinka or Auschwitz were—

Of course we knew. I was the last district; without me these trains couldn't reach their destination ... .

Did you know that Treblinka meant extermination?

Of course not!

You didn't know?

Good God, no! How could we know? I never went to Treblinka. I stayed in Krakow, in Warsaw, glued to my desk.

You were a ...

I was strictly a bureaucrat!

Document source: Letter dated June 28, 1943,
Auschwitz administrator Karl Bischoff wrote up a tally of
all the cremations, burning of corpses, performed on a single day.

481. Which best helps explain the passage in the context of the historical period it describes?

(A) Germany forced more than 7 million people other than Jews into labor camps or jobs to support the war.

(B) World War I or the Great War was, up until that time, the bloodiest war in history, causing tremendous suffering and death to soldiers.

(C) Political conflicts before and during World War II lead to various forms of genocide and ethnic violence.

(D) During Kristallnacht in 1938, Jews throughout Germany and Austria were beaten and killed.

482. The previous text document acts as historical evidence for which of the following statements?

(A) The Nazis were using the smoke from the crematoriums to hide the murders they had committed.

(B) The Allies started World War II and later used their victory to place all blame on the Germans.

(C) Crematoriums were a more efficient way of disposing war dead than mass graves.

(D) The Holocaust, or systematic murder of Jews before and during World War II, is an indisputable fact.

THE WAY BACK

—Political cartoon.

483. The Marshall Plan was developed to

(A) Create a tariff-free common market in Europe

(B) Rebuild the economies of Europe after World War II

(C) Bring about the unification of Europe

(D) Increase Europe's dependence on the United States

484. Which was a strong motivation for the Marshall Plan in Europe?

(A) The return of the Nazi party in England and Germany

(B) The fall of the Berlin Wall and reunification of Germany

(C) Fear of economic hardships leading to extremist politics

(D) The Vietnam War's effects on domestic opinion in Germany

Through our protective measures of 13 August 1961 we have only safe-guarded and strengthened that frontier which was already drawn years ago and made into a dangerous front-line by the people in Bonn and West Berlin. How high and how strongly fortified a frontier must be, depends, as is common knowledge, on the kind of relations existing between the states of each side of the frontier ... We no longer wanted to stand by passively and see how doctors, engineers, and skilled workers were induced by refined methods unworthy of the dignity of man to give up their secure existence here and work in West Germany or West Berlin.

—1962 brochure from the
German Democratic Republic (GDR), published
in English for foreign distribution.

There are many people in the world who really don't understand, or say they don't, what is the great issue between the free world and the Communist world. Let them come to Berlin. There are some who say that communism is the wave of the future. Let them come to Berlin. Freedom has many difficul-ties and democracy is not perfect, but we have never had to put a wall up to keep our people in, to prevent them from leaving us ... . Freedom is indivisible, and when one man is enslaved, all are not free. When all are free, then we can look forward to that day when this city will be joined as one and this country and this great Continent of Europe in a peaceful and hopeful globe. When that day finally comes, as it will, the people of West Berlin can take sober satisfaction in the fact that they were in the front lines for almost two decades. All free men, wherever they may live, are citizens of Berlin, and, therefore, as a free man, I take pride in the words "Ich bin ein Berliner.

—President John F. Kennedy's speech in June, 1963
when he visited Berlin.

485. The readings above are best understood in the context of which of the following historical events

(A) The rise of Islamic fundamentalism
(B) The Cold War years
(C) The European Union
(D) The increase in illegal migration

486. The second reading by President Kennedy differs from the first reading from the GDR in that it

(A) takes a stand against illegal immigration to Berlin
(B) agrees that the Berlin Wall is keeping the peace
(C) opposes the Berlin Wall as antithetical to freedom
(D) supports the Communist idea of a divided Berlin

EXTREMISTS' RISE TO POWER IN RUSSIA

From Outset of Revolution They Have Thwarted Efforts of Moderate Governments.

SAPPED KERENSKY'S RULE

Supported Premier Only When the Kornlloff Movement Filled Them with Apprehension.

—New York Times headline, November 9th, 1917.

487. The issues referred to in the headlines above are best understood in the context of

(A) World War I
(B) The rise of Fascism
(C) The Russian Revolution
(D) The Great Depression

488. It can plausibly be argued that the seizure of power in Russia by radical socialists and Communists in 1917 marks the beginning of

(A) The mandate system
(B) The Cold War
(C) World War I
(D) The League of Nations

The famine of 1932–1933 was the most terrible and destructive that the Ukrainian people have ever experienced. The peasants ate dogs, horses, rotten potatoes, the bark of trees, grass—anything they could find. Incidents of cannibalism were not uncommon. The people were like wild beasts, ready to devour one another. And no matter what they did, they went on dying, dying, dying … .

There was no one to gather the bumper crop of 1933, since the people who remained alive were too weak and exhausted. More than a hundred persons—office and factory workers from Leningrad—were sent to assist on the kolkhoz; two representatives of the Party arrived to help organize the harvesting … .

That summer (1933) the entire administration of the kolkhoz—the book-keeper, the warehouseman, the manager of the flour mill, and even the chairman himself—were put on trial on charges of plundering the kolkhoz property and produce. All the accused were sentenced to terms of seven to ten years, and a new administration was elected … .

—*The History of a Soviet Collective Farm* by Fedor Belov.

489. Which of the following acts as context for the reading above?

(A) The problems of totalitarian rule in the Soviet Union

(B) The overreliance on agriculture as a food source

(C) The damage done by the Nazi German invasion

(D) The dangers of the Cold War between the superpowers

490. Which Soviet policy contributed greatly to the tragedy described above?

(A) De-Stalinization

(B) Glasnost

(C) Collectivization

(D) Detente

—Soviet propaganda poster issued in Uzbekistan, 1933, "Strengthen working discipline in collective farms."

491. Based on the image above, the Soviet Union instituted which of the following changes?

(A) The implementation of Communist economic policies in rural areas

(B) The banishment of refugees from central Asia to eastern Europe

(C) The increase in population through centralized family planning

(D) The ending of payments to the old aristocracy from czarist Russia

492. Based on the image above, which of the following was a commonality of totalitarian regimes in the twentieth century?

(A) Use of the elderly as a revolutionary force

(B) Television and radio propaganda

(C) Private ownership of industry and factories

(D) Persecution of minorities and scapegoats

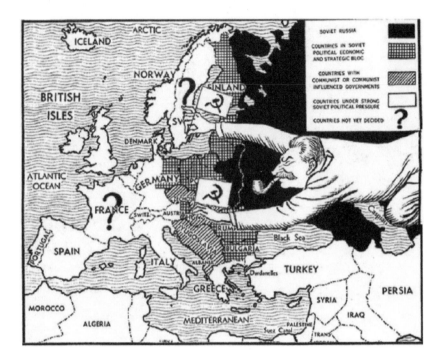

493. After World War II, the Soviet Union established satellites in Eastern Europe in order to achieve which of the following?

(A) Support the remaining Fascist governments in Eastern Europe
(B) Preserve entrepreneurship in Eastern Europe
(C) Create a buffer against future invasion from the West
(D) Establish democratic governments in Eastern European nations

494. One major cause of the Cold War was the

(A) Trade competition between imperial powers
(B) Differences in ideology between the United States and the USSR
(C) Differences in how to best promote literacy throughout the world
(D) Determination of the United States to maintain political control of Eastern Europe

495. What post–World War II development does the map above most accurately reflect?

(A) Creation of new military alliances
(B) Migration patterns
(C) Industrialized versus unindustrialized nations
(D) Protestant and Catholic countries

The most important one was the belief, which went back to [Vladimir] Lenin, that capitalists would never be able to cooperate with one another for very long. Their inherent greediness—the irresistible urge to place profits above politics—would sooner or later prevail, leaving communists with the need only for patience as they awaited their adversaries' self-destruction.

—Historian John Lewis Gaddis in his book
The Cold War: A New History.

496. Which of the following best represents the historical argument made by John Lewis Gaddis?

(A) World conflicts were inevitable given the capricious nature of capitalism.

(B) The Cold War resulted in the emergence of two superpowers by the end of World War II.

(C) World War I resulted in a wave of decolonization in Africa, Asia, and the Americas.

(D) The Cold War soon gave way to a hot war between the United States and Russian armed forces.

Work Time Needed to Buy Goods and Services, 1982

Goods and Services	Soviet Union	United States
White bread (2.2 pounds)	17 minutes	16 minutes
Sirloin steak (2.2 pounds)	182 minutes	79 minutes
Chicken (2.2 pounds)	185 minutes	16 minutes
Fresh milk (1 quart)	22 minutes	6 minutes
Potatoes (2.2 pounds)	7 minutes	7 minutes
Oranges (2.2 pounds)	92 minutes	10 minutes
Bath soap	20 minutes	4 minutes
Aspirin	246 minutes	5 minutes
Lipstick	69 minutes	30 minutes
Gasoline (3 gallons)	210 minutes	36 minutes
Newspaper	3 minutes	3 minutes
Blue jeans	46 hours	3 hours
Washing machine	165 hours	47 hours
Gas Bill (1 month)	39 minutes	290 minutes
Telephone call (local)	1 minute	2 minutes
Haircut	37 minutes	63 minutes
Car (medium sized)	88 months	8 months
Rent (1 month)	12 hours	56 hours

—Radio Library Research Supplement, 1982.

497. Based on the chart above, which of the following conclusions can be made about the Soviet Union compared to the United States?
(A) Trade goods were imported from wealthy Western countries.
(B) Basic necessities were more affordable than consumer goods.
(C) Goods like aspirin were within easy reach of all Soviet citizens.
(D) The cost of a newspaper and magazine was vastly different.

498. Which of the following was a result in the Soviet Union of the conditions outlined in the chart above?
(A) Economic stagnation and shortages of consumer goods
(B) Trade tariffs and other barriers to interaction with the world
(C) An increase in the world price of petroleum and heating gas
(D) A rise in the standard of living for workers and peasants

"Russians" song & lyrics by Sting

In Europe and America, there's a growing feeling of hysteria
Conditioned to respond to all the threats
In the rhetorical speeches of the Soviets
Mr. Khrushchev* said we will bury you
I don't subscribe to this point of view
It would be such an ignorant thing to do
If the Russians love their children too
How can I save my little boy from Oppenheimer's deadly toy**
There is no monopoly in common sense
On either side of the political fence
We share the same biology
Regardless of ideology
Believe me when I say to you
I hope the Russians love their children too
There is no historical precedent
To put the words in the mouth of the President
There's no such thing as a winnable war
It's a lie we don't believe anymore
Mr. Reagan*** says we will protect you
I don't subscribe to this point of view
Believe me when I say to you
I hope the Russians love their children too
We share the same biology
Regardless of ideology
What might save us, me, and you
Is if the Russians love their children too

*Russia's leader in the 1950s & 1960s
**The atomic bomb
***America's leader in the 1980s

499. Which of the following provides historical context for the lyrics above to the song "Russians"?

(A) The US policy of containment of communism
(B) The arms race between the US and the USSR
(C) The use of science in the Green Revolution
(D) The friendship between Communist Russia and China

500. References to lyrics like "there's no such thing as a winnable war" refer to which aspect of the Cold War?

(A) NATO or North America Treaty Organization

(B) DMZ or demilitarized zone

(C) MAD or mutually assured destruction

(D) SALT or Strategic Arms Limitation Agreement

ANSWERS

Chapter 1

1. (D) The Chinese Han viewed the Mongols as a barbarian people who had no right to rule over them and therefore considered the Yuan dynasty as illegitimate. The Mongols refused to adopt Chinese ways such as Confucianism and the civil service exams, and the Chinese eventually threw them out of China.

2. (B) While the Chinese were obviously upset by the military conquest of the Mongols over the Song dynasty, it was both their foreignness and disdain for Chinese culture and ways that set many Chinese, especially the Confucian educated scholar-gentry class, to reject Mongol Rule. The Mongols in turn distrusted the Chinese and refused them high offices in running the government. They used many foreigners in the government, especially Persians but famously Marco Polo.

3. (A) A court fight over the treasure fleet voyages emerged between Confucian scholars, who saw little value in them, while the court eunuchs promoted them and fellow eunuch Zheng He, who led the voyages.

4. (A) The Chinese were reported to have visited the East Coast of Africa and even been given a giraffe as a gift for the Chinese emperor, who lived what must have been a lonely life in Beijing.

5. (C) Scholars have divided the study of China into dynasties as a way to understand this civilization. Other East Asian civilizations like Japan are also studied in this way.

6. (B) The Mandate of Heaven was developed in the classical era as a way to explain and justify why the ruling dynasties were replaced by other dynasties.

7. (B) During the Song dynasty Chinese cities saw a profusion of trade until the Mongol onslaught in the twelfth century.

8. (C) Confucian tradition teaches that merchants who do not produce anything or govern are little better than parasites and therefore are not respected as a social class.

9. (A) Islam was introduced into China by the eighth century by traders and migrants. X'ian as the endpoint of the Silk Road was a cosmopolitan urban center of Muslim, Christian, and even Jewish communities. The long established contact between Chinese cultures and these newer belief systems encouraged a blending of cultures.

10. (C) Islam established a presence in some Chinese cities by the eighth century during the postclassical era.

11. (C) Scholars and government officials were schooled and tested in Confucian classics, which encourage them to look down on other belief systems.

12. **(A)** One argument against Buddhism by Confucian scholars was its foreign origin in India. References such as "cult of barbarians" and "did not speak the languages of China" show clear ethnocentrism.

13. **(B)** Shinto was the indigenous belief system of Japan. Primarily animist in origin and form, its State Shinto form in the late nineteenth and early twentieth centuries began to stress the divinity of the emperor.

14. **(A)** Buddhism came to Japan from Korea and China and from monasteries and royal patronage, and it spread slowly with another imported belief system, Confucianism, and coexisted with indigenous Shinto beliefs.

15. **(B)** Many aspects of Chinese culture, such as Buddhism, Confucianism, Daoism, and the writing system, were introduced to Japan from the fourth to the eighth century.

16. **(C)** Chinese Mahayana Buddhism was influential in both Korea and Japan

17. **(B)** Japan was not politically unified till late in the sixteenth century. Previously, central Japan was often a battleground for control by various clans.

18. **(A)** The code of the Japanese warriors was Bushido, which translates as the "way of the warrior." This code was repurposed in the late nineteenth century as Japan embarked on imperialistic ventures in Asia.

19. **(D)** For the Japanese samurai, the sword was considered the most important weapon. Skill at the bow and the spear were also prized but not to the extent of the sword.

20. **(B)** The Mongol invasions of Japan in 1274 and 1281 failed, and this marked the last time that Japan faced a serious outside threat until the nineteenth century with the arrival of the Americans in 1854.

21. **(B)** The failed Mongol invasions of Japan later contributed to a Japanese belief in their special role in the world and fear of outsiders in the island nation.

22. **(D)** India was a great cultural influence on Southeast Asia. This can be seen in Southeast Asia's religious traditions, architecture, dance, and writing system.

23. **(A)** Angkor Wat was originally a Hindu temple complex but was converted to and remains a Buddhist temple complex and monastery.

24. **(A)** Chinese traders, similar to the Europeans in the Early Modern Era, often had relationships with local women that were both intimate as well as business related.

25. **(B)** In Southeast Asia, societies were generally not strict patriarchies and women had a fair amount of autonomy and independence.

26. **(A)** Buddhism, like Christianity, offers the option of a monastic lifestyle as a show of devotion.

27. (B) Mahayana Buddhism was more influential in East Asia including Vietnam, whereas most of Southeast Asia was influenced by Theravada Buddhism.

28. (C) Like many religions, Islam coexisted with indigenous belief systems in many areas of the world, but this was most pronounced in Southeast Asia and West Africa.

29. (B) Sufism refers to the practices or a sect of Islam that was less doctrinaire than many forms of Islam. It was often found on the margins of the Islamic world such as southeastern Europe in the Balkans and India and was an effective missionary movement that helped spread the religion.

Short-Answer Question

30. Answers for this short-answer question (SAQ) may include how the Franks were Crusaders who tried to wrest control of the so-called Holy Land from the local Muslims around the city of Jerusalem in the Middle East.

31. Answers for this short-answer question (SAQ) may include how the two sides are using the same place of worship. In fact, the Templars chastise a fellow Christian for being rude to Usamah Ibn Munqidh. The fact that they are from different religions and cultures is undoubtedly shown in a positive light. This is a great reading to counter the popular "clash of civilizations" concept when thinking about the Crusades.

32. This reading is set in what is sometimes referred to as the Holy Land. Famously, Christians and Muslims fought each other in the Crusades from the eleventh to the thirteenth centuries. During this time European Christians, who were full of religious fervor, sought to gain control of the Holy Land since it was sacred to them. However, they were eventually defeated, and the area reverted to Muslim control. Other incidents in history saw a Christian and Muslim divide, but as the reading shows there was also plenty of nonviolent interaction, such as trade and learning between the two communities.

33. (B) During the Abbasid dynasty the Islamic cities of Baghdad and Cordova were great centers of learning, especially scientific learning in astronomy, optics, and navigation.

34. (D) Before the year 1200, Baghdad was perhaps the most sophisticated city on the planet. Only Chinese urban centers would have rivaled it.

35. (A) Networks of caravanserai were stretched over Southwest Asia/Middle East to provide for the basic needs for traveling merchants and promote overland trade.

36. (C) When the Europeans realized their long-term goal of finding an all-water route to Asia, the Middle East began to slowly lose its profitable role as the middle man. Caravanserai began to diminish in importance.

37. (C) A decrease in the number of workers due to deaths caused the remaining workers to feel empowered to higher wages for their services.

38. (A) Both the Mamluk and European governments realized the contagious nature of the bubonic plague and took steps to quarantine the infected and limit public interactions.

39. (A) The Columbian Exchange, with its infusion of New World foods like potatoes, corn, and chilies, transformed the diets of most of the world.

40. (B) Arabic script has been a cultural continuity in the region for centuries, even among non-Islamic populations.

41. (C) A bias toward a European perspective is pervasive throughout many scholarly disciplines, even outside Europe.

42. (B) In East Asia, the study of history is divided into dynastic periods such as the Ming in China, the Tokugawa in Japan, or the Yi in Korea.

43. (C) From a Eurocentric point of view, the beginning of the "Middle Ages" in the Middle East would correspond to that of Europe, which would be the fall of the (Western) Roman Empire.

44. (D) Silk Roads passed through the central Asian heartlands of the Mongol Empire.

45. (C) The Mongols conquered the territory that is now Korea, which was for centuries a Chinese tributary state.

46. (A) The map clearly shows the Russian cities of Kiev and Moscow in the area that was under the domination of the Golden Horde.

47. (A) The Mongol expansion stopped in Eastern Europe, in what constitutes present-day Poland. Italy was never directly threatened.

48. (D) The image shows Persian or Turkish musicians on the back of a camel that inhabits the western (non-Han Chinese) areas that had long contact and trade with peoples west of China. The fact that the piece was made in China shows the links between these areas of the world.

49. (A) Camels requiring less water than horses and built for a desert climate were ideal for transportation.

50. (A) Europeans feared the Mongols as barbarian warriors similar to the Huns who contributed to the fall of the Roman Empire. Descriptions such as Paris's would have solidified this feeling.

51. (D) Marco Polo as a traveler with his father and uncle were accepted as merchants, and his long time in the East had given Marco a positive view of the Mongols as well as other peoples of the East.

52. (C) The Pax Mongolica term is used to describe the eased communication and commerce the unified administration helped to create and the period of relative peace that followed the Mongols' vast conquests.

53. (A) Passports, caravanserai, and border patrols are methods that the state used to promote trade.

54. (B) The Mongols were very open to new ideas from other civilizations, whether it was new military technology such as siege machines or religions such as Islam or Tibetan Buddhism.

55. (D) Until the arrival of the Portuguese in the late fifteenth century, the trade in the Indian Ocean was largely done by Muslim merchants, which also explains why Islam expanded from the East Coast of Africa to the archipelagos of Southeast Asia.

56. (A) The Delhi sultanate borrowed heavily from Persian culture but used Arabic writing as it was the script of the prophet Muhammad and the Koran.

57. (B) While Muslim had been in India since the eighth century, they were either in small numbers as raiding parties or merchants in port cities. The Delhi sultanate was the first permanent Islamic rulers to establish themselves.

58. (C) The towering height of the Qutb Minar and its use of carved stones from nearby Hindu temples were meant to demonstrate the primacy of Islam.

59. (D) Sufism was popular in some areas of the Muslim world, especially in countries where Islam was not overwhelmingly the majority religion. Sufism can be seen as a form of accommodation to different faiths.

60. (B) Sufism is a focus on a spiritual or aesthetic form of Islam rather than on strict doctrines. Sufis are known to dance, sing, and compose poetry. In countries that practice a more fundamentalist form of Islam, Sufis are often outlawed and disowned.

61. (A) One of the challenges facing many religions including Islam is the existence of variations in belief and practices across the world.

62. (B) Phrases such as "source of legitimacy for their rule" "gained recognition" and "political alliances" show how political considerations were important in the conversion to Islam. Conversion was of a top-down nature.

63. (A) The phrase in the early part of the excerpt stating how "They did not ... give up their religious ... traditions" shows how Islam coexisted with previous belief systems.

64. (D) The Sahara Desert lies in the northern third of the African continent, and the local peoples like the Berber or the Tuareg were able to successfully navigate these geographic barriers.

65. (C) Choice **(A)** is accurate for some but not all of postclassical black Africa. Choices **(B)** and **(D)** are not accurate descriptors of the same.

66. (A) Integration of West, central, eastern, and southern Africa into world trade was achieved via Muslim contact as well as trans-Saharan and Indian Ocean trade networks.

67. (D) Ibn Battuta was an older Islamic jurist who throughout his travel journals demonstrated a critical eye for practices he felt were un-Islamic or communities he felt were less than observant.

68. (A) Ibn Battuta was upset at the casual gender relations and wanted more separation between genders who were not family. Terms like "shocked" and "amazed" demonstrate his displeasure.

69. (A) Prior to the discovery of gold in the Americas, Africa was a key source of gold for Europeans.

70. (C) West Africa was known for its trade of salt for gold in equal amounts due to the geographic disparities in various areas of Africa.

71. (B) Mansa Musa was famous for his journey to the Islamic holy cities of Mecca and Medina, and his lavish spending and actions inadvertently devastated the economies of the regions through which he passed.

72. (C) Great Zimbabwe in southern Africa was a thriving agricultural and trade center in the postclassical era, but its achievements were later denied by European settlers who claimed it had to have been founded by a Mediterranean society.

73. (D) Like many other famous archaeological sites, Great Zimbabwe was abandoned and the reasons remain unclear. Scholars are still investigating the exact causes, which include shifts in trade routes, political instability, and climate change.

74. (C) Choice (C) makes little sense, while the others are standard reasons why defensive walls are built in castles, fortresses, or around cities.

75. (D) The Incas developed quipu to keep records, although their exact use is still being Investigated.

76. (B) The Incan system for record keeping, called the quipu, was indigenous to the Americas and not influenced by any outside cultures.

77. (C) The pyramids of the Meso-Americans were not used as palaces because they would have been impractical but were used solely for religious practices such as human sacrifices and offerings. The building of these structures was done by the Mayans as a form of taxation and religious observance that glorified the rule of the Mayan dynasties.

78. (A) The Aztec pyramids, like other Meso-American structures, were built by a semicoerced form of labor called corvée, which was also a form of taxation. This form of labor was also used extensively in many other civilizations in world history.

79. (C) No large animals appropriate for domestication existed in the "New World." Despite this, Native American civilizations accomplished remarkable degrees of architectural achievements using only human muscle power.

80. (A) The Incas' empire was founded in the mountainous city of Cuzco and spread along the Andes Mountains north to Colombia and as far south as Chile.

81. (C) The Incan empire was primarily located in the Andes Mountains. They overcame difficult geography to stretch their empire from the modern nation of Colombia down to Chile.

82. (B) China has long had a number of areas that use terrace or step farming as a way to increase agricultural output for its large population.

83. (D) Potatoes, corn, and beans were the staple crops of the Americas and due to the Columbian Exchange spread to become staple foods in many areas of the world.

84. (B) Mita or corvée extracts labor from the natives as a form of obligatory public service or tribute.

85. (C) The Aztecs were an aggressive empire who conquered and dominated neighboring states from which they received regular tribute

86. (A) The Codex Mendoza may not be accurate since it was written two decades after the Spanish conquered the Aztecs.

87. (A) The non-Aztec people will eagerly join the Spanish in defeating their hated overlords.

88. (C) The Inuit people adapted to Greenland by relying on fish, fowl, and mammal food sources that they could catch or hunt. Their weapons, tools, clothes, and watercraft were carefully engineered for the environment, whereas the Greenland Vikings were better suited to warmer climates and farming.

89. (B) The Greenland Viking settlements died out by the 1400s and scholars still debate the various theories as to why. Some such theories are climate change, the Black Death, and the inability to adapt to a new environment.

90. (C) There is no evidence that Austronesian seafarers made it past Easter Island to the West Coast of South America.

91. (A) Bantu-speaking peoples dominate much of the southern half of Africa, where the language originated, while Austronesian languages spread from Easter Island to Madagascar.

92. (C) The Austronesian outrigger canoe is perfectly suited for island hopping across the Pacific Ocean. Also, their voyages within recent history without charts or navigational tools are awe-inspiring. Furthermore, we have linguistic proof of their ocean prowess.

Document-Based Question

93. A document-based question essay requires a 5-6 paragraph essay that directly addresses the question with a thesis with an argument and areas of specificity or roadmap. Answers will vary on the impact of the Black Death or bubonic plague in the mid-fourteenth century but will probably start with the high mortality in many areas of Afro-Eurasia. Answers may then address the economic impact of trade declining with shops being closed. It should address the acute labor shortages with the resulting rise in prices for items like bread. This in turn led to a demand for higher wages for laborers. The Black Death also saw a rise in religious fervor, with many people blaming the sinfulness of the people as a cause of the calamity. One such example of religious fervor was the violence against Jews. There were also advancements in medical knowledge, with people practicing social distancing that later developed into quarantining, and changes in art like the danse macabre or dance of death. Some students may add more information and context outside the documents like the rise in dissatisfaction of the Catholic Church, a rapid bounce back in the economy, and the decline of feudalism.

94. (B) The image of the farmers in the forefront doing agricultural work shows the farming/ agricultural basis of the European economy.

95. (D) The images show lords and peasants fulfilling different roles and occupying different levels of society.

96. (B) Serfdom was a major institution within European feudalism since the fall of the Western Roman Empire.

97. (D) Both images show huge castles in the background, which were controlled by the nobles.

98. (B) In return for loyalty and military service, nobles would receive fiefs from their overlords, which include land, houses, castles, and serf peasants.

99. (C) The fall of the Western Roman Empire and the lack of a strong centralized government brought about an economic and social system known as feudalism. This was similar to the situation in early Japan where there was no central authority until the Tokugawa shoguns united the country.

100. (B) Japan also developed a feudalistic system of government and social system of daimyo lords and samurai warriors.

101. (B) The chart of Hanseatic League trade clearly shows various amounts of exports and imports. This demonstrates the League's success.

102. (D) Hanseatic League trade provided the economic basis for the cultural flowering that sprung from Northern German towns, England, and the Low Countries. This was similar to Mediterranean trade contributing to the Italian Renaissance.

103. (A) Viking raids largely ended by the end of the eleventh century and Hanseatic League trade grew at the same time from German towns who entered into a commercial and defensive confederation of merchant guilds and market towns.

104. (A) The bubonic plague caused a labor shortage that put severe stress on the old feudal relationship and ushered in a wage labor system.

105. (D) The bubonic plague predates this declaration by three years and the shortage of workers persuaded workers to push for wage laborers.

106. (A) The slow introduction of wage labor brought about the end of feudalism with its system of coerced labor.

107. (C) Throughout the postclassical era (600–1450) the Church and monarchs regularly clashed over issues, especially lay investiture over who had the right to appoint clerical positions.

108. (D) The reoccurring lay investiture crisis weakened the alliance between the papacy and the various Western European monarchs.

109. (D) The Byzantine borrowed from the earlier Roman system of both secular authority as well as divine authority. Also, a breakdown of the term caesaropapism will reduce it to parts that help with its definition.

110. (A) The Byzantine Empire was a huge influence on Russian religion, writing system, calendar, architecture, and imperial system.

111. (A) Constantinople was founded by Greek settlers and its had long been a great center of trade and culture due to its location on the Bosporus Straits between the Black and Mediterranean seas dividing Europe from Asia.

112. (B) The Great Schism of 1025 brought a final rupture in the Christian Church that had its origins in Roman times when the Empire was divided into Western and Eastern halves and the linguistic differences of Latin and Greek.

113. (C) Neither Scandinavia, India, nor sub-Saharan Africa is adjacent to the choke point between the Black and Mediterranean Seas that made Byzantium such a key trade hub in the ancient and postclassical world.

114. (A) Benjamin Tudela, a Jewish rabbi speak positively about the city in glowing terms and mentions the "all sorts of merchants" from Europe, North Africa, and the Middle East.

115. (B) After the Second Crusade in 1187, the Islamic warrior Saladin regained control over Jerusalem and the Middle East and was never seriously threatened by European Crusaders.

116. (C) The fall of Constantinople is considered a major turning point in world history, from the ending of the Roman Empire to the triumph of Islam.

117. (A) The Great Schism in 1054 between the two main branches of European Christianity caused a cultural divide that later led to political distrust.

118. (D) Russia was forced to pay regular payments of valuable goods to the Golden Horde (Mongols) after being defeated.

119. (A) One of the theories for Russia's relationship with the West is that the long years of Mongol domination caused it to fall behind the West and be removed from key developments and trade.

120. (B) According to scholars, the game of chess originated in India and diffused westward to the Islamic Middle East and North Africa, where it was exposed to Europeans there and in Spain.

121. (D) The movement of the Lewis chessmen from Arctic Circle, Norway, and the Hebrides was primarily by sea, which was the quickest way to move goods. The Indian Ocean trade network was well established at this point in history.

122. (C) The Lewis chessmen were carved from walrus tusks and were traded long distances. Only highly priced items were worth the effort of movement over tough environments. For example, staple foods were rarely shipped through the North Sea but animal furs were.

123. (B) Medieval Europeans had a limited understanding of the wider world and that limited knowledge would have been strongly influenced by Christianity.

124. (A) Europeans began to have a wider world view due to the Crusades, increased trade, and early exploration.

125. (C) The map only shows Europe, Africa, and Asia and omits the Americas and Antarctica due to a lack of knowledge of those areas.

Chapter 2

126. (A) The use of awe-inspiring mountains hidden by mists, cut by hidden streams with the diminutive size of humans and the inclusion of poetry in the top left of the painting that uses a metaphor of a traveler for a journey of one's life make clear reference to Daoism.

127. (D) Paintings, calligraphy, and poetry complement one another and were the provenance of the scholar class in traditional China.

128. (B) The Portuguese were the first Europeans to reach China, and they were under strict restrictions based on their outsider status and merchant activities.

129. (A) The Chinese were always suspicious of non-Chinese, probably due to their experiences in the northwest frontier, where nomadic tribes had long posed a threat. Confucianism also contributed to Chinese ethnocentrism or sinocentrism.

130. (B) There has long been trade and cultural diffusion between China and the Middle East, and this contact continued into the Islamic era.

131. (C) Demand for Asian trade goods drove the European Age of Exploration.

132. (A) The distance to Asia and Chinese tough regulations on foreign trade made it profitable for Europeans to copy manufactured Asian goods.

133. (B) The excerpt, undoubtedly written by a Confucian scholar, is tolerant of Buddhism and Daoism but is dismissive of the new religion being spread by Christian missionaries.

134. (B) Despite the efforts of Jesuit and other Christian missionaries and the fears of the Chinese elites, Christianity did not have many followers.

135. (D) The Jesuits was one of the main responses to the threat posed by the Protestant Reformation. Jesuits were highly trained and aggressive in their missionary work.

136. (B) The Jesuits had little initial success in China but when they began to dress in scholar's robes, grow their beards, and learn the Chinese language, they had more success, especially with higher classes.

137. (A) In the Americas, the Jesuits found societies that suffered demographic losses and disruption, so had no reason to adapt to local conditions. They were never an important factor in southern Africa or the Netherlands. They were in India but never adapted to local tastes in their dress or approach.

138. (D) Filial piety, or respect for one's elders and superiors, is one of the main pillars of Confucianism.

139. (A) The Qing dynasty underwent considerable Sinification to appear to Chinese and lessen any resistance to their rule.

140. (A) The pronouncements in the Sacred Edict are typical of Chinese dynastic government at this time in history.

141. (C) The Yuan or Mongols ruled China directly and not as a tributary state like the early Russian state in Kiev. However, they kept separate from the native Chinese, ended civil service exams and did not adopt Chinese culture, seeing it as inferior to their own.

Document-Based Question

142. Answers should address the extent to which China was open to the outside world. Students may write about how some documents indicate a tough attitude towards outsiders in making them adhere to restrictions and protocols such as the kowtow. Other documents show xenophobic attitudes especially towards Christian missionaries. On the other hand, students should see how, in all of the documents, there is consistent interaction between China and Europeans. Students may point out the willingness of the European missionaries and merchants to adapt to Chinese norms.

143. (C) In 1600, the daimyo Tokugawa Ieyasu was able to establish their domination over the other daimyo contenders and establish their descendants as shoguns. Therefore, the large number of samurai involved in the previous decades of warfare suddenly became unnecessary. Many samurai became ronin, or masterless samurai.

144. (B) European fighting men utilized gunpowder weapons increasingly by the Early Modern Era, and this led to a similar decline in the power of the nobles and lords.

145. (D) With the advent of peace and stability, the samurai class lost their economic security if not their official status.

146. (A) The Tokugawa shogunate was fearful of both a European takeover, as had happened in the Philippines, and also cultural influences such as Christianity, particularly Roman Catholic Christianity, which promoted loyalty to the European pope.

147. (B) With the exception of the Dutch trading at the port city of Nagasaki, the amount of knowledge of the world entering Japan was quite limited.

148. (C) Japan in the early seventeenth century began to severely restrict contact with the outside world. With the exception of diplomatic and trading missions occasionally by the Chinese and Koreans, only the Dutch were allowed to trade at the port of Nagasaki and then only one ship per year. The Spanish and Portuguese were not allowed upon pain of death.

149. (A) The Tokugawa shogunate heralded in a time of peace and stability despite being isolated largely from the world. Internal trade boomed and culture blossomed.

150. (B) The Pax Tokugawa was most similar to the Northern Renaissance in terms of its economic prosperity and cultural flowering.

151. (B) Daimyo were the feudal lords and held fiefs or domains under the authority of the shoguns and emperors.

152. (D) Statements of being loyal and selfless are essential aspects of Confucianism, which was introduced into Japan in the Postclassical era.

153. (B) The lines "To follow our nature is called the Way" is a clear reference to Chinese Daoism and, in fact, the world "Dao" translates to "the Way."

154. (C) Chinese influences in Vietnam include a shared respect for education and the scholar-gentry class.

155. (A) Joint-stock companies such as the VOC or East India Company aggressively engaged in armed trading throughout the Indian Ocean and in Southeast Asia against both Muslim merchants and other European powers.

156. (D) Despite Confucian and Islamic influences, women in this region of the world maintained some status and independence.

157. (B) The sweet potato, an import from South America, was smuggled into China and later promoted by officials in Fujian province.

158. (B) The introduction of New World foods into the Old World contributed to population increases in not only China but also areas like Ireland and Russia.

159. (C) The movement of people, goods, and ideas throughout the world is named after the famous European explorer who helped usher in a new age of world history.

160. (A) Early modern monarchs often had scribes, poets, and bards write exceedingly flattering verse to promote the rule of the monarch.

161. (B) Ottoman sultans were expected to expand the boundaries of the empire, and Suleiman was very successful at this, with extensions into Arabia, North Africa, Mesopotamia, Hungary, and he twice conducted sieges against the European city of Vienna.

162. (D) Islamic calligraphy and minarets are well-known examples of Islamic design, and their presence indicates not sharing of space between religions in this temple but a replacement.

163. (A) After the fall of the Ottoman Empire, Kemal Ataturk began a secularization program that had included the Hagia Sophia mosque and other landmarks such as the Ottoman palaces. The current Turkish government however has recently moved towards reestablishing it as a mosque, thus ending a century of secularization.

164. (A) Gunpowder weaponry and technology gave these states the military edge over their opposition.

165. (C) The Muslim Mughals, being in a minority, generally practiced toleration toward their Hindu subjects and cooperated with local Hindu Rajput rulers.

166. (D) The Janissaries were an intriguing aspect of Ottoman rule. Similar to the Mamluks in Egypt, they often achieved a level of social mobility, but legally they were subject to the wishes of the sultans.

167. (B) Young boys who were taken to serve the Ottoman state could be chosen for a number of positions in the devshirme system. Most famous role to be chosen was as Janissaries.

168. (A) Many young boys collected in the devshirme system later ended up serving the Ottoman states as court officials, Janissary generals, and in a few cases viziers. It was felt that the attainment of high positions would have helped their birth families.

169. (B) The Safavid dynasty was distinctive in its practice of Shia/Shiite Islam, which helped fuel its conflict with the Ottomans and continues to be a defining characteristic of Iran today.

170. (A) The split in Islam was due to Mohammad's succession. Shia believe that it should fall to the descendants of Ali, whereas Sunni believe it should fall to whoever is most capable of promoting the religion.

171. (B) Vasco da Gama's journey by water to India in 1498 eliminated the need for the land-based trade route, known as the Silk Road. This over time weakened the economies of the Ottomans and Safavids.

172. (D) Many regional world powers, including these three, tended to ignore threats posed by rising Western power until it was too late and they had been forced into unfavorable trade relations or outright domination.

173. (B) The Mughal emperor Akbar was famous for his religious meetings in which clergy members of various faiths discussed spiritual matters.

174. (A) Akbar's descendant, Aurangzeb, was notorious for his reimposition of the non-believer tax and destroying Hindu temples.

175. (D) The Muslim Mughals were members of a minority faith in a sea of Hindus and other faiths such as Sikhs, Jains, and Parsis.

176. (C) The Islamic empires (Ottoman, Safavid, and Mughal) were also known as the "gunpowder" empires, which they used to gain and maintain control.

177. (A) All three "gunpowder" empires were ruled by warriors who adopted Islam, but only the Safavid practiced Shia Islam.

178. (B) The author of the Rotario mistook Hindus for Christians due to a lack of understanding. They had little knowledge of Hindus and Hinduism. However, they recognized almost immediately some local Muslims and attacked them.

179. (A) Since the Crusades, Europeans had long desired a route to Asia that was quicker and cheaper than the Silk Road route. With the monopolization of the Eurasian land and Mediterranean Sea route by Venetians and Ottomans, European sought an alternative route.

180. (C) The priest caste in Hindu society are known as the Brahmins, while the other choices are all main castes in Hindu society.

181. (D) The Portuguese Age of Exploration in Asia resulted in only controlling port cities like Macao in China and Goa in India, whereas the Spanish Age of Exploration resulted in the colonization of large areas in the Americas.

182. (B) Phrases such as "I am neither in temple nor in mosque" and "Hindus and Muslims alike have achieved that End" demonstrate that the Bhakti movement was ecumenical in its outlook.

183. (A) Sikhism is a syncretic faith that blended aspects of Hinduism and Islam.

184. (A) The iconic Taj Mahal acted as a mausoleum and is now famed for its beauty and incorporation of Islamic design concepts.

185. (B) Monumental architecture such as palaces, castles, gardens, mausoleums, and even churches are meant to enhance a ruler's or a dynasty's stature.

186. (C) With the exception of Mongolia, most of central Asia converted to Islam and adopted many aspects of Islamic and Persian culture.

187. (A) The area that used to be the Yarkent Khanate is now western China's Xinjiang province and the "Stan's" like Tajikistan and Kazakhstan come under Russian and later Soviet Union domination.

188. (B) The fifteenth century saw an expansion of Europe to the Americas, Africa, and Asia. Merchants and missionaries used maritime trade winds to facilitate their travels to these parts of the world.

189. (C) The monsoons are seen as both a blessing and a curse since they enable agriculture to flourish yet also bring flooding.

190. (B) Muslims must pray towards the Holy City of Mecca five times a day, so knowledge of the correct direction is vital to the correct religious observance. It also helped with navigation and trade.

191. (B) In the Postclassical world, the most educated centers of learning were located in cities that were needed to support scholars who could devote themselves to study, learning, and teaching.

192. (D) The line "they had no knowledge whatever of such articles" indicates that this society was not connected with the larger Afro-Eurasian trade networks where spices and gold were highly valued. This was the same in the Americas. In fact, feathers from exotic birds were more highly prized than gold and silver.

193. (A) The Age of Discovery was motivated about finding an all-water route to Asia for cheaper trade goods to cut out the middle men in the Middle East and Mediterranean Sea.

194. (A) The well-known practice of using fellow Africans in the slave trade was a way to avoid European and American responsibility for the horrors of the Atlantic slave trade.

195. (C) The most physically arduous part of an enslaved person's journey was walking from the interior to the coast. However, the Middle Passage was probably the most barbarous aspect due to the cramped and unsanitary conditions.

196. (B) The trade in African slaves, European manufactured goods, and American crops dominated the trade relations in the Atlantic world in the Early Modern Era.

197. (B) The estimated mortality rate was 10 percent during the Middle Passage. This was certainly the most horrific part of the journey for these unfortunates.

198. (C) The Indian Ocean slave trade was smaller, but lasted longer and was less harsh than, the Atlantic Slave trade

199. (B) Mita labor or corvee extracts labor from the natives as a form of obligatory public service or tribute.

200. (A) The tribute such as caged exotic birds that can be seen at the bottom of the picture was a long standing practice in Meso-American civilizations.

201. (C) Without Indian allies, there were key moments in the battle of Tenochtitlan and at other times where the European victory would have been lost.

202. (A) While guns were not the only factor in the success of the Spanish, their unexpectedness, loudness, and shock value played a key role at key moments in the battles.

203. (C) Gunpowder was first developed in China, and gun technology, although probably developed in the Middle East, was later defused back to China. China was more familiar with cannons than hand-held gunpowder weapons, but the latter did exist.

204. (B) The isolation of the Americas from the rest of the world kept the Americas from developing any resistance to the introduction of diseases from Afro-Eurasia.

205. (A) All of these areas suffered catastrophic damage from the diseases with the exception of Asia, which is part of the Old World and had built up some immunity.

206. (B) The treaty was negotiated after the initial voyages of the Age of Exploration to avoid conflict between the two nations. Because they were Catholic countries, the Pope arbitrated the negotiations.

207. (C) For centuries, a strong continuity of Europe has been claiming, conquering, and dominating non-European land. Some scholars argue that this impulse began with the Crusades. Others argue that it was later when Europeans acquired a higher level of technology.

208. (A) The merging of different religious aspects into one faith is common throughout world history. In the case of the Americas, it was inevitable that some aspects of pre-Columbian faith would remain and be blended with the dominant faith of Christianity.

209. (B) The mountain above the Bolivian city of Potosi was responsible for an estimated 60 percent of the world's silver during the second half of the sixteenth century.

210. (A) Casta paintings reflect the rigid social class system that developed in Spanish colonial Americas.

211. (D) The conquest of the Americas and the Atlantic slave trade helped create Latin American society with its harsh inequalities. This in turn led to long-term political insecurity and unrest.

212. (D) European settlers to Latin America tended to be young men without families who then intermarried with the local indigenous women and produced mixed race offspring, such as the so-called mestizos and mulattoes.

213. (B) The Commercial Revolution intensified and greatly expanded world trade. The well-known triangular trade network was just one aspect of the Commercial Revolution.

214. (A) European nation-states' trade operated with mercantilist laws in order to increase their nation's wealth in relation to other nation-states. The sentence about subsidizing the slave traffic in order to stimulate sugar plantation economy demonstrates mercantilist thinking.

215. (B) While the sugar plantations of the Caribbean Island, taken together, made up the main destination of enslaved Africans, the sugar plantations of Brazil's Atlantic coast attracted more slave ships than any other single colony on its own. The British 13 colonies were never a major destination in the slave trade compared with points farther south.

216. (A) Polynesian settlement starting in the 1200s had a significant effect on the amount of tree cover in New Zealand.

217. (C) A subset of Austronesians who settled in the Pacific areas of New Zealand, Hawaiian islands, and Easter Island are called Polynesians.

218. (B) The use of architecture to lay out the vanishing lines of perspective is one of the essential elements that make this painting a masterpiece.

219. (A) The artist painted no religious figures despite depicting 21 individuals.

220. (B) The artist Raphael only painted figures from the Classical era and some of his contemporaries, including himself, from the Early Modern Era. Combined with his boastful title he tried to show a strong connection between the two eras and discounted any achievement from the Postclassical Medieval era.

221. (B) The artist Raphael, like other Italian Renaissance artists, was captivated by the Greco-Roman era but dismissive of the preceding European Medieval era.

222. (A) Renaissance humanism promoted the use of vernacular languages.

223. (B) A marked increase in literacy due to the invention of the movable type printing press led to later demands for literature and scripture in vernacular languages.

224. (C) The scholar Erasmus clearly supports increasing the access of scripture by printing them into languages other than Greek and Latin.

225. (B) The printing press with its movable type helped usher in the modern world and, some say, the Renaissance.

226. (B) The Northern Renaissance paintings were less religious than even Italian Renaissance paintings, which were less religious than European Medieval paintings.

227. (C) After the Black Death, the peasants were still tied to the land and had to fulfill certain feudal requirements but were increasingly part of the monied economy.

228. (C) Peasants had more rights than slaves and serfs but still owed labor and or crops to their landlord who was usually a nobleman.

229. (A) Early Modern European peasants had much more freedom than their ancestors before the Black Death due to an initial shortage of labor and the increasing use of money.

230. **(D)** Medieval and early modern European rulers, like rulers long before them, had a close and mutually supportive or symbiotic relationship with religion and established belief systems.

231. **(A)** Johann Gutenberg's printing press spread Luther's ideas far and wide, and any attempt against him would have made him a martyr and maybe spread his ideas even farther.

232. **(C)** The scale and elaboration of monumental architecture is beyond its functionality and strongly reflects the government that orders or facilitates its construction. It nearly bankrupted the state because it was built to a scale to house many of the most powerful aristocrats in France so he could keep them in check.

233. **(B)** Building monumental architectural structures and controlling all aspects of government is indicative of an absolute monarch. Louis XIV was known as the "Sun King" since he was the center of the "French universe," reflecting the new knowledge of the era.

234. **(A)** Kings and their states with increasing taxation, were able to provide the financial backing for authors, artists, craftspeople, and explorers as well as scientists, all of whom increased the prestige and glory of the monarchs.

235. **(D)** Despite great cultural flowerings in both China and the Islamic Middle East, an orthodoxy had set in these societies and discouraged intellectual pursuits, which were seen as of little value. The ending of the voyages of the Chinese explorer Zheng He is a famous example.

236. **(B)** The emphasis on gold and silver and a favorable balance of trade are key aspects of mercantilism.

237. **(D)** The impetus for monarchs was to control as much as possible from the Early Modern Era to the nineteenth century.

238. **(D)** The Little Ice Age refers to a time during the fourteenth to the nineteenth centuries when there was a general falling of temperatures.

239. **(B)** While Europe's population steadily increased during this time period, Iceland's population contracted or dwindled.

240. **(B)** Ivan III was the first of the Russian leaders who refused to pay tribute to the Mongols and used the nascent Russian state to resist their domination.

241. **(C)** In the image, one of the soldiers is clearly shown with an arquebus, or early musket. Also, the reading mentions muskets.

242. **(D)** Russia's vast territories and undeveloped transportation network necessitated allowing the boyars great latitude in local affairs in return for allegiance and tax revenues.

243. **(A)** Russian serfs were ethnically the same as boyars, while the end of the Silk Road trade had no impact on serfdom, and Russia abhorred Mongol practices and customs.

244. (B) Czar Peter I was intent on a program of modernization, especially in shipbuilding for a modern navy, the construction of St. Petersburg, which could act as a "window to the West," and controlling the boyars or nobles through the tables or ranks, but he is also famously remembered for his opposition to the long beards that were symbols of Russian nobles.

245. (B) Throughout history, clothing and appearance have had symbolic importance. Sometimes they were seen as old fashioned or opposed to change, whereas during the Ottoman era, the fez was seen as a more modern hat than turbans, which were signs of status, towering, and time consuming to adorn.

246. (D) Regarding world trade, Russia played to its own strengths, supplying resources that its vast territory could produce in bulk.

247. (A) The goods listed on the left are in a raw or unfinished state while the goods on the right have been processed or are handcrafted.

248. (D) The economic theory of mercantilism stipulates that colonies provide their mothercountry with raw materials and in turn are provided with manufactured goods.

249. (B) Joint-Stock companies such as the Dutch East India Company (VOC) and the British East India Company were the main engines for exploration, trade, and colonialism in the Early Modern Era.

250. (D) As the image shows, there are no ranks of oars for the Iberian ships who sailed the Atlantic Ocean as well as the Mediterranean Sea, which was where galleys with oars were primarily used.

251. It challenges the idea that the Americas were a "New World," distinct from the Old World. The Europeans did not know what they had come upon, so it cannot be said that they knew they discovered anything in 1492.

252. Europeans were ignorant of where they were and what they had actually claimed as theirs. The Americas were not shown on maps to be distinct from the Old World till much later.

253. Columbus called the native peoples "Indians" because he believed he was in Asia. Europeans did not reach many areas of the Americas and the Pacific Ocean till much later.

Chapter 3

254. (C) Traditional Chinese society, like most societies, was male dominated or patriarchal. However, the practice of footbinding defines China at this time as a strict patriarchy.

255. (D) Footbinding was a traditional practice reaching back centuries in China. Its demise came about through a variety of factors, but the arrival of the West played a key role, especially via missionaries who sought to institute major changes in Chinese society.

256. (A) Korea, like other East Asian countries, was impressed by Western technology but was reflexively dismissive of the larger European culture.

257. (B) Yi Hangno used the phrase "the world is a big place" to indicate that distance and geography in general kept these regions apart for much of history.

258. (A) The introduction of New World crops such as corn and sweet potatoes led to more food being produced. This was also helped by the intensification of farming on hillsides and in less-settled areas like Szechuan province.

259. (B) The big increase in China's population and its interaction with the outside world led to a growing diaspora of Chinese outside the mainland. By 1911, there were Chinese communities scattered across the world.

260. (D) The Opium War highlighted the disparity in military superiority between China and the West. The Chinese forces were ineffective against British steam-powered warships with modern guns.

261. (A) Hong Kong remained a British colony till 1997 and even today has a distinct identity different than the rest of China.

262. (A) After losing the Opium War in 1842, China was forced to open up more to the world.

263. (B) When China signed the Treaty of Nanjing, it agreed to open up more ports to European traders. This signaled a big shift in the balance of power between China and the West.

264. (B) The mid- to late nineteenth century saw a weakened China that was unable to control its own sovereignty. This period is what some Chinese call the "Century of Humiliations."

265. (A) The continent of Africa was divided up before, during, and after the Berlin Conference of 1884–1885 in what was called the "Scramble for Africa."

266. (A) In the 1850s Japan opened up due to US Commodore Matthew Perry's visit and begun a series of reforms in foreign policy and trade. Japan also began to threaten China's territorial integrity.

267. (D) According to Confucian precepts, merchants produce nothing yet live off the work of others, so therefore, they were traditionally regulated to the lowest level of society including in Japan.

268. (C) The position of the emperor in China and Japan differed in that there was no shogun in China and the emperor in theory wielded enormous power; however, in reality the imperial bureaucracy held huge power.

269. (B) The port at Nagasaki was open for trade and ships from China, Korea, and Holland were allowed to enter. So-called "Dutch learning" was steadily entering Japan and translated. Its dissemination, however, was limited.

270. (C) East Asian nations believed that their cultures were vastly superior to Western but were interested in European science and technology, especially military.

271. (C) Since Japan was largely closed off for many years, information about the actual governing of the nation was very limited.

272. (A) Commodore Perry's mission was a major turning point in Japanese history and brought many profound changes to the nation and the world.

273. (B) The closure of Japan came to an abrupt end soon after Perry's visit in 1853 and would soon provide an impetus for the modernizing reforms under the emperor Meiji.

274. (A) Japan's changes in the Meiji era are often compared to the lack of reforms in China during the same period. The 100 Days of Reform are a point in fact.

275. (D) Historians now challenge the idea of Japanese modernization as a direct result of the arrival of the Americans. Many of the precursors of modernization were already in place in Tokugawa Japan.

276. (B) The two figures standing on the right have adopted a Western style of dress, or more specifically a military cadet style of dress. This was a time of increasingly Western influence on Japan, especially in military and economic affairs.

277. (D) Samurai status was demonstrated daily by the exclusive right to carry two swords. This practice was outlawed throughout the 1870s and then samurai status itself was eliminated in 1879.

278. (D) Industrialization of the textile industry used female labor largely due to their low salaries and the belief in appropriate types of industries for females.

279. (B) This individual being from a rural area and a member of the Buddhist clergy, was most likely sympathetic to the plight of the young women. This would make him a reliable source for a historian studying this period.

280. (A) As was common during the second wave of imperialism, local customs, dress, and hairstyles were slow to change.

281. (B) The scene in the newspaper would be a common one in Asian ports in this time period as Asia and many other parts of the world were incorporated into the economy of the world.

282. (B) The language used by Napoleon to these troops is meant to ameliorate any bad feelings or rebelliousness in the local population.

283. (C) The invasion of Egypt marks the beginning of the Modern age. It saw the beginning of the end of the Ottoman rule and introduced modern inventions such as the printing press and rifles. It also helped Egypt become more integrated into the world economy.

284. (C) The accidental discovery by a French officer in Napoleon's army opened up hieroglyphics that had been indecipherable for centuries.

285. (C) In Islamic Sunni tradition the human figure is never depicted and any image of the prophet Muhammad or of Allah is considered highly disrespectful. In Shia Islam, depicting the human form is allowed, as in the case of Persian miniatures.

286. (B) The introduction of the printing press by Napoleon's army into Egypt in 1798 would challenge both the monopoly of the scribes on the written word and the sultanate's control over information.

287. (D) Mamluks could not mount an effective resistance to the French Invasion of 1798 and were a disruptive force in Egypt for decades. In the Ottoman Empire proper, the Janissaries refused to modernize to rifles and more effective European battle tactics. Finally, they rebelled and actually killed a sultan.

288. Crop production using forced labor was similar to sugar plantations in the West Indies where slave labor was used, or to grain production in Russia where serfdom was common.

289. Crop production in Khedive Egypt under Muhammad Ali was different from many areas of the world. For example, many areas of the world, such as tea production in China or coffee production in Latin America operated under a more free-market system where growers chose to participate.

290. This is a very open-ended question where students can list many answers, such as crop production under a Communist system or a more intense capitalist system in the twentieth century.

291. (A) Turkish Muslims were officially the elite due to their religion and language but social realities tested this status. Many Christian and Jewish Ottomans were able to use their connections to take advantage of the burgeoning trade.

292. (B) Similar to efforts in Japan, Russia, and China, the Ottoman Empire made efforts to adapt to changes in the world, especially their apparent weakness relative to the West.

293. (D) The Ottoman's poor performance during the Crimean War and the increased exposure to Western powers encouraged the Ottomans to reform.

294. (B) The Tanzimat Reforms from the 1830s to 1870s removed the legal inequality against Christians and Jews and other minorities. These were part of modernization efforts after Ottoman losses in the Crimean War.

295. (A) Subject peoples such as Slavs and Arabs demanded more autonomy and even independence. This was part of a global process of rising nationalism in the nineteenth century.

296. (C) The Great Game was about territorial claims and strategic advantage in central Asia between the Russian and the British empires. It was the backdrop for the famous novel *Kim* by Rudyard Kipling.

297. (A) The Great Game, where Britain and Russia competed for control over central Asia, was very similar to European competition for colonies in Africa.

298. (C) Persia was caught between the big power rivalry of Russia and Great Britain, and even though it was never militarily conquered, it was forced to accept unfair treaty conditions known as capitulations.

299. (D) The Persian capitulations to European powers became a rallying cry among Persians and are still taught in Iranian classrooms as an example of Western attempts at domination.

300. (B) The Seven Years' War was a global conflict fought in India as well as North America, the Caribbean, and Europe. Though the British East India Company was an arm of the British government, it was now unchallenged on the Indian subcontinent.

301. (B) The British East India Company, with the help of native forces or sepoys, defeated the French in a decisive battle at Plassey in 1757. This battle was part of a larger contest that is known in world history as the Seven Years' War, or in America as the French and Indian War.

302. (A) The use of the phrase "Firmly relying ourselves on the truth of Christianity" shows the arrogance of the conquerors. This assumption and others like it will later grate on Indian sensibilities.

303. (C) The British East India Company was increasingly seen as insensitive toward Indian belief systems. The most notorious example of this involved a new type of rifle that used animal grease (reportedly from pork or beef fat) to insert the cartridge down the barrel. This helped cause the Sepoy Mutiny or Uprising.

304. (B) A shift starting in the 1830s and increasing after the Sepoy Rebellion moved the British away from working with locals to paternalistic rule over inferior natives.

305. (C) Mercantilist thought ordained that colonies like India should benefit their mother countries. This ideology remained strong even when more capitalist and laissez-faire attitudes became popular in Britain.

306. (C) The fact that the speaker spoke in London and presumably in the English language shows that he was British educated and had the means to travel such a distance. This group was fostered in colonial societies and was essential to the smooth running of the colonial venture.

307. (D) All of the choices capture the mix of divide and conquer, paternalism, and racism that characterized the colonial relationship.

308. (A) A marked increase in women and children joining their European family members who were stationed in Asian colonies took place increasingly in the nineteenth century as transportation and health services improved.

309. (C) In the seventeenth and eighteenth centuries about one-quarter to one-third of Europeans died after two years due to disease. By the nineteenth century the number had fallen considerably, and with improved transportation, it was common for women and even children to join their family members.

310. (D) This famous image of slave ships brought home to many people the inhumane conditions associated with the trade in human beings.

311. (B) Slavery in the Atlantic world came to an end in the nineteenth century as a result of the abolition movement.

312. (A) Despite Laird's statements about moral superiority, he was closer to the true causes of British exploration when he spoke of the steam engine.

313. (B) Laird's statements are almost a textbook definition of social Darwinism with his assumptions of white superiority and the "dark corners" of Africa.

314. (D) The Berlin Conference in 1884 was an attempt to bring order to the Scramble for Africa and avoid hostilities between European powers.

315. (C) African representatives were notoriously not invited to Berlin. Furthermore, borders between African colonies and later nations would disregard ethnic and linguistic group territories.

316. (B) There is a strong historical connection between the production of sugar and the Atlantic slave trade.

317. (D) While Britain ended slavery in 1833, France in 1848 and America in 1865, slavery continued in the Spanish and Portuguese empires till the 1880s and sadly still exists in some forms in corners of the world.

318. (C) Europeans made large use of native troops, who could be trained in modern weapons and tactics, plus had the benefit of knowing the land, peoples, and languages and were vastly cheaper and lived longer than European troops.

319. (A) European armies, especially Britain, used native troops in India. In 1857, some of them revolted against British East India Company rule due to religious insensitivities.

320. (B) European powers built railroad and other infrastructures for their own benefit. Despite the new capitalist ideology, they still adhered to the idea that colonies existed for the benefit of the mothercountries.

321. (A) Social Darwinism proposed the idea that the more powerful nations had a "right" to exploit weaker ones.

322. (A) European nation-states' trade operated with mercantilist laws in order to increase their nation's wealth in relation to other nation-states.

323. (A) The American colonies were long upset with mercantilist ideas and practices. The famous Boston Tea Party was one such demonstration of their anger.

324. (D) Many French soldiers were demoralized by both the conditions of fighting in Haiti, with its high death toll due to disease, plus the contradiction of their goals in Haiti with Republican ideals that they had been raised on.

325. (D) The British antislavery movement was just beginning in the 1780s and had not had much influence beyond England and the newly freed American colonies.

326. (A) The abolition movement had been growing since the 1780s in the West, and supporters of the slave trade such as planters felt a need to advocate for themselves and their economic interests.

327. (D) Europeans choose to believe self-serving ideas, such as that Africans were better off being enslaved and thus were more "civilized" by their proximity to Europeans.

328. (D) Some leaders, like Bernardo O'Higgins, became dictators after achieving independence from Spain. They differed significantly from the North American independence leaders like George Washington and James Madison.

329. (B) The legacy of the conquest plus slavery led to a new strict social class system where racial origins were a determining factor.

330. (B) Latin America had weak political institutions such as independent courts and a lack of universal suffrage. This continued into the twentieth century up until the 1980s.

331. (D) The wars of Independence were not social revolutions and this stifled political ambitions of the non-Creole majority. This combined with the infighting among the Creoles produced numerous revolutions and coup d'états.

332. (C) The viewpoint of the Qing government toward the so-called "coolies" did not discourage them from migrating in search of better opportunities.

333. (A) The sale of guano mirrors other Latin American exports like tin, copper, sugar, bananas, and coffee in that they are for export to Europe and North America and have contributed, some say, to a "neocolonialist" relationship with the world economy.

334. (A) Interdependence means a dependence of two or more things on one another; this was definitely increasingly the case for the world economy in the nineteenth century. It is also related to the idea of globalization, which is not a twenty-first-century phenomenon.

335. (B) The Diaz regime (1876–1911) oversaw many improvements in Mexico but these were limited to urban areas, involved crony capitalism and foreign domination of some industries, like oil production.

336. (D) While there were clear gains during the Porferio era, the advancement of democracy was not one of them.

337. (C) Western sailors and missionaries brought the first deadly diseases to the Hawaiian islands, and the population was nearly halved within decades.

338. (B) The geographic isolation of indigenous peoples left them unprepared for the onslaught of Western intrusion into their lands, especially their immune systems.

339. Various answers are acceptable for the document-based question. Correct answers might refer to how this event later impacted political thought and the Enlightenment. For example, known Enlightenment thinkers such as Voltaire, Rousseau, and Immanuel Kant questioned the cause for the disaster. Specifically, Voltaire pushed back on the knee-jerk reaction of some religious authorities like Gabriel Malagrida that the people of Lisbon were facing God's wrath for their sinful ways. Students may also address how the government reacted to the disaster in an organized and very modern way with urban planning and a questionnaire.

340. (B) The Enlightenment was an intellectual movement in Europe during the late seventeenth and eighteenth centuries emphasizing reason and knowledge rather than religion and tradition. The printing of an encyclopedia was an attempt to catalog and build upon all existing knowledge that could facilitate human progress.

341. (A) The Enlightenment was a major cause of the American, French, Haitian, and Latin American political revolutions that came after.

342. (A) Inequality among the different social classes in France is considered to be one of the main causes leading to the Revolution in 1789.

343. (C) Within the Third Estate (bourgeoisie, peasants, and urban poor), only the bourgeoisie's condition was improved by the French Revolution and Napoleonic reforms.

344. (A) Many clergy in the Catholic Church refused to take the oath in the Civil Constitution of the Clergy, which the Pope had spoken out against and many felt would have subordinated the Church to the new state.

345. (D) Hilaire Beloc was a historian writing from a Catholic perspective. His bias is evident in his very negative descriptions of the French Revolution's actions toward the Church, which he sees as "persecution," "cruelty," and a "failure."

346. (A) Adam Smith's seminal work observed factory conditions where changes in production in a pin factory increased output.

347. (B) The division of labor was a key component for industrialization since it sped up the manufacturing process and led to greater output.

348. (A) The Scientific Revolution led to the Industrial Revolution by the practical application of science in technology.

349. (C) Britain had the right geography, government support, and infrastructure to encourage industrialization. It also had the right social conditions in a middle class that sought opportunities in industrialization.

350. (C) Thomas Malthus warned of the dangers of overpopulation due to the ability of the world's population to always exceed its ability to produce sufficient food. The only ways to keep the population in check were famines, diseases, and war.

351. (B) The Irish Potato Famine seems to demonstrate an instance where a population is not able to be sustained by the food production. In fact, Malthus predicted that Ireland would suffer "a check" on its population.

352. (A) As machines got too big to be accommodated inside houses, factories were built to handle their large sizes. Also, as demand increased for more labor, workers were not part of family units.

353. (C) With the invention of the machines that were not dependent on water or wind, factories were moved to the cities, hence urbanization.

354. (D) Smiles's use of terms like "over-government" and phrases like "Heaven helps those who help themselves" clearly show his view in the debate about government's role in helping the less fortunate.

355. (C) The new capitalist class promoted the values of laissez-faire and minimal government involvement in the economy. The old paternal yet condescending attitude of the landed class slowly gave way.

356. (D) The potato was introduced in the sixteenth century from South America due to its ease of use and ability to thrive in a temperate but wet climate. It also helped Ireland's population grow to high levels.

357. (C) The economic changes brought about by the mid-nineteenth century were being felt in formerly peripheral areas of the world.

358. (B) Many people lay the blame for the deaths and depopulation of Ireland at the door of Britain and its promotion of laissez-faire/capitalism, which had taken hold of Britain's ruling class since the repeal of the Corn Laws in the early 1840s.

359. (A) The unemployment created by the invention of labor-saving machines led some workers to take out their frustrations on the machines and those who owned them.

360. (C) Karl Marx saw history as a constant struggle between the "haves and have nots." He predicted that workers would overthrow the bourgeoisie and create a worker-run state.

361. (B) Germany entered the race for an overseas empire later than other nations and felt overshadowed by Britain's large navy.

362. (A) Social Darwinism was a popular concept in the nineteenth century and was used to justify imperialism. They added to and/or replaced other beliefs such as religious bigotry that were more common in earlier eras.

363. (B) Russian serfdom lasted decades or even centuries longer than in the rest of Europe. It was widely held to be an anachronism, even in Russia in the decades preceding its abolition.

364. (A) Historians argue that its late industrialization and small middle class, widespread illiteracy, and poor performance in the Crimean War and later Russo-Japanese War were a result of the long history of serfdom.

365. (D) Russia was intent on being an industrial power, and that required goods that could be bought and used for industrial and business users.

366. (B) Russia's industrialization program was impressive but its late entry meant it was far behind other nations. It will not be until the 1940s in World War II that Russian industrial output reached Western levels.

367. (D) The assassination of czar Alexander II in 1881 led to a wave of repression against suspected radicals and non-Russians like Jews. It was felt that non-Russians were a threat to the state. This was part of a pattern throughout Russian history and continued even into the Communist era.

368. (B) Many Jews fled the Russian empire, and America was a preferred destination, particularly through Ellis Island in New York. This was one of the great diasporas and had profound implications for world history.

369. (C) The British East India Company and other joint-stock companies brought many previously isolated areas of the world into one global economic system.

370. (A) This painting has an interesting composition with divide between East and West, the top and bottom and the light and dark halves. Its location in the British East India Company headquarters presents an extremely benign view of the company's activities.

371. (D) The British East India Company, like the Dutch East India Company (VOC), was one of the first international companies and ended up being involved in numerous incidents as a semibranch of British foreign policy. It was not, however, involved in the Congress of Vienna, which was a diplomatic endeavor.

Chapter 4

372. (D) By 1900, China was in danger of being carved up the way Africa was during the Congress of Berlin in 1884. The defeat of China in the Boxer Rebellion soon led to competing territorial claims by outside powers.

373. (A) A weakened China after the Boxer Rebellion almost immediately became prey for foreign powers, and the competition among them soon led to hostility and war.

374. (C) Students were the most active groups in both events in Chinese history. It is interesting that the call for democracy and other reforms were among their demands.

375. (B) When the provisions of the Versailles treaty became known in China, students and intellectuals erupted in anger that endangered the life of some members of their diplomatic delegation.

376. (A) Efforts by educated Chinese and Western missionaries since the late nineteenth century had begun to reduce the practice of footbinding by 1919.

377. (D) Karl Marx theorized that in an industrial society the workers or proletariat would eventually rise up and overthrow the capitalist or bourgeoisie class. Mao saw the revolutionary potential in the peasant class. This is known as Maoism.

378. (B) Mao believed that the landlord class would have to be eliminated throughout China and that violence was necessary.

379. (B) The Great Leap Forward program (1958–1961), with its push for industrialization over agriculture, occurred at the same time as natural disasters such as floods and landslides.

380. (D) Stalin's forced collectivization caused a major famine where millions starved. Whereas this has long been seen as deliberate by Ukrainian nationalists, the famine in China was not seen as deliberate.

381. (B) Both the Soviet Union and Mao's China used the Soviet realism style in its propaganda posters. This encouragement of women was consistent with the Communist ideology that stressed equality.

382. (D) As we have seen throughout world history, women's struggle has been an uphill battle and no less so in Communist-leaning nations. Still, the gains made by Chinese women within three generations were remarkable.

383. (B) Many revolutionary rulers such as Lenin, Stalin, Hitler, and Ataturk had cults of personality during and after their rules. Mao's cult was particularly strong and remains so today.

384. (B) The cult of Mao Zedong was at its apex during China's Cultural Revolution when Red Guards used the position and ideas of Mao to punish dissenters and class enemies.

385. (A) Events in the Soviet Union under the leadership of Mikhail Gorbachev sparked a desire for change in both China and Eastern Europe.

386. (C) The banning of an image, writing, or idea is a form of censorship, and China, like many nondemocracies, has a long history of such actions. In the early 2000s Western companies like Google acquiesced to China's demands that this image not be shown in China.

387. (B) China, unlike the Soviet Union, has successfully undergone massive economic changes but no political changes, as it is ruled undemocratically by the Chinese Communist Party. Russia, however, is increasingly becoming an authoritarian state under Vladimir Putin.

388. (A) The image that shows a strong Russian sailor and ship delivering a devastating blow to stereotypically drawn Japanese sailor and ship was typical of European propaganda before this conflict. The impact of the Japanese defeat on Russia would be one of world history's great upsets and gave encouragement to non-Europeans all over the world and be a harbinger for World War II in Asia.

389. (C) The fact that by 1904 major powers were fighting over China's territory while China could just look on helplessly shows China's weakened state.

390. (C) The depiction of the methods and weapons of war shows a clear militaristic bent that was all too common at the time in the world.

391. (A) Due to increased world trade and economic integration, the effects of the Great Depression were felt around the world and not just in America and Europe.

392. (A) The Pacific theater required land, air, and sea forces due to the many islands, archipelagos, and mainland campaigns.

393. (C) The topography of Southeast Asia and the Pacific Islands is largely made up of rainforest or jungle conditions and was challenging for US and Allied soldiers.

394. (B) Propaganda and censorship were the norm during wartime even for democracies. A photo such as this was feared for its depiction of dead US forces, which might diminish public support for the war.

395. (D) Japan's loss was a turning point in its foreign relations. While the Communist takeover of China and North Korea has put stress on its commitment to Article 9, overall this new stance is very popular with the Japanese people.

396. (C) Following World War II, Japan, with its inclusion of a "no war" clause into its constitution, does not engage in aggressive actions and only maintains a small armed force for defensive purposes only.

397. (A) Since 1949, the United States followed a policy of containment of Communism, and that was the prime rationale for America's involvement in the Korean War. This idea would later be expanded into the so-called "domino theory," which saw Communism expanding all over Asia if it was not checked.

398. (C) At Yalta Conference in 1945, the Allies agreed to the division of both Germany and Korea with much less thought given to the latter.

399. (A) Vietnamese nationalists under Ho Chi Minh hoped to avoid a conflict with both the French and Americans after the war was over. The wording of the document was deliberately chosen for that purpose.

400. (C) The opening of the Declaration with the lines "All men are created equal. They are endowed by their Creator with certain inalienable rights; among these are Life, Liberty, and the pursuit of Happiness" shows a clear influence of the Enlightenment—specifically the American experience of the struggle for independence.

401. (D) As industrialization became state policy in many Asian nations, workers were drawn from the agricultural sector, which was also being mechanized.

402. (B) Following Japan as a model, many Asian nations began to focus on an export-driven economy. These nations became known as the "Asian Tigers" or "Tiger Cubs."

403. (C) Indonesia, Thailand, and Malaysia are all nations in Southeast Asia. These nations have been referred to as the "Tiger Cubs."

Short-Answer Question

404. Answers may include the forced nature of the land reform program, the role of war as a catalyst for the change or the interaction of economic and social factors for the loss of landlords' status when they lost their primary economic holdings.

405. Answers may include the differences in the use of violence to achieve the land reform. With the exception of Japanese settlers, land reform in South Korea was largely peaceful, while instances of violence in China were common. Another difference is the impetus for this change. While the Chinese Communists began this process as early as 1927 in China, in South Korea, America encouraged land reform.

406. Answers may include explanations of why land reform was forced from above, such as its striving for social equality as more important than respect for traditional authority, and also how wars bring change to nations that are often unexpected. How the Americans in the mindset of an emerging Cold War sought land reform as a way to stave off a Communist-inspired revolution.

407. (D) It's fair to say that the Chinese Communist Party has put striving for egalitarianism on the proverbial back burner for the time being. Also, if there is a new class, it is probably a relatively affluent middle class that has been created due to modernization.

408. (D) The Morgenthau memoirs remain a powerful indictment against Turkey for its denial of culpability for the genocidal acts committed by the Turkish government during World War I. At the time, the United States was not at war against the Ottomans and had little reason to lie or exaggerate.

409. (C) Rising nationalism led to a push for many groups to establish ethnic states out of the Ottoman Empire. By 1915, groups such as the Greeks, Serbs, Romanians, and Bulgarians had already broken away to form new nations.

410. (A) The current policy of the Turkish government was that there was no plan of extermination of Armenians and any killings that took place were an unfortunate part of the messiness of war and were, in fact, the acts of bandits and not government policy.

411. (A) The mandate system was established after the Versailles treaty and based on the secret wartime agreement, the notorious Sykes-Picot negotiations in 1916.

412. (B) The Arab revolt against the Ottomans was encouraged by Britain, through their officer on the ground, the famous Lawrence of Arabia. The Arabs were promised self-rule in the Hussein-McMahon correspondence.

413. (C) The rise of Fascism and Nazi aggression in Europe had a profound impact on the security of Jewish life. However, strict immigration laws closed off many avenues for fleeing Jews. Many chose British-controlled Palestine, which was also illegal, but there were strong historic ties to the Holy Land.

414. **(A)** The two competing yet justifiable claims by Israelis and Palestinians make this conflict one of the most intractable in the world today.

Document-Based Question

415. Answers will vary but should address the different and competing national desires of the three main groups—the Allies (Britain and France and the Americans), the Jews, and the Arabs. Students may notice the clashing views of the idealistic Americans with the imperialist desires of their former allies, Britain and France. Students should also see the incompatible aspirations of the Jews, who desired a nation with the indigenous Arabs, who felt they were also promised a state of their own. Students may discuss the differences among correspondence, declarations, secret treaties, and articles in the League of Nations, and if so, this is the type of angle that may earn them the complexity point.

416. **(B)** With no history of secular government, Middle Easterners have struggled with Islam's correct role in Middle East state and society to this very day.

417. **(C)** In the mid-twentieth century, the driving force in the Middle East was nationalism and this is clear in the reading. However, by the 1970s, Islamist forces like the Muslim Brotherhood and the Iranian Revolution were challenging secular governments across the Middle East.

418. **(D)** This United Nations resolution was adopted unanimously by the UN Security Council on November 22, 1967, in the aftermath of the Six-Day War. It has remained the basis for peace talks ever since and was adopted by the Palestinian people.

419. **(C)** The conflict in the Holy Land has changed over the years from 1967 with no signs of ending but switches from periods of crisis to periods of relative calm.

420. **(B)** The rise in nationalism among non-Westerners led to a desire for them to control the resources within their own nations as well.

421. **(C)** Nationalization by non-Western nations was very common. It was encouraged by the spread of Communism and nationalism in the developing of the so-called Third World.

422. **(D)** The invasion ultimately destabilizes the nation, which will later lead to the rise of the Taliban with its strict observance of Islam.

423. **(C)** The geography is Afghanistan is almost the opposite of Vietnam in that it is very dry, has sparse vegetation, and lies at a high altitude.

424. **(B)** Indian nationalists like Nehru never failed to point out the negative effects of British rule and even nonpartisan Indian thinkers like Mukerjee mention the massive unemployment of a traditional Indian industry.

425. **(D)** The forced integration of formerly isolated economies like Japan or semi-isolated economies like India often had negative local consequences. This could be called an earlier wave of globalization.

426. (B) The Sepoy Rebellion of 1857 was the last organized mass movement of anti-British feeling till Amritsar.

427. (D) The Amritsar, or Jallianwala Bagh massacre of 1919, was a major turning point in Indian nationalism. The idea of demanding independence was previously limited to a small group of Indian elites.

428. (C) Gandhi's Salt March in 1930 is a famous example of a colonized people strenuously resisting a colonial power yet not resorting to physical violence.

429. (A) British military officers were opposed to yielding any colony back to the colonized subject peoples.

430. (B) The movement of people after the partition of India was one of the largest migrations in world history.

431. (B) The violence of the partition of India and Pakistan had long-term causes dating back to the period of British colonial rule and further back to Hindu resentment of Muslim domination in the Mughal era.

432. (D) Through the use of science and technology, technocrats and scientists sought to increase the food supply.

433. (C) India's vibrant democracy has had many problems, but they have been successful in averting famines.

434. (C) The Bangladeshi Nationalist Party was rejected by the West Pakistani, thereby initiating a crisis that later led to the partition of Pakistan.

435. (B) Pakistan was founded as a state for Muslims albeit in two halves. But making Urdu the only official language and other issues caused the Bengalis to chafe under West Pakistani control.

436. (B) With the exception of a few areas such as Ethiopia and Liberia, Africa was under the control of European powers since the nineteenth century.

437. (C) Postal systems, like other aspects of modernity, were established in the twentieth century.

438. (B) This parable encouraged colonized people to seek independence and decolonization after decades or even centuries of rule by outsiders.

439. (D) Korea was colonized by Japan from about 1890 till 1945 when it lost in the Second World War. Anti-Japanese feeling in Korea still dominates its relations with its eastern neighbor.

440. (B) British West Africa had the slightest edge on Sumatra, another British colonial territory.

441. (D) As seen in the chart, the exponentially increasing amounts of palm oil being exported from the colonial territories show how Europeans exploited its colonies.

442. (A) European settlers often expropriated or bought the best land for themselves and displaced the original inhabitants, who often moved to marginal areas, drifted to the cities, or became landless laborers for the settlers. This process was common in colonized countries from Ireland to Malaysia.

443. (B) The building of railroads during the colonial period had a huge impact on African urbanization till this day.

444. (D) The FLN in Algeria and the Mau Mau in Kenya expressed the anticolonial sentiment in their nations through the use of violence and were met in turn with overwhelming violence by the colonial authorities, leading to numerous deaths.

445. (A) World War II forever changed the relationship between colonizer and colonized, especially in Africa. Decolonization was largely inevitable.

446. (C) By the early 1960s, most nations in Africa were free of European rule. It was overwhelmingly a peaceful transition with the exception of nations like Kenya and Rhodesia (Zimbabwe).

447. (B) Apartheid is the Afrikaner word for the South African policy of strict racial segregation that existed from 1948 to the 1990s.

448. (B) South Africa's apartheid regime was based on a stricter implementation of laws that harkened back to ideas of social Darwinism and scientific racism from the colonial era.

449. (D) South Africa ended its apartheid regime in the early 1990s and when it held elections, Nelson Mandela was elected president of the nation, traveling the common road of "prisoner to president" in decolonization.

450. (C) The Nationalist Party that negotiated independence in 1960 ruled an apartheid state where the majority black population could not vote.

451. (B) The mention of the employment in the Americas and the revolutionary violence in Europe were clear factors that promoted migration to the Americas.

452. (B) The image shows a strong stream from the Iberian nations of Spain and Portugal. The latter was a Portuguese colony for centuries.

453. (C) Since the Monroe Doctrine, Latin American nations have had to navigate their relationships with the United States through difficult times, especially during the Cold War era.

454. (B) The United States maintained an isolationist policy in Europe but was quite interventionist in the Americas and Asia. Understanding the friction that the interventions caused, President Roosevelt promoted the "Good Neighbor" policy toward Latin America.

455. (A) The poverty and inequality of prerevolutionary Mexico was the main cause of the revolt and kept it going for 10 long years.

456. (B) Foreign-controlled companies owned by Americans in Mexico or the British in China caused a groundswell of antiforeign sentiment that was one of the main causes of the revolutions in those countries in 1910.

457. (D) When France and the Low Countries fell to the Nazi blitzkrieg, Britain was said to have "stood alone." This claim is only partly true in that Britain had many parts of the empire behind it as well and many nations contributed armed forces and volunteers.

458. (B) The war against Fascism immediately brought up the irony of nonwhite peoples fighting for imperialist states like Britain and France.

459. (C) The coup d'état in Chile in 1973 was just one of the more infamous setbacks for democracies in Latin America. Sadly, the coup received the approval of the president of the United States, Richard Nixon at the time.

460. (A) The United States saw the Cuban Revolution as a direct threat even before the Cuban Missile Crisis. No longer was the spread of Communism limited to Eurasia; it was only 90 miles off the Florida Keys. Therefore, the United States was determined to be more vigilant in its policy of containment. It regularly backed antidemocratic governments in Nicaragua, Guatemala, and a number of other Latin American countries.

461. (A) Ever since Lenin had said that "imperialism was the highest stage of capitalism," Communists had expressed support for decolonization. Communist states like Cuba were active in their support.

462. (D) It was in the island nation of Cuba in the Americas rather than in African states where missile bases were discovered and led to a crisis that almost brought the two armed camps to warfare.

463. (D) Australia and New Zealand were primarily populated by settlers from the British Isles, and loyalty to the mother country was strong.

464. (A) Australia and New Zealand fought with Britain in the Boer War, World War I, World War II, and Korea. Their participation in World War I was felt as a coming of age for many people in the twentieth century.

465. (C) The introduction of nonindigenous species into previously isolated regions can damage those areas forever.

466. (A) Australia's rabbit-proof fence, the Great Wall of China, and the Berlin Wall seem expedient at the time to some but rarely fulfill their promise.

467. (A) Indian troops as well as African, Australian, New Zealand, Canadian, West Indian, and Irish troops joined the British side during World War I.

468. (B) Trench warfare was generally a static form of warfare compared to World War II, which saw blitzkrieg attacks by German forces and surprise attacks by the Japanese.

469. (B) World War I and other total wars involved the mobilization of all resources as well as public opinion, which can both be seen in the poster.

470. (C) Women's heavy participation in World War I was seen as justification for women's suffrage in many Western nations.

471. (B) Yeats wrote this poem with the postwar unrest in mind, especially in Russia, Germany, and his native Ireland.

472. (D) In nations like Germany, Austria-Hungary, Russia, and the Ottoman Empire, their monarchs were forced to abdicate.

473. (B) Fascism promotes imperialist aggression as good for the nation in terms of power but also for the benefit of the people's "vitality."

474. (C) This easy question asks students to find the commonalities in the interwar era.

475. (C) As part of the Versailles treaty strict limits were placed on Germany's armed forces. They were not allowed to have an air force or tanks and their navy and size of the army was severely shrunk as can be seen in the chart as well as the graphics on the map.

476. (D) It is widely argued that punishing Germany helped Adolf Hitler and the Nazis rise to power. Although the treaty was unpopular with most Germans, the propaganda value of Germany's victimhood helped them win the elections of 1933.

477. (C) Studying the dates and noticing trends are important in answering this question.

478. (C) The Allies made Germany pay financially, territorially, and in other ways for World War I and this weakened its economy.

479. (B) African Americans went to war with the goals of what they called Double Victory, a fight against Fascism and militarism abroad and a fight against racial injustice at home. These goals were also sought by non-Europeans as they sent millions to fight for the imperial powers.

480. (D) In a true total war situation, racial segregation brings inefficiency and betrays the idea that the people of a nation are needed to fight the enemy.

481. (C) The killing of Jews and other groups was preceded by decades or even centuries of antisemitism and bigotry. The Nazi party in Germany scapegoated Jews for the economic and other problems the nation faced in the aftermath of the defeat in World War I.

482. (D) The mountains of evidence and admissions of former German officials expose the outrageous lies in Holocaust denials.

483. (B) The United States wanted to have a strong trading partner and Cold War concerns were important as well in the plans to rebuild Europe.

484. (C) Understanding the insidious impact of the Great Depression on European political life, the United States was concerned about economic recovery, especially in light of the looming Cold War.

485. (B) The fall of the Berlin Wall in 1989 heralded the end of communism in Eastern Europe and a de-escalation of tensions between America and the Soviet Union. The USSR ended within two years in 1991.

486. (C) US president John F. Kennedy's famous speech takes strong issue with the idea of a wall to keep East Berliners trapped behind the Iron Curtain and helped it become an iconic symbol of Communist oppression.

487. (C) In late 1917, Russia was rocked by a second revolution, this time by Bolsheviks, a radical group of Communists under their leader Vladimir Lenin.

488. (B) Some historians place 1917 as the start of the Cold War due to the radical economic policies advocated by Russian Communists. However, other scholars see the start as events in World War II such as the Yalta agreement or Red Army liberation of Eastern Europe.

489. (A) The Great Ukrainian Famine (1932–1933) or the Holodomor is seen by many people as a man-made disaster and an attack on the Ukrainian people.

490. (C) Stalin's collectivization removed any personal initiative for Russian peasants to grow more crops. Coupled with the sale of grain to pay for the industrialization and anti-Ukrainian feeling, these factors all led to a severe shortage of food.

491. (A) The Soviet regime forcibly imposed collective farming, which alienated some prosperous farmers, the so-called kulaks. These enemies were then eliminated in the antikulak campaigns.

492. (D) Stalin's persecution of so-called "kulaks" or well-off peasants mirrored the actions other totalitarian regimes like Nazi Germany, Fascist Italy, or Khmer Rouges' Cambodia.

493. (C) According to some scholars, a continuity in Russian history is a xenophobic attitude toward foreign ideas and fear of foreign invasion.

494. (B) There are numerous causes of the Cold War including geopolitical, leaders' personalities, and overreactions to escalating events. However, probably the most common explanation is ideological, which can be argued began in 1917.

495. (A) When the United States and its Western allies saw the Soviet Union's grip tighten on Eastern Europe, it created the military alliance NATO. In turn, the Soviet Union created the Warsaw Pact of its satellite nations shown in the map.

496. (A) Lenin and other Communists believed that imperialism was the highest form of capitalism and World War I was caused primarily by imperialist desires. The war did not change the economies of any of the participants except for Russia; therefore, more wars would follow.

497. (B) Throughout the Communist world, basic goods were kept within reach of the working classes and peasantry. This helps to explain the popularity of these regimes, particularly in Cuba.

498. (A) By the 1970s, the economic problems in the USSR were hard to ignore and the premier Mikhail Gorbachev attempted to reform the system.

499. (B) Lyrics "Oppenheimer's deadly toy" and "winnable war" are a clear reference to the competition in both conventional and nuclear arms that the US and the Soviet Union engage in during the postwar era.

500. (C) MAD is an acronym that is used frequently to describe the Cold War. It is based on the theory of deterrence, which holds that the threat of using strong weapons against the enemy prevents the enemy's use of those same weapons.

CREDITS

Page 16: The American military in Haiti in 1920. Source: Times Wide World Photos.

Page 19: First Image is own by Sean McManamon. Second image is from LoC Reproduction Number: LC-DIG-ppss-01285.

Page 29: Detail of a scroll painting, "Along the River During the Qingming Festival" by Zhang Zeduan.

Page 32: Taken from the Asia for Educators website. http://afe.easia.columbia.edu/ps/japan/shinran.pdf

Page 52: "Dance of Sufi Dervishes." Unknown author, from the illustrated book *Divane Hafez Shirazi*, circa 1480.

Page 72: Woodcuts of the Danse Macabre. Figure 1: *Danse Macabre* by Michael Wolgemut, 1493. Figure 2: Woodcut, *The Abbess* by Holbein, 1549.

Page 75: Two medieval illustrations (*August, June*) in the *Book of Hours* by Pol de Lumbourg, circa 1412–1416.

Page 81: https://andersonsclasses.weebly.com/uploads/2/6/0/9/26093804/world_civ_-_chapter_4_-_toward_a_new_world.pdf page 4

Page 85: A History of the Crusades: Their Rise, Progress and Results. https://lccn.loc.gov/03009770, Image 133.

Page 87: Photo by Sean McManamon.

Page 92: This image was donated to Wiki commons by the Metropolitan Museum of Art in NYC.

Page 125: Library of Congress, https://www.loc.gov/resource/ppmsca.12199/; https://www.loc.gov/resource/gdclccn.04024471v1/?sp=268&r=-0.021, 0.973,1.347,0.503,0

Page 129: Sketch from *The last journals of David Livingstone in Central Africa, from 1865 to his death*. London, 1874. The encryption reads "Slavers revenging their losses."

Page 132: Drawing showing Cortez and La Malinche meeting Moctezuma II, 1519, from the "Lienzo de Tlaxcala," which was created by the Tlaxcalans to remind the Spanish of their loyalty to Castile and the importance of Tlaxcala during the Conquest, ca. 1550.

Page 133: Images from *The General History of the Things of New Spain* by Fray Bernardino de Sahagún: The Florentine Codex. Book XII: The Conquest of Mexico, 1577]. https://www.loc.gov/item/2021667857/.

Page 135: https://web.archive.org/web/20210125031349/http://www.reformation.org/dudum-siquidem.html

Page 140: *School of Athens* by the artist Raphael, circa 1509 to 1511.

Page 142: "Peasant Dance" by Pieter Bruegel.

Page 143: *Luther Before the Diet of Worms*, 1521, painted by Anton von Werner.

Page 148: "Standing on the Ugra River," 1480. Miniature in Russian chronicle, sixteenth century. "And our men had beaten many foes with arrows and muskets, and their arrows had fallen between our men, and had nobody hurting, and had repelling them off the shore."

Page 161: *China: The Cake of Kings … and Emperors*, in Le Petit Journal, 1898.

Page 164: Illustration of a microscope in a 1787 book, *Various Accounts from the Dutch*.

Page 166: *Steam train between Tokyo and Yokohama* by HIroshige, 1875.

Page 170: The port of Hanoi in Indochina in 1891 from French newspaper *Le Monde* illustrated.

Page 172: Hilye, a calligraphy panel that describes the physical appearance of the Prophet Muhammad by Kazasker Mustafa İzzet Efendi (1801–1876).

Page 182: Magazine sketch called Christmas in India, in *The Graphic*, 1881.

Page 183: Diagram of a slave ship from the Atlantic slave trade. From evidence delivered before the British House of Commons in 1790 and 1791.

Page 187: French Senagalese Soldiers. Image 23. https://www.loc.gov/resource/gdcwdl.wdl_20061/?sp=23&r=-0.174,0.328,1.16,0.433,0

Page 198: Radio interview with Mark Molesky, in his book, *This Gulf of Fire: The Destruction of Lisbon, or Apocalypse in the Age of Science and Reason*, recorded on November 2, 2015.

Page 201: Map of Lisbon, 1786, showing its reconstruction plan that was uses a grid system, supposed to help in any future disaster situation. https://lccn.loc.gov/2021668347

Page 204: Cover page of the Encyclopedia or a Systematic Dictionary of the Sciences, Arts and Crafts, edited by Denis Diderot and printed in 1751.

Page 205: Jackson J. Spielvogel, *World History.* New York: Glencoe/McGraw-Hill, 2003 (adapted).

Page 220: Cartoon in *Puck*, an American magazine published in 1900 in the aftermath of the Boxer Rebellion in China.

Page 228: Boy's kimono, 1933, courtesy of Sam Perkins.

Page 256: James Killoran et al., The Key to Understanding Global History, Jarrett Publishing Co. (adapted)

Page 271: Memorial book on the ANZAC forces in World War I. *The Anzac Book,* London, New York: Cassell, 1916.

Page 273: https://www.loc.gov/item/16015303/.

Page 277: Photo by Sean McManamon.

Page 285: New York Times headline, November 9, 1917.

NOTES

NOTES